RUBY ON RAILS™
P O W E R !
The Comprehensive Guide

By Aneesha Bakharia

THOMSON

COURSE TECHNOLOGY™

Professional ■ Technical ■ Reference

ISBN-10: 1-59863-216-7
ISBN-13: 978-1-59863-216-3

Library of Congress Catalog Card Number: 2006923475

Printed in the United States of America

07 08 09 10 11 PH 10 9 8 7 6 5 4 3 2 1

THOMSON

COURSE TECHNOLOGY

Professional ■ Technical ■ Reference

Thomson Course Technology PTR, a division of Thomson Learning Inc.
25 Thomson Place
Boston, MA 02210
http://www.courseptr.com

Publisher and General Manager, Thomson Course Technology PTR:
Stacy L. Hiquet

Associate Director of Marketing:
Sarah O'Donnell

Manager of Editorial Services:
Heather Talbot

Marketing Manager:
Mark Hughes

Acquisitions Editor:
Mitzi Koontz

Marketing Coordinator:
Meg Dunkerly

Project Editor:
Sandy Doell

Technical Reviewer:
John Flynt

PTR Editorial Services Coordinator:
Erin Johnson

Copy Editor:
Gene Redding

Interior Layout Tech:
Digital Publishing Solutions

Cover Designer:
Mike Tanamachi

Indexer:
Sharon Shock

Proofreader:
Heather Kaufman Urschel

This book is dedicated to my Grandmother, who looked after me before I started school, took me on many great holidays, and raised eight children.

Acknowledgments

I would like to thank:

- ❋ My grandmother, Rada; my dad, Abdulah; and my mum, Juleka; also, my aunts, Kulsum, Julie, Hajira, and Shaida; my uncles, Ebrahem, Rashid, and Cassim; and my cousins, Celine, Zaeem, and Tess for their continued support and encouragement.

- ❋ Acquisitions editor Mitzi Koontz for her continued support and patience.

- ❋ Project and copy editor Sandy Doell for her direction, flexibility, close attention to detail, and enthusiasm.

- ❋ Copy editor Gene Redding and technical editor John Flynt for their excellent feedback and suggestions.

- ❋ Digital Publishing Solutions, Heather Kaufman Urschel, and Sharon Shock, for their diligence in creating the final product.

- ❋ Madonna for making great music to listen to while writing.

- ❋ Special thanks to Emi Smith.

About the Author

Aneesha Bakharia is a web developer and accomplished author. Aneesha specializes in creating dynamic database-driven web sites. She has a Bachelor of Engineering degree in Microelectronic Engineering and various postgraduate qualifications in multimedia, online course development, and web design. In addition to *Ruby on Rails Power!: The Comprehensive Guide*, she has written several other books for Course Technology PTR, including *Microsoft Visual C# 2005 Express Edition Programming for the Absolute Beginner, Dreamweaver UltraDev Fast & Easy Web Development, JavaServer Pages Fast & Easy Web Development,* and *Microsoft C# Fast & Easy Web Development.* Aneesha lives in Queensland, Australia. She is fluent in C#, Java, JavaScript, ASP.NET, JSP, HTML, XML, Ruby, Ruby on Rails, and VB.NET.

TABLE OF Contents

❄ ❄ ❄

} Introduction

Welcome to Ruby on Rails Power!

Thank you for purchasing this book. *Ruby on Rails Power!: The Comprehensive* Guide provides an introduction to both the Ruby language and the Ruby on Rails framework. Ruby on Rails is feature-rich, easy to learn, and powerful. It certainly is a great time to learn to develop database-driven web applications. I hope this book inspires you to author the next successful Web 2.0 application.

How This Book Is Organized

Here's a look at the way this book is organized and a brief overview of each chapter. You'll also find appendixes with quick reference guides for both Ruby and Ruby on Rails.

Chapter 1: Getting Started

In Chapter 1, we install Ruby, Ruby on Rails, and the MySQL database server. You will learn about Model View Controller architecture, the key components in Rails (Active Record, Action Controller, and Action View) as well as the benefits that Rails brings to web development. The traditional "Hello World" application will be built in Rails. We also create a simple Rails application that displays random images.

Chapter 2: Ruby Essentials

Ruby, an object-oriented, interpreted language, powers the Ruby on Rails framework. An understanding of the Ruby language and its capabilities and syntax will make learning Rails a breeze. In Chapter 2, you'll learn about data types, conditionals, loops, data structures (arrays and hashes), classes, and exceptions. We will also cover Embedded Ruby (ERb), which allows Ruby code to be embedded within an HTML file and interpreted.

Chapter 3: Prototyping Database-Driven Applications with Rails

Chapter 3 illustrates the power and simplicity that Rails brings to web development. In Chapter 3, we will prototype three practical applications: a contact list, FAQ manager, and weblog. The Rails scaffold generator will be used to create a starting point for each application, which we can then customize.

Chapter 4: Active Record

Active Record is a crucial Rails component and is responsible for mapping object properties columns (or fields) in a database table—this is known as object-relational mapping (ORM). Active Record makes it easy to insert, update, delete, and search for data in a database without writing native queries in SQL. We also look at migrations—a feature in Rails that allows us to create and alter the tables and columns in a database. A migration is even able to undo the changes made to a database. This means that we are able to revert to a previous version of the database at any time.

Chapter 5: Action Controller

In Chapter 5, we'll learn to process posted forms, retrieve environment variables, render templates, and redirect requests, as well as store data within a cookie or session. We will also take a look at storing data temporarily between requests in the flash. Finally, we cover routing rules—how request URLs get mapped to controllers and actions.

Chapter 6: Action View

Action View is responsible for displaying templates that belong to a controller's action. Within a template, we are able to format the data retrieved from a database as well as provide a forms-based interface for a user to maintain the data. In this chapter you'll learn to use helpers, layouts, and partials. You will also learn to associate form fields with an Active Record model.

Chapter 7: Web Services and RESTful Applications

In this chapter you'll learn to process and generate XML from within a Rails application. You will learn to use web services (REST, XML-RPC, and WSDL) exposed by the popular photo sharing web site Flickr and the Google search engine. We will also cover adding both a REST and a traditional web service API to an existing Rails application.

Chapter 8: AJAX and Rails

This chapter begins by first explaining AJAX and the `XMLHttpRequest` object. AJAX is tightly integrated into the Rails application framework. Rails uses the Prototype and Scriptaculous libraries behind the scenes. Numerous helpers that add AJAX support to a Rails application are explained. Finally, we cover Rails JavaScript (RJS) templates. RJS files (`.rjs`) map to an action, are written in Ruby (not JavaScript), and are able to alter multiple page elements at the same time.

Chapter 9: Flex on Rails

In Chapter 9, we look at building rich interfaces using Adobe Flex. The declarative MXML syntax and interface controls are first covered. Rails provides a great back end for Flex. We will build a database-driven application with a Flex front end to view and maintain employee details.

Chapter 10: E-mail, Image Processing, and Graphing

In Chapter 10, we look at adding functionality to a Rails application by using existing Ruby libraries. We learn to send e-mail using TMail; process images with RMagick; and generate bar, pie, and line charts with Gruff.

Chapter 11: Rails Plug-Ins

Rails plug-ins place a plethora of functionality at your fingertips. In this chapter you'll learn to add commenting, version control, and tagging to an Active Record model. The `acts_as_ferret` full text search plug-in, which is based upon Lucene, will be covered. We even look at converting a view to PDF format. Bookmark, Article, and Note manager applications are created in this chapter.

Chapter 12: Filters, Caching, and Active Support

In Chapter 12, we look at miscellaneous Rails features. Filters are methods that can be executed before or after an action within a controller. We will use filters to log the duration of actions and add authentication to an application. Instead of always dynamically generating content, we look at caching content that rarely changes in order to improve performance. Finally, we cover the Ruby language extension included in Active Support.

Chapter 13: Testing and Debugging

In this chapter, you'll learn to use Ruby's unit testing framework, namely `Test::Unit`, as well as write unit tests to test Active Record models, functional tests, with which we test the actions within a controller, and integration tests to test functionality that spans multiple controllers. We also look at techniques to debug a Rails application.

Chapter 14: Designing Rails Applications

In the final chapter, we build two practical applications in Ruby on Rails—a wiki and a forum. The wiki stores a new version after each edit. Users of the wiki can easily create new pages as well as view a history of edits and even revert to a previous version. Wiki markup is also supported. The forum allows messages to be threaded and is based in `acts_as_nested` set.

 Note

The source code for each chapter can be downloaded from the Course Technology Web site: http://www.courseptr.com/downloads.

1 } Getting Started

In 2004, Ruby on Rails emerged from obscurity. It was a time when something just felt wrong with current web development frameworks and technologies. Web development had become a tedious task. So much time was being wasted on the plumbing that held an application together that critical functionality was often neglected. Web application frameworks were just overly complex and extremely time consuming to configure. Ruby on Rails solved all these problems and made web development feel natural and fun again.

In this chapter you'll learn how to:

※ Install Ruby, Ruby on Rails, and MySQL

※ Create a Ruby on Rails project

※ Explore the directory structure of a Ruby on Rails project

※ Understand the Model View Controller (MVC) architecture

※ Create the traditional Hello World first application

※ Create a Rails application that displays random images

※ Explore the Ruby on Rails API documentation

Ruby on Rails Fundamental Concepts

A lot of web frameworks and technologies existed and were well established when Rails (see Figure 1.1) was first introduced by David Heinemeier Hansson in 2004, yet Rails was able to easily redefine web development. The aim behind Ruby on Rails was to simplify web development and improve programmer productivity. Core Rails concepts and techniques have managed to inspire numerous clone frameworks in just about every popular language. Let's review these fundamental concepts:

※ **Conventions over configuration.** Rails comes pre-configured with defaults. You don't need to spend hours editing the parameters in an XML file to get up and running. You just need to spend a little time learning conventions to reap the productivity rewards. This in no way means that Rails is not configurable. Rails is very flexible but constraints are liberating.

❋ **Start with a specific, well-defined directory structure.** In a Rails application there is a specific place for everything, including models, views, controllers, images, style sheets, JavaScript, and configuration settings. This illustrates the convention over configuration idea. Instead of wasting time thinking about where something trivial like JavaScript should be placed, just accept the predefined directory structure and get on with the functional requirements of your application.

❋ **Use Ruby.** Rails is built using Ruby. Ruby is fully object-oriented. Ruby also has a very concise and expressive syntax. You will learn more about Ruby and its impressive features in Chapter 2, "Ruby Essentials."

❋ **Use the Model View Controller (MVC) architecture.** The Model View Controller architecture is a natural fit for web applications and is fully implemented by Rails. Rails has the simplest and most intuitive MVC implementation I have ever seen.

❋ **Employ metaprogramming concepts.** *Metaprogramming* is when you use code to generate code. Rails includes script generators to create stub files for you. The `rails` generator, for example, creates a new project with the Rails predefined directory structure. There are also script generators to create the required files for models and controllers within your application.

❋ **Don't Repeat Yourself (DRY).** Rails promotes code reuse. Rails provides practical ways to abstract code so that it can be used in multiple places. This is aided in part by the MVC architecture.

❋ **Embrace Web 2.0 and AJAX.** AJAX-enhancing a web application with Rails is an absolute breeze. The Prototype and Scriptaculous JavaScript libraries are both included with Rails. You don't even have to know JavaScript; using Rails helpers and Rails JavaScript templates (RJS) you just need to know Ruby.

❋ **Built-in unit, functional, and integrations testing.** Writing test cases is advocated as part of the development process. When you use a script generator to create a new controller or model, stub files for unit and functional test cases also get generated. Comprehensive tests will help you to detect errors when an enhancement is made to an application.

❋ **Object-relational mapping.** Rails makes accessing relational databases a breeze with Active Record, which smartly maps table fields to Ruby objects automatically. No XML configuration files need to be edited.

❋ **Server lifecycle aware.** Rails is the first framework to understand the different environments that developers work in. Rails knows that as a developer you will mostly likely work code on a development server, transfer code to a staging server for testing, and finally, if all is working according to plan, deploy your application to a live production server. Details for each environment are stored within the Rails application and are easily edited in a human-readable data format.

❋ **Developer productivity.** Rails simplifies routine tasks leaving heaps of time to concentrate on functionality and usability. Rails inspires developers to add that final finishing touch to their application.

Figure 1.1
The Ruby on Rails web site.

The Model View Controller Paradigm

Model View Controller (MVC) is a way of separating an application intro three components: the model, the view, and the controller. MVC was first invented by Trygve Reenskaug all the way back in 1974. The MVC paradigm is a perfect match for web development. Business logic inter-mixed with database access code makes it difficult to maintain, debug, and extend web applications. The MVC paradigm allows for clean separation of business logic (the controller), data (the model), and the formatting of data for display and user interaction (the view).

❋ The *model* manages the data, which is usually stored in a database. The model both retrieves and inserts data into the databases, and enforces any associated business rules. The Active Record component in Ruby on Rails creates models.

❋ The *controller* maps user input requests to a matching command or action. The action in Rails is a method, which is able to interact with the model, perform required calculations, and pass the results to the view. Action Controller is responsible for routing `get` and `post` requests to their corresponding action or method.

The *view* is responsible for displaying data. A view should not contain complex processing logic. A view should only be responsible for formatting and displaying the data variables passed to it from the action. Action View displays the .rhtml templates, which contain embedded Ruby code. The view is actually the user interface. The view could contain links that call other actions. Forms that are used to enter and update data are also displayed by the view. Actions are also able to process data entered into a form and submitted.

Active Record is in charge of Object/Relational Mapping (ORM). Active Record provides an object-oriented wrapper around a database. Database tables are mapped to classes. This means that fields within a table are referenced as the properties of a class. Active Record also provides class methods for performing operations on the data such as save and find. Unlike other ORM libraries, Active Record requires no complex configuration and is able to infer mappings based on conventions used in naming tables and fields. Active Record makes Rails the most productive framework for database-driven web sites.

Note

The controller and view components in Rails are so interconnected that they are packaged together and called Action Pack.

Installing Ruby, Rails, and MySQL

You are keen and eager to get started, but before you can create database-driven web sites with Rails you will need to install Ruby, Ruby on Rails, and MySQL. We will be installing these packages on Windows. If you have a Macintosh or Linux computer, the screen shots will look different. You will also need to download the appropriate binaries for your platform as well.

Note

Other items to include on your shopping or download list:

* **A good text editor.** Programming requires editing code—lots of code almost every day. If you are using a Mac, TextMate (http://macromates.com/) is an excellent choice. RadRails (http://www.radrails.org/) is a good cross platform editor for Rails that is based on Eclipse. Any text editor that you are comfortable with will suffice. Syntax highlighting (Ruby, HTML, JavaScript), code block indentation, and auto-completion will help improve your productivity.

* **Version control.** Popular choices for version control are CVS or SubVersion. A version control repository stores changes and allows you to revert to previous versions. You can even review a list of all changes made, called a *history*. You can also manage your software releases on different branches. Remember to commit changes to your repository regularly.

> **Note**
>
> InstantRails is approximately 50 MB and installs Ruby, Rails, and MySQL all at the same time.

Installing Ruby

Download the latest stable One-Click Ruby Installer for Windows from http://rubyinstaller.rubyforge.org/. The One-Click Ruby Installer is an executable file (.exe). Install Ruby by double-clicking on the executable. You can simply follow the onscreen instructions (see Figure 1.2) accepting the default settings.

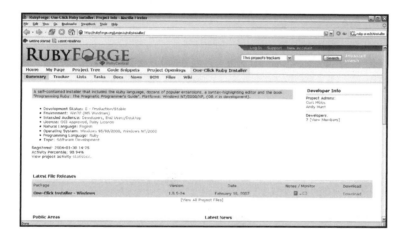

Figure 1.2
The One-Click Ruby Installer.

> ❄ **Note**
>
> The command prompt is going to be your new best friend if you are a Windows user. If you are a Linux user, the command prompt is already an old acquaintance. Throughout this book, we'll need to use the command prompt to install applications, create new Rails projects, and even generate skeleton MVC code. The command prompt looks different on each platform, so to make the examples cross-platform, the command prompt will be represented by the $ symbol. Figure 1.3 shows the Windows command prompt.

After Ruby is installed, we can try some Ruby code to make sure it is working. Ruby contains an interactive shell called irb. Irb can be started from the command line by typing:

```
$ irb --simple-prompt
```

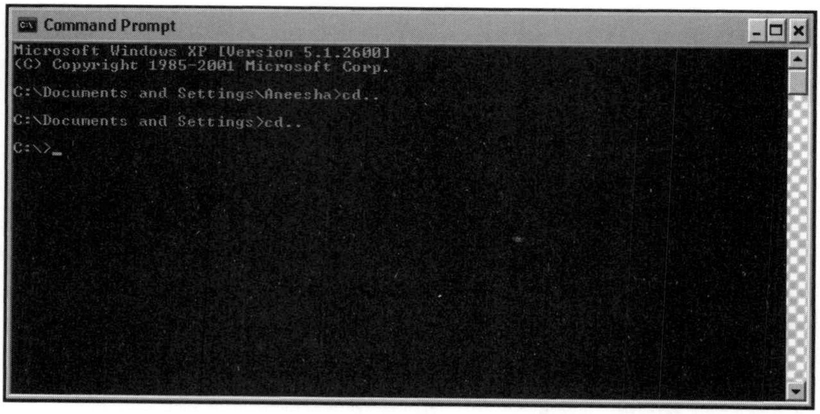

Figure 1.3
The Windows command
prompt.

Irb allows you to type Ruby code at the command prompt and have the code evaluated when you press the Enter key. We can now try some simple Ruby code snippets in irb:

```
$ 1 + 1
=> 2
$ "hello".reverse
=> "olleh"
```

Exit irb by typing:

```
$ exit
```

Installing Ruby on Rails

Now that Ruby is working, we are ready to install Rails. Ruby contains a package manager call RubyGems. RubyGems is able to download software packaged into the gem format from RubyForge. RubyGems operates from the command line. The install command will install Rails:

```
$ gem install rails --include-dependencies
```

RubyGems will also install the libraries that Rails requires. This includes Rake, Action Mailer, Active Record, and Active Pack.

You can use this command line gem to update to the latest version of Rails (see Figure 1.4):

```
$ gem update rails --include-dependencies
```

Installing MySQL

MySQL is a popular database that has successfully served as the data source for numerous popular sites developed in Rails. Active Record has no database-specific code, but for databases

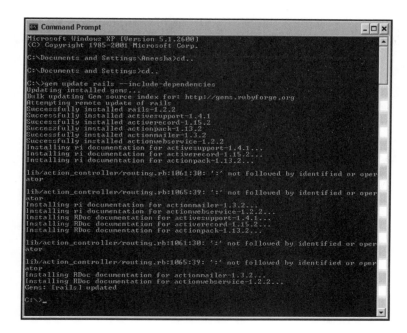

Figure 1.4
Using gems to install Rails.

other than MySQL, you will need to install a database driver. To save you this trouble it is recommended that you use MySQL.

The latest stable MySQL release can be downloaded from http://dev.mysql.com/downloads/mysql/. Run the installer and accept the defaults. The Configuration Wizard will be displayed. Make sure you choose a secure root password. Failing to enter a root password could result in serious security breaches.

A graphical interface to create databases and tables and to inspect your data will also be a valuable asset. HeidiSQL (http://www.heidisql.com/) and SQLyog (http://www.webyog.com/en/) are two open source options. SQLyog is shown in Figure 1.5.

Creating a Ruby on Rails Project

A Ruby on Rails project must follow a specific directory structure. The `rails` generator script runs from the command line prompt and creates the required folders, config files, and scripts. The name of the project or application that is to be created must be passed to the `rails` generator script. The `rails` generator script saves us from having to create our own version of the Rails project structure. This is advantageous because we won't need to re-create our version each time Rails gets an update. The `rails` command is built in, and each time it is run, the current Rails installation is used. I'd rather run one command rather than manually copying and customizing a previous project.

Figure 1.5
Using SQLyog as a GUI interface to MySQL.

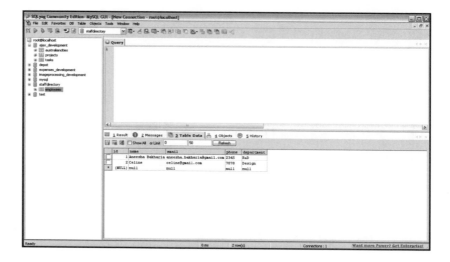

Type the following at the command prompt to create a project called `my_first_app`:

```
$ rails my_first_app
```

Exploring the Ruby on Rails Directory Structure

Ruby on Rails provides a skeleton or starting point source code structure. The `rails` generator script creates a directory that is named after the project's name. Within the project directory a series of files and directories are created. Every file or folder that is created is logged to the console. Here is an extract of the log that printed when `my_first_app` was created—only directories are listed:

```
create
create   app/controllers
create   app/helpers
create   app/models
create   app/views/layouts
create   config/environments
create   db
create   doc
create   lib
```

```
create   lib/tasks
create   log
create   public/images
create   public/javascripts
create   public/stylesheets
create   script/performance
create   script/process
create   test/fixtures
create   test/functional
create   test/integration
create   test/mocks/development
create   test/mocks/test
create   test/unit
```

Let's take a peek at what is inside the most important folders:

❉ The *app folder* is where your application code goes. Rails splits your application into three interacting components: models, controllers and views. This is depicted in the app subfolder structure.

❉ The *config folder* stores configuration settings. It contains numerous files that store configuration details. The most important is database.yml, which specifies the databases to be used in development, testing, and production. The Rails environment structure (environment.rb) and action router (routes.rb) are also found in this folder.

❉ The *db folder* provides a place to store database creation and manipulation scripts.

❉ The *generated documentation* that RubyDoc produces is placed in the doc folder.

❉ The *log directory* contains error logs. There is a log file for each environment (development.log, test.log, and production.log). A server.log file is also placed here.

❉ The *public directory* is where you would place static HTML web pages. There are subfolders for your images, JavaScript files, and style sheets. The JavaScript subfolder contains the .js files for the Scriptaculous and Prototype frameworks.

❉ The *script folder* contains the generator scripts. There are scripts to start the Webrick web server as well as generate models and controllers. We will be using these scripts in just about every chapter of this book.

❉ The *unit, functional,* and *integration test* cases are placed in the test folder. Chapter 13, "Testing and Debugging" covers testing.

Using the Webrick Web Server

Ruby on Rails comes with its own web server—Webrick. A Webrick server can be started for each Rails project. The `script/server` generator is used to create a Webrick server that runs on port 3000 by default. Type `cd my_first_app` to navigate to the newly created folder for your project and at the command prompt type:

```
$ ruby script/server
```

Webrick will display the following within the console window:

```
=> Booting WEBrick...
=> Rails application started on http://0.0.0.0:3000
=> Ctrl-C to shutdown server; call with --help for options
[2006-10-14 14:49:08] INFO  WEBrick 1.3.1
[2006-10-14 14:49:08] INFO  ruby 1.8.4 (2006-04-14) [i386-mswin32]
[2006-10-14 14:49:08] INFO  WEBrick::HTTPServer#start: pid=5472 port=3000
```

We can now view our Rails project from within a web browser with the following URL: http://localhost:3000/. We have not added any code to our project, but we are already able to view the Rails "Welcome aboard" page. In Figure 1.6 the "About your application's environment" link has been clicked and version numbers of all the components are displayed.

Figure 1.6
The Rails Welcome aboard page.

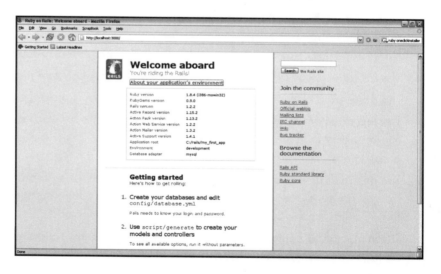

Flip back to the console window where Webrick was started. Each page request is reflected within the console—even the Firefox request for a favicon and required `.js` files. A *favicon* is an icon that is displayed to the left of the URL in the address bar. Firefox makes a request for an icon called `favicon.ico` for each new domain encountered:

```
127.0.0.1 - - [14/Oct/2006:14:54:18 E. Australia Standard Time]
"GET / HTTP/1.1" 200 7552
- -> /
127.0.0.1 - - [14/Oct/2006:14:54:20 E. Australia Standard Time]
"GET /javascripts/prototype.js HTTP/1.1" 200 55149
http://localhost:3000/ -> /javascripts/prototype.js
127.0.0.1 - - [14/Oct/2006:14:54:21 E. Australia Standard Time]
"GET /javascripts/effects.js HTTP/1.1" 200 32871
http://localhost:3000/ -> /javascripts/effects.js
127.0.0.1 - - [14/Oct/2006:14:54:21 E. Australia Standard Time]
"GET /images/rails.png HTTP/1.1" 200 1787
http://localhost:3000/ -> /images/rails.png
127.0.0.1 - - [14/Oct/2006:14:54:21 E. Australia Standard Time]
"GET /favicon.ico HTTP/1.1" 200 0
- -> /favicon.ico
127.0.0.1 - - [14/Oct/2006:14:55:49 E. Australia Standard Time]
"GET /rails/info/properties HTTP/1.1" 200 896
- -> /rails/info/properties
127.0.0.1 - - [14/Oct/2006:14:55:55 E. Australia Standard Time]
"GET /rails/info/properties HTTP/1.1" 200 896
- -> /rails/info/properties
```

Webrick can be started on a port other than 3000. You simply need to use the -p flag to set the port. The following example starts Webrick on port 80:

```
$ ruby script/server -p 80
```

Press Ctrl+C to shut down the Webrick server. Help options are also available by typing **–help** while the console window has focus.

❄ **Note**

Webrick is an ideal server to use while developing, but you will need to consider alternatives within your live production environment.

Controllers, Actions, and Views

We can now have some fun and see the Rails framework in action (no pun intended). We will be creating a Rails version of the traditional Hello World application. We will start by using `script/generate` to create a controller called Greeting:

```
$ ruby script/generate controller Greeting
```

The following log of files is output to the console:

```
exists   app/controllers/
exists   app/helpers/
create   app/views/greeting
exists   test/functional/
create   app/controllers/greeting_controller.rb
create   test/functional/greeting_controller_test.rb
create   app/helpers/greeting_helper.rb
```

The `greeting_controller.rb`, `greeting_controller_test.rb`, and `greeting_helper.rb` files have been created. The methods or actions in a controller need to link to a view. Rails creates a folder for you to store the views that belong to a specific controller in the `app/views` directory.

We passed Greeting to `script/generate`, but it converted the name to lowercase and added a _controller suffix. This is a Rails convention. The _controller suffix must be added to all controllers. The `greeting_controller.rb` file contains a class called `GreetingController`. The class that is associated with a controller starts with a capital letter and is suffixed with `Controller`.

We can now edit the `app/controllers/greeting_controller.rb` file and add an index action. To add an action we simply need to add a method called `index`:

```
class GreetingController < ApplicationController
    def index
    end
end
```

Save the `app/controllers/greeting_controller.rb` file, start Webrick up and view http://localhost:3000/greeting in a web browser. Oops—we get a Template is missing error as shown in Figure 1.7. Rails seems to be looking for `/app/views/greeting/index.rhtml`. This is the view template that corresponds to the index action.

The `index` method does not contain any code. Actions automatically link to a view template with a matching name. We have not yet created the `/app/views/greeting/index.rhtml` file.

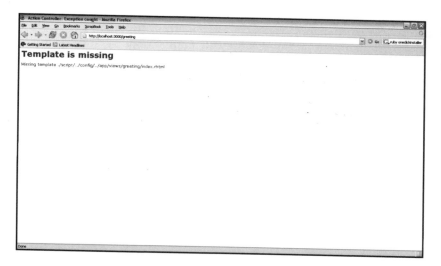

Figure 1.7
The Template is missing
error message.

We just want to print Hello World, so instead of creating an `index.rhtml` template file, we will just use the `render_text` method:

```
class GreetingController < ApplicationController
    def index
            render_text "Hello World"
    end
end
```

> ❄ **Note**
>
> Parentheses are not mandatory, but can be used to pass parameters to a method in Ruby. These two method calls are therefore semantically correct and equivalent:
>
> ```
>     render_text "Hello World"
>     render_text("Hello World")
> ```

Hurray! We just need to reload the http://localhost:3000/greeting URL and the Hello World message will be displayed. We did not even need to restart Webrick—our changes to the index action were automatically picked up once the page was refreshed. This is surely going to make development a lot easier. Ruby allows full object-oriented support without any need for compiled classes.

We could enter http://localhost:3000/greeting/index to display the response of the index action. In this case both the controller and action are included in the URL path. If only a controller is present in the URL path, Rails will look for an index method and the corresponding `index.rhtml` template.

We will now create the `app\views\greeting\index.rhtml` template file. The `app\views\greeting\` folder has already been created by `script\generate`. Files with the .rhtml extension are able to include Ruby code. We need to remove the `render_text` method from the `index` method or the `app\views\greeting\index.rhtml` file won't be retrieved when the index action is called.

The `app\views\greeting\index.rhtml` file:

```
<html><head>
<title>Hello World</title>
</head>
<body>
<h1>Hello World</h1>
</body>
</html>
```

Refresh the http://localhost:3000/greeting/ URL, and the Hello World message will be displayed with more emphasis.

Using Embedded Ruby (ERb)

We can use the <%= and %> delimiters to insert the result of an expression in an .rhtml template. View templates files (i.e., files with .rhtml extensions) are processed by ERb. ERb stands for embedded Ruby.

In Ruby we can get the current time by calling the `Time.now` method. We will use the <%= and %> delimiters to dynamically render the current time (see Figure 1.8):

```
<html>
<head>
<title>Hello World</title>
</head>
<body>
<h1>Hello World</h1>
The current time: <%= Time.now %>
</body>
</html>
```

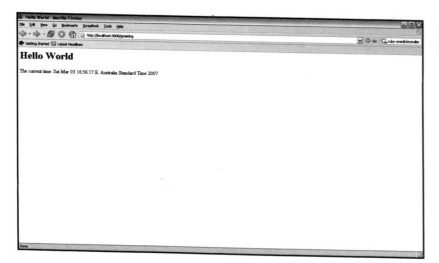

Figure 1.8
Dynamic output with ERb.

In ERb the <% and %> delimiters allow Ruby code to be placed within an .rhtml file. In this example, a loop writes Hello World to the screen five times (see Figure 1.9):

```
<html>
<head>
<title>Hello World</title>
</head>
<body>
<%
5.times do
%>
<h1>Hello World</h1>
<%
end
%>
The current time: <%= Time.now %>
</body>
</html>
```

Instance variables set within an action are available for use in the corresponding view. In the index action we set an instance variable called @message. The @message variable can then be displayed by the index (or index.rhtml) view. The @message is set to Hello World. We also set the @current_time variable:

Figure 1.9
Hello World times five.

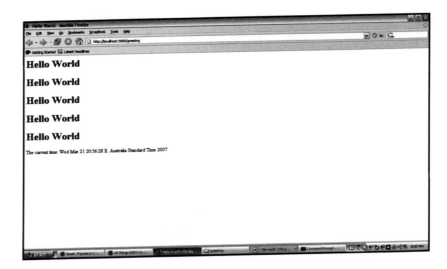

```
class GreetingController < ApplicationController
      def index
                @message = "Hello World"
                @current_time = Time.now
      end
end
```

After the action is executed, the corresponding view is displayed. Now we can use the <% and %> delimiters to display the @message and @current_time variables in the index.rhtml view:

```
<html>
<head>
<title><%= @message %></title>
</head>
<body>
<%
5.times do
%>
<h1><%= @message %></h1>
<%
end
%>
The current time: <%= @current_time %>
```

```
</body>
</html>
```

Linking to Actions

Let's add some more actions to the Greeting controller. The action we add will be called say_goodmorning and say_goodafternoon. Both methods are included in the app/controllers/greeting_controller.rb file:

```
class GreetingController < ApplicationController
    def index

    end

    def say_goodmorning

    end

    def say_goodafternoon

    end
end
```

We need corresponding app\views\greeting\say_goodmorning.rhtml and app\views\greeting\say_goodafternoon.rhtml templates. We won't make a mistake again and call the actions without a view template because we know a Template is missing error message will be produced.

The app\views\greeting\say_goodmorning.rhtml file:

```
<html>
<head>
<title>Good Morning </title>
</head>
<body>
<h1>Good Morning</h1>
</body>
</html>
```

The `app\views\greeting\say_goodafternoon.rhtml` **file:**

```
<html>
<head>
<title>Good Afternoon </title>
</head>
<body>
<h1>Good Afternoon</h1>
</body>
</html>
```

The `say_goodmorning` action is accessed via http://localhost:3000/greeting/ say_goodmorning. The `say_goodafternoon` action is accessed via http://localhost:3000/ greeting/say_goodafternoon. How do we include a link in one template that is able to request that another action be displayed? We could include a direct link within our template file:

```
<a href="/greeting/say_goodmorning">Say Good Morning</a>
```

Several issues are associated with direct or hard coded links. If the way Rails handles routing to controllers and actions changes or you restructure your application, the hard coded links will need to be fixed manually. Rails, however, provides a `link_to()` helper method with the sole purpose of inserting dynamic links to controllers and their associated actions. We could now rewrite the link to the `say_goodmorning` action as:

```
<%= link_to "Say Good Morning", :action => "say_goodmorning" %>
```

The `link_to` method is placed within the `<%` and `%>` delimiters. The first parameter is the text to be displayed in the hyperlink. The second parameter specifies the action to link to. A colon is placed in front of the word action—this is a Ruby symbol and can be read as "the item named action." The `=>` operator assigns the name of the actions (a string) to `:action`. This is a keyword parameter and is used extensively in helper methods. This is useful when a number of optional parameters can be passed to a helper method.

Displaying Random Images

We are going to build an additional project, just to reinforce the controller and view concepts covered in this chapter. We will display a randomly selected image each time a page is requested. Our controller will be called `RandomImage`, and the action to display the random image, show.

We start by creating a new controller:

```
$ ruby script/generate Controller RandomImage
```

The `app/controllers/random_image_controller.rb` **file and** `app/views/`
`random_image` **folder are created. We can now edit the** `random_image_controller.rb`
file. The `RandomImageController` **class has been created. We will insert the** `show` **action:**

```
class RandomImageController < ApplicationController
    def show
    end
end
```

The `show` **action maps to the** `show.rthml` **template. We will need to create this file and place it
within the** `app/views/random_image` **folder. Within the view we need to select and display a
random image. We have five images and have saved them to the** `/public/images` **folder. We
will store the names of the images in an array, generate a random number between 0 and 4, and
then display the image that corresponds to the random number. Here is the Ruby code:**

```
images = ["image1.jpg", "image2.jpg", "image3.jpg", "image4.jpg", "image5.jpg"]
random_no = rand(5)
random_image = images[random_no]
```

This code can be inserted between the `<%` **and** `%>` **delimiters in the** `show.rthml` **file:**

```
<html>
<head>
<title>Random Image</title>
</head>
<body>
<h1>Random Image</h1>
<%
images = ["image1.jpg", "image2.jpg", "image3.jpg", "image4.jpg", "image5.jpg"]
random_no = rand(5)
random_image = images[random_no]
%>
<img src="/public/images/<%= random_image%>">
</body>
</html>
```

Code mixed with HTML in the view is both hard to read and maintain. The code to randomly select an image should be placed within the controller. The `random_image` instance variable will still be available to the view:

```
class RandomImageController < ApplicationController
    def show
        @images = ["image1.jpg", "image2.jpg", "image3.jpg", "image4.jpg",
"image5.jpg"]
        @random_no = rand(5)
        @random_image = images[random_no]
    end
end
```

Our view now only needs to reference the `random_image` variable where the image must be inserted:

```
<html>
<head>
<title>Random Image</title>
</head>
<body>
<h1>Random Image</h1>
<img src="/public/images/<%= random_image%>">
</body>
</html>
```

Generating Your Own Ruby on Rails API Documentation

The Rails API documentation is available from http://api.rubyonrails.org. This is a handy resource to view documentation of individual Rails components (Active Record, Action Pack, Action Mailer, etc.) and Rails helper methods (e.g., `h()`). It might, however, not be practical to view the documentation online.

We start by creating a new Rails application. This is done by typing **rails** at the command prompt followed by the name of the application. After a folder has been created and populated with the predefined Rails directory structure, follow these instructions, to be typed at a command prompt to generate a local copy of the API:

```
$ rails sample_app
$ cd sample_app
$ rake rails:freeze:gems
```

```
$ echo >vendor/rails/activesupport/README
$ rake doc:rails
```

Building the documentation will take a few minutes. Once complete the generated documentation will be placed within the doc/api directory. You can copy this directory to a new location and then delete the sample_app project. Figure 1.10 show the Rails API documentation being viewed locally.

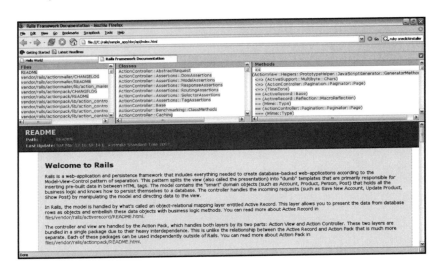

Figure 1.10
The Ruby on Rails API documentation.

Joining the Rails Community

Ruby on Rails has a vibrant and active user base. The mailing list provides a way to keep up with current developments and tool announcements. If you are ever stuck or have a bug you just can't fix, the mailing list is a great place to ask for assistance. There is also a Ruby on Rails weblog and podcast. The Ruby on Rails podcast, hosted by Geoffrey Grosenbach, is both entertaining and informative.

Mailing list: http://groups.google.com/group/rubyonrails-talk

Ruby on Rails weblog: http://weblog.rubyonrails.com/

Ruby on Rails Podcast: http://podcast.rubyonrails.org/

Ruby on Rails Wiki: http://wiki.rubyonrails.org/rails

Conclusion

In this chapter you learned to install the key software elements required to get you started and even built a very simple Ruby on Rails application. It is quite easy to see why Rails has not only received so much publicity but is also used to develop numerous popular Web 2.0 sites. In Chapter 2, "Ruby Essentials," we delve into Ruby, the language that powers Rails. Working knowledge of Ruby will help you to better understand and enhance your Rails applications. In Chapter 3, "Prototyping Database-Driven Applications with Rails," the fun really begins when we start to use Rails to power a database-driven site.

2} Ruby Essentials

The first public release of Ruby was made by Yukihiro "Matz" Matsumoto in 1995. Ruby is a cross between Small-Talk and Perl. Ruby popularity began to soar after the release of the Ruby on Rails full stack web framework in 2004. Programmers from around the world then began to appreciate Ruby's powerful, yet simple, syntax. Ruby is fully object-oriented but also supports the functional and procedural paradigms. Ruby is also an interpreted language, which means that compilation is not required. This chapter introduces you to the Ruby language and provides many examples for you to try. A thorough understanding of Ruby will help you build more powerful Rails applications.

In this chapter you'll learn how to:

* Understand the Ruby language syntax
* Use the Interactive Ruby shell (irb)
* Understand Ruby data types
* Perform string and mathematical operations in Ruby
* Use conditionals and loops
* Use the array and hash data structures
* Organize code with classes and methods
* Handle exceptions
* Use Embedded Ruby (ERb)

Ruby Syntax

An example Ruby program is shown in Figure 2.1. The Ruby code prints a counter variable to the console 10 times using a `while` loop. This is a very simple code snippet, but it does highlight the essence of Ruby language syntax. From this simple code example we note that:

❋ Ruby files have a `.rb` extension.

❋ The `;` character does not need to be placed at the end of each line.

❋ The `#` character is used to denote a comment.

❋ The equal-to sign (=) is used to assign a value to a variable.

❋ Variables don't need to be declared as a specific data type before they are used.

❋ The `begin` and `end` keywords mark the `while` loops code block. The `{` and `}` matching braces are not required.

❋ Strings are enclosed in quotation marks.

❋ The `puts` method prints a string to the console.

Figure 2.1
Dissecting Ruby language syntax.

Interactive Ruby: irb

Interactive Ruby (irb) is a Ruby shell program that evaluates Ruby code and prints the result to the console. irb is a great learning tool as it allows you to enter Ruby code and immediately see output as well as errors. Let's use irb to experiment with the Ruby language. We start irb at the command prompt:

```
$ irb --simple-prompt
```

We need to press Enter at the end of each line of code. irb makes a handy calculator:

```
>> 1 + 1
=> 2
>> 100 * 3
=> 300
```

The `puts` method is used to write text to the console:

```
>> puts "Hello"
Hello
=> nil
```

The `puts` method does not return a value, so a `nil` object or simply `nil is displayed` are the result.

We can get irb to deliver a personalized greeting. The `gets` method captures keystrokes until the Enter key is pressed. The keystrokes captured by the `gets` methods can be assigned to a variable, in this case called `name`. The `#{...}` syntax is used to insert the value stored in a variable in a string before it is output.

```
>> puts "Please enter your name:"
=> Please enter your name
>> name = gets
Aneesha
>> puts "Hello #{name}"
```

> ❊ **Note**
>
> You will encounter occasions when you need to enter lengthy lines of Ruby code. It is very easy to enter multi-line Ruby statements in irb; we can make lines *wrap around* by placing a backslash (\) at the end of each line. This technique is shown in the example that follows.
>
> ```
> >> puts "This is a very long " \
>         "sentence that spans two lines"
> ```

We can exit irb at any time by entering the `exit` keyword.

```
>> exit
```

Using the Ruby Interpreter

While irb is a great tool for testing Ruby one liners and experimenting with Ruby syntax, it does not replace the need to use the Ruby interpreter. The Ruby interpreter is run from the command prompt and executes programs stored in a file. There are over 20 command line switches for the Ruby interpreter. Table 2.1 lists the most important and useful command line switches.

Create a new text file called `rubyexample.rb`. This program will ask the user to enter their name and then print a customized greeting to the console. Enter the following lines of code and save the file:

```
puts "Please enter your name:"
name = gets
puts "Hello #{name}"
```

We can now use the Ruby interpreter to check the file for syntax errors:

Table 2.1 Summary of Ruby Command Line Switches

Switch	Description
-c	Check a program for syntax errors. The program is not executed.
-w	Display warning messages while a program is being executed.
-e	Executes the code provided between quotation marks.
-v	Displays Ruby version information and displays warnings.
-1	Forces a newline character to be printed to the console after all output statements.
--version	Displays the Ruby version number.

```
$ ruby -cw rubyexample.rb
```

If "Syntax OK" is returned, we are ready to execute our simple program by typing the following at the command prompt:

```
$ ruby rubyexample.rb
```

Variables, Constants, and Assignment

The equal-to sign (=) is used to associate a value with a variable—known as an assignment operator. Variables don't need to be declared in Ruby and can store strings, characters, whole numbers, and decimals. A variable gives you the ability to meaningfully name or label the data you will use in a program. Once variables are assigned a value, you can include the variable in any of the code that follows. You can also update the value stored in a variable at any time.

Using irb, we will create a variable called city and use assignment operator (=) to assign a string value of "Brisbane" to the variable.

```
>> city = "Brisbane"
=> "Brisbane"
```

We can use puts to print the contents of the variable to the irb console:

```
>> puts = "I live in sunny " + city + "."
I live in sunny Brisbane.
=> nil
```

The value stored in a variable can be changed by assigning a new value to an existing variable. Here the variable called city will be changed from "Brisbane" to "Sydney":

```
>> city = "Sydney"
=> "Sydney"
>> puts = "I live in " + city + "."
```

```
I live in Sydney.
=> nil
```

It is very important that you name your variables appropriately as this will make both writing and debugging your code easier. Descriptive variables are also very useful to other developers who may help to fix or enhance the code that you write. In Ruby, variables must begin with a lowercase letter. This is a Ruby convention.

Constants are used to store fixed values that are not meant to be changed while a program is being interpreted. A value must therefore only be assigned to a constant once. The first letter of the name of a constant must be in uppercase. This is the Ruby convention to denote a constant.

You can change the value of a constant, but Ruby will display a warning message:

```
>> Pi = 3.12
=> 3.12
>> Pi = 3.12222
(irb) warning: already initialized constant Pi
=> 3.12222
```

Objects and Data Types

In Ruby everything is an object, even simple data types. Strings, integers, and floats are all objects. Objects have methods that can be called via dot (.) notation. Some examples:

```
>> a_string = "This is a string."
>> a_number = 5
>> a_floating_point_number = 0.5
```

Let's use the `class` method to determine which classes our objects belong to:

```
>> a_string.class
=> String
>> a_number.class
=> Fixnum
>> a_floating_point_number.class
=> Float
```

We can also use the `is_a?` method to check if a variable is an instance of a particular object:

```
>> a_string.is_a?(String)
=> true
>> a_string.is_a?(Float)
=> false
```

The `to_*` methods are handy when you need to convert data types. An integer can be converted to a string using the `to_s` method. A string can be converted to an integer using the `to_i` method.

```
>> 5.to_s
=> "5"
>> "5".to_i
=> 5
```

There is even a method to list all of the methods that an object can call. Surprisingly this method is called `methods`. Table 2.2 displays the sorted list of methods available to string objects.

```
>> "A string".methods
>> "A string".methods.sort
```

Strings

Text entered by a user or read in from a file is represented by the string class in Ruby. The string class provides various useful methods for manipulating and processing textual information (see Table 2.2). Strings are enclosed in quotations marks. Here are some examples:

```
>> name = "Celine"
"Celine"
>> sentence = "This is a sentence."
"This is a sentence"
>> paragraph = "This is a paragraph. This is the 2nd line in a paragraph."
"This is a paragraph. This is the 2nd line in a paragraph."
```

Table 2.2   String Manipulation Methods

Method	Example	Result
capitalize	"hello".capitalize	"Hello"
upcase	"hello".upcase	"HELLO"
downcase	"HELLO".downcase	"hello"
swapcase	"HeLLo".swapcase	"hEllO"
strip	"Hello".strip	"Hello"
lstrip	"Hello".lstrip	"Hello "
rstrip	"Hello".rstrip	"Hello"
chop	"Hello".chop	"Hell"
chomp	"Hello/n".chomp	"Hello"
reverse	"olleh".reverse	"hello"

The methods in Table 2.2 all return a new string and don't alter the original string. There are, however, bang (!) equivalents for each method which do alter the original strings. We'll get a better understanding of bang (!) methods once we try a few examples in irb.

```
>> city = "brisbane"
=> "brisbane"
>> city.capitalize
=> "Brisbane"
>> puts city
=> "brisbane"
>> city.capitalize!
=> "Brisbane"
>> puts city
=> "Brisbane"
```

As you can see, the `capitalize` method has not changed the contents of the variable called `city`. The `capitalize!` method has, however, updated the value stored by the `city` variable.

The plus sign (+) is used to concatenate strings together:

```
>> "Good " + "Morning"
=> "Good Morning"
```

If a variable is enclosed in quotation marks, we can even assign a numeric value to it as a string and use the `to_i` method to convert the data back to an integer:

```
>> "3" + "4"
=> "34""
>> num = "1"
=>"1"
>> num.to_i + 5
=> 6
```

Multiplying a string by a number:

```
>> "Hello" * 3
=> "HelloHelloHello"
```

The interpolation operator (#{...}) allows variables and expressions to be inserted in strings and evaluated before the string is output. Here is an example:

```
>> name = "Aneesha"
=>"Aneesha"
```

```
>> puts "Hello #{name}"
=> "Hello Aneesha"
```

Certain characters, such as a backslash (\) and a quotation mark ("), need to be escaped within a string:

```
>> "This string has a backslash \\ and a quotation mark \"."
```

Ruby also supports textual data enclosed in single quotes. Interpolation is not supported in strings enclosed in single quotes. The interpolation operator is simply printed out. In strings enclosed in single quotes, only the single quote needs to be escaped.

```
>> 'Let\'s try to print a variable "#{name}"'
=> 'Let's try to print a variable "#{name}"'
```

Mathematical Operations

A large percentage of the programs that you write will need to perform mathematical calculations in some form or another. Table 2.3 displays the mathematical operators available within the Ruby language. As expected, addition, subtraction, multiplication, and division are all supported. Table 2.3 also shows the modulus (%) and exponent operators (**).

Table 2.3   Mathematical Operators in Ruby

Operator	Description
+	Addition
–	Subtraction
*	Multiplication
/	Division
%	Modulus
**	Exponent

Simple addition, subtraction, multiplication, and division in the irb shell:

```
>> 234 + 334
=> 568
>> 560 – 60
=> 500
>> 500 * 2
=> 1000
>> 1000 / 2
```

```
=> 500
>> 3/2
=> 1
```

Hold on—3/2 is not equal to 1. The correct value answer should be 1.5. What is going on? Ruby returns the integer component when two integers are divided. If we wanted a floating point number returned, one of the values in the expression would need to be a float.

```
>> 3.0/2
=> 1.5
```

The +, −, *, and / operations can be used with variables. Table 2.4 shows the Ruby shortcut syntax for adding, subtracting, multiplying, or dividing from a variable. We can try these out in irb:

```
>> x = 5
5
>> x += 2
7
=> x ** 3
343
```

Table 2.4   Shortcut Syntax for Performing Mathematical Operations on Variables

Example	Shortcut	Meaning
x = x + 4	x += 4	Add 4 to x
x = x - 4	x -= 4	Subtract 4 from x
x = x * 4	x *= 4	Multiply x by 4
x = x / 4	x /= 4	Divide x by 4
x = x % 3	x %= 3	x modulo 3
x = x ** 3	x **=3	x cubed (x * x * x)

Generating Random Numbers

Some web sites display a random quote, product, or image. This is a simple yet powerful technique to provide dynamic and interesting content to regular web site visitors. A random number generator is required to reproduce this concept. In Ruby we just need to call the rand method to generate a random number between 0 and 1. Each time we call rand a different number is returned to 15 decimal places.

```
>> rand
=> 0.462668225169182
```

```
>> rand
=> 0.343490909078823
>> rand
=> 0.872672369927781
```

If we pass an integer value to the rand method, it will return random integer (whole number) values from 0 to 1 below the specified integer. This means that if we only had five images, we could use rand(5) to generate a random number between 0 and 4 and display the appropriately numbered image.

```
>> rand(5)
=> 0
>> rand(5)
=> 2
>> rand(5)
=> 3
>> rand(5)
=> 1
>> rand(5)
=> 4
```

Conditional Processing

In our daily lives we constantly need to make decisions. Computer programs would be almost useless if they could not be programmed to evaluate expressions, make decisions, and execute the appropriate code. Ruby provides operators to make comparisons (see Table 2.5). Comparison operators return either a true or false value. The results returned by a comparison operator can then be used by an if statement to determine whether a code block should be executed. This is indeed powerful as your code no longer needs to be linear and can respond to changing conditions.

Table 2.5   Comparison Operators in Ruby

Symbol	Description
==	Equal
!=	Not equal to
>	Greater than
<	Less than
>=	Greater than or equal to
<=	Less than or equal to

Let's use irb to perform some simple equality comparisons:

```
>> "one" == "one"
=> true
>> "one" == "two"
=> false
>> 1 == 1
=> true
>> 1 == 2
=> false
>> 1 == 2
=> false
>> 1 == "1".to_i
=> true
>> 5 < 10
=> true
>> 344 > 4
=> true
```

Next we will execute the code within an `if` and `end` code block if an expression returns a true value. The `==` operator is used to compare the value stored in the variable x with the integer value of 10. If x is equal to 10, some text will be printed to the console. If x is not equal to 10, the line will be skipped and code execution will resume after the end keyword.

```
if x == 10
      puts "The variable x is equal to 10."
end
```

Placing the `then` keyword after the comparison allows us to shrink this code to one line:

```
if x==10 then print "The variable x is equal to 10."
```

We could also use a `;` instead of the `then` keyword.

```
if x==10; print "The variable x is equal to 10."; end
```

The `else` clause and the code that it wraps will be executed if the expression evaluated by the `if` clause is false. There can be only one `else` clause used in conjunction with an `if` statement.

```
x = 5
if x == 10
      print "The variable x is equal to 10."
```

```
else
      print "The variable x is not equal to 10."
end
```

Multiple elsif clauses can follow an if code block. The elsif clause allows additional conditions to be evaluated and an appropriate code block to be executed. In the example that follows, if, elsif, and else clauses are used.

```
x = 5
if x == 10
      print "The variable x is equal to 10."
elsif x == 5
      print "The variable x is equal to 5."
else
      print "The variable x contains a value other than 10 and 5."
end
```

The case statement comes in handy when evaluating the same variable in each elsif statement. The case statement provides simplified syntax instead of re-evaluating the variable for each elsif clause. The when keyword replaces the elsif keyword and no comparison operators are required. Here is an example of using case to evaluate the variable x against values and execute the appropriate code block.

```
x = 5
case x
when 5
      puts "x is equal to 5"
when 1
      puts "x is equal to 1"
else
      puts "No match"
end
```

Loops

Looping constructs allow blocks of code to be executed a predefined number of times or until a condition becomes true. If we wanted to output Hello World five times, we could copy and paste the code five times. If we wanted to print a customized greeting for 50 people it would simply not be practical to copy and paste each line 50 times, especially if we then had to alter the greeting. The simplest loop in Ruby is the times do loop. Here we print Hello World 5 times:

```
5.times do
      puts "Hello World"
end
```

The do loop requires a counter variable; n is used in the example below. Each time the loop is executed, the counter variable must be incremented. The do loop iterates until the break if clause becomes true.

```
n = 1
loop do
      n = n + 1
      puts "Loop iteration #{n}"
      break if n > 9
end
```

The while loop requires a counter variable but first checks whether a counter variable has exceeded the required iterations (condition is true) before commencing with the next iteration. The counter variable must be incremented within each loop iteration.

```
n = 1
while n < 11
      puts "Loop iteration #{n}"
      n = n + 1
end
```

Ruby allows us to place the while keyword and evaluate the condition at the end of the loop iteration:

```
n = 1
begin
      puts "Loop iteration #{n}"
      n = n + 1
end while n < 11
```

Arrays

An *array* is a fundamental data structure in Ruby that is used to store and process similar data in an automated manner. An array usually contains a set of values that can be accessed via an index. Arrays usually store data of the same type, but arrays in Ruby are able to store different data types. Arrays are easy to implement and very efficient.

There are two ways to create an array in Ruby:

```
numbers = Array.new
```

or

```
numbers = []
```

Arrays are dynamic in Ruby and don't need to be initialized to a predefined size or data type. Elements can also be added or removed as required. Some examples:

```
# An array that stores mixed data types - integers, strings and floats
messages = [1,2,"three",4.0]
# An array storing numeric data
numbers = [1,2,3,4,5,6]
# An array that stores Strings
name = ["Madonna", "Aneesha", "Celine"]
# An array that stores decimal values
x_coordinates = [1.0, 3.4, 35.6, 24]
```

Each element in an array has a unique index. The index is used to reference an element so that it can be updated, retrieved, or removed. The index count in an array starts at 0. Let's create an array that stores Australian cities and then display the first element (referenced as 0).

```
cities = [ "cairns", "brisbane", "sydney", "perth", "adelaide" ]
puts cities[0]
```

The array is a Ruby object and has many useful methods. The `sort` **method rearranges the elements in an array so that they are in alphabetical order:**

```
>> cities.sort
=> ["adelaide", "brisbane", "cairns", "sydney", "perth"]
```

The `reverse` **method inverts the order of the array:**

```
>> cities.reverse
=> ["perth", "sydney", "cairns", "brisbane", "adelaide"]
```

We can determine how many elements are in an array with the `length` **method:**

```
>> cities.length
```

The +, −, and * operators can be used on arrays:

```
# Using + to add an element to an array
cities + ["gold coast"]
# Using - to remove an element
```

```
cities - ["sydney"]
# Using * to repeat the elements is an array
cities * 2
=> ["adelaide", "brisbane", "cairns", "sydney", "perth", "adelaide",
"brisbane", "cairns", "sydney", "perth"]
```

The unshift method is used to add an element at the beginning of an array in index position 0:

```
>>numbers = [1,2,3,4]
>>numbers.unshift(0)
=> [0,1,2,3,4]
```

The push method adds an element to the end of an array:

```
>>numbers.push(5)
=> [1,2,3,4,5]
>> numbers.push(6,7,8)
=> [1,2,3,4,5,6,7,8]
```

We can use two less than signs (<<) to do the equivalent push:

```
an_array << 5
```

Two strings can either be concatenated with the concat method or the + symbol:

```
>>[1,2,3].concat([4,5,6])
>>numbers + [4,5,6]
```

Checking if an array is empty:

```
>> numbers.empty?
```

We can even check if an array contains an element with a certain value:

```
>> numbers.include?(1)
```

It is not uncommon for arrays to contain duplicate values, which can easily be removed with the uniq method:

```
>> [1,2,2,3,4,5,5,6].uniq
=> [1,2,3,4,5,6]
```

The each do code block iterates over all elements and stores the value of the current element in the variable between the pipe characters. This is handy when we need to print all elements.

```
cities.each do |city|
     puts "Australia has a city called " + city
end
```

The `each_with_index` code block does exactly as its name implies. It takes both index and element value variables between the pipe characters. We can now print out an elements index as well.

```
cities.each_with_index do |i,city|
     puts "Australia has a city called #{i}= " + city
end
```

Hashes

A *hash* is another popular data structure in Ruby. A hash is very similar to an array except a hash does not store elements by index. Each element in a hash must have a unique key. The key is used to reference the elements for retrieval, modification, or removal.

This is the syntax for creating a `post_codes` hash that associates a postal code (hash value) with a city name (hash key).

```
post_codes =
{
     "Brisbane" => 4000,
     "Mt Gravatt" => 4122,
     "Carindale" => 4152
}
```

We can then use the key to retrieve the post code:

```
puts "Enter a Suburb in Brisbane:"
suburb = gets.chomp
puts "The post code is " + post_codes[suburb].to_s
```

Adding a new key value pair is very simple:

```
post_codes["Kelvin Grove"] = 4065
```

The hash is an object and as such has many useful methods. The `keys` method prints all keys in the hash while the `values` method outputs all the values:

```
>> post_codes.keys
>> post_codes.values
```

We can also determine the number of keys in a hash and find out if a certain key exists:

```
# Check if a post code for Carindale exists in the post_codes hash
>> post_codes.has_key?("Carindale").to_s
# Determine the size of a hash
>> puts post_codes.size.to_s
```

We can also use the each_key and the each_value **code blocks to iterate over either the key or values of a hash. The** each **code block gives us access to both the key and value:**

```
# using each_key
post_codes.each_key do |key|
     puts key
end
# Using each_value
post_codes.each_value do |val|
     puts val
end
# Using the each code block to print both keys and values
post_codes.each do |key,val|
     puts "#{key} - #{val}"
end
```

In the following example a hash is inverted. Inverting a hash turns the keys into the values and the values are in turn made into the keys. We can now enter a post code and retrieve the matching city's name.

```
post_codes.invert.each do |key,val|
     puts "#{key} - #{val}"
end
```

 Note

The Ruby API documentation is a handy reference and is located at: http://www.ruby-doc.org/. Consult the API for a full list of available objects and methods.

Functions

Code placed within a function can be reused or called from multiple places within the same script. A function is not associated with an object and can be called generically—this is what distinguishes a function from a method. The def keyword is used to create a function. The name of the function must be placed after the def keyword. The end keyword is used to close the code block.

A function that prints Hello to the console:

```
def greet_me
     puts "Hello"
end
```

Calling the function multiple times:

```
# Call the greet_me function for the first time
greet_me
# Call the greet_me function for the second time
greet_me
```

Functions can also take parameters or arguments that can be used within the code block. This function takes an argument called name so that a personalized greeting can be displayed:

```
def greet(name)
     puts "Hello #{name}"
end
```

Ruby provides two ways to call a function and pass parameters to it:

```
# Call the greet function for the first time and pass name
greet("Daniel")
# Call the greet function without parentheses
greet "Sandy"
```

Reusing Code

Once a function is added to a Ruby file, it can't be called from another Ruby script. If you would like to reuse your functions in multiple scripts, they need to be placed in a file that will serve as a code library. The code library that contains the functions can then be reused. The require keyword is used to specify a file that must be included in the current script.

```
require 'functions.rb'
puts "Please enter the temperature in Celcius:"
puts "The temperature in Fahrenheit is: " + calctemp(gets)
```

Classes and Methods

Ruby is an object-oriented language. Even simple data types are objects in Ruby. Ruby allows you to design your own classes from which object instances can be created. A class encapsulates methods and attributes or properties. A class serves as a blueprint for creating object instances.

Every class must have an `initialize` method, which sets the default attribute values. Within a class object or instance, variables are prefixed with the @ symbol.

We are going to model a simple `Employee` class. Initially the `Employee` class will only have a single attribute, called `first_name`, but additional attributes will be added as the section progresses. All objects created from the `Employee` class will have access to the `first_name` instance variable.

The `Employee` class:

```
class Employee
    def initialize(first_name)
        @first_name = name
    end
end
```

The `Employee` class contains a single method called `initialize`, which sets `@first_name`. Now we can create our first object instance by using the new method and passing it an employee's first name. The new method is known as a constructor.

```
employee1 = Employee.new("Aneesha")
```

The `employee1` object has been created. We can now add a method to access or read the `first_name` attribute that was set with the constructor.

```
class Employee
     def initialize(first_name)
          @first_name = first_name
     end
     def first_name
          @first_name
     end
end
employee1 = Employee.new("Aneesha")
puts employee1.first_name
```

This can further be simplified by using an `attr_reader`. The `first_name` method is replaced by `attr_reader :firstname`.

```
class Employee
     attr_reader :first_name
     def initialize(first_name)
          @first_name = first_name
```

```
        end
end
employee1 = Employee.new("Aneesha")
puts employee1.first_name
```

Next we will set the `first_name` attribute to be a blank default value and create a method to set the attribute:

```
class Employee
      attr_reader :first_name
      def initialize
            @first_name = ""
      end
      def first_name =(first_name)
            @first_name = first_name
      end
end
employee1 = Employee.new
employee1.first_name = "Aneesha"
puts employee1.first_name
```

We can simplify the setting and attribute syntax by using an `attr_writer`. The `attr_writer` is used to specify the instance variable that can be updated instead of using a method.

```
class Employee
      attr_reader :first_name
      attr_writer :first_name
      def initialize
            @name = ""
      end
end
employee1 = Employee.new
employee1.first_name = "Aneesha"
puts employee1.first_name
```

The `attr_accessor` is handy if the instance variables require both read and write access. The `attr_accessor` keyword has helped us to reduce the code required for each instance variable that required read and write access by five lines:

```
class Employee
      attr_accessor :first_name
      def initialize
            @first_name = ""
      end
end
employee1 = Employee.new
employee1.name = "Aneesha"
puts employee1.name
```

We can now complete our `Employee` class by adding `email`, `phone`, and `department` as additional attributes. The example that follows illustrates Ruby's powerful syntax and the ease with which it allows you to create new classes. Object-oriented programming has never been easier.

```
class Employee
      attr_accessor :first_name, :email, :phone, :department
      def initialize
            @first_name = @email = @phone = @department = ""
      end
end
employee1 = Employee.new
employee1.first_name = "Aneesha"
employee1.email = "aneesha.bakharia@gmail.com"
employee1.phone = "2341"
employee1.department = "Marketing"
puts employee1.first_name
puts employee1.email
puts employee1.phone
puts employee1.department
```

Ruby's inbuilt objects have a `to_s` method to print output to a string. This is a standard convention used in Ruby. We are going to extend the `Employee` class to incorporate a `to_s` method that will neatly print an `employee` object's attributes.

```
class Employee
      attr_accessor :first_name, :surname, :email, :phone, :department
      def initialize
            @first_name = @surname =  @email = @phone = @department = ""
```

```
      end
      def full_name
            @first_name + " " + @surname
      end
      def to_s
         "      " + @first_name + "\n" + \
         "      " + @email    + "\n" + \
         "      " + @phone   + ", " + @department
      end
end
employee1 = Employee.new
employee1.first_name = "Aneesha"
employee1.surname = "Bakharia"
employee1.email = "aneesha.bakharia@gmail.com"
employee1.phone = "2341"
employee1.department = "Marketing"
puts employee1.full_name
puts employee1.to_s
```

Handling Exceptions

Sometimes unexpected events occur while a program is executing. A file that is being written to may have been changed to read only; while sending a network request, the network may go down; or dozens of other unexpected events may occur. Without providing code to deal with these errors, Ruby will print an exception message to the console and terminate. This is not user friendly and makes your program look unprofessional.

A `ZeroDivisionError` occurs when an attempt is made to divide a number by 0. This type of exception could easily occur if a user entered a number that was then used as the denominator. We can simulate a `ZeroDivisionError` exception in irb:

```
>>10/0
=> ZeroDivisionError: Divided by Zero
```

The `ZeroDivisionError` exception from the Ruby interpreter:

```
$ ruby dividebyzero.rb
dividebyzero.rb:7:in `/': divided by 0 (ZeroDivisionError) from
dividebyzero.rb:7
```

Ruby provides a simple and effective mechanism to deal with unexpected errors that occur while a program is being interpreted. This mechanism is known as exception handling and relies upon the `rescue` clause. An exception is a special object, an instance of the `Exception` class, e.g. `ZeroDivisionError`. The `rescue` clause is able to detect that an exception has occurred and deal with it in an appropriate manner or terminate the application if necessary.

Using the `rescue` clause is very easy; we simply need to add a `rescue` clause. The code that handles the unexpected behavior in the `rescue` clause is then placed in the `rescue` clause. The following code implements a `rescue` clause:

```
# Rescue an exception
num1 = 10
num2 = 0


begin
        puts num1/num2
rescue
        puts "An exception occurred"
        exit
end
```

We could also explicitly only handle a `ZeroDivisionError`:

```
# Rescue a Divide by Zero exception
num1 = 10
num2 = 0
begin
        puts num1/num2
rescue ZeroDivisionError
        puts "An divide by zero exception occurred."
        exit
end
```

Multiple `rescue` clauses are used to deal with different exceptions that may occur. Table 2.6 contains a list and descriptions of common exceptions.

```
begin
        puts num1/num2
rescue ZeroDivisionError
        puts "A divide by zero exception occurred."
        exit
```

```
rescue IOError
      puts "An IO Error has occurred."
      exit
rescue
      puts "An exception has occurred."
      exit
end
```

Table 2.6   Common Exceptions

Exception	Description
RuntimeError	The RuntimeError is the default exception.
NoMethodError	The method of function being called does not exist.
NameError	The method or variable is not available.
IOError	An error has occurred while reading or writing to an output stream.
TypeError	A method is passed an argument of incorrect type
ArgumentError	An incorrect number of parameters are passed to a method or function.

Embedded Ruby

Embedded Ruby (known as ERb), written by Seki Masatoshi, allows Ruby to be embedded with textual documents and used as a template engine. Although it is possible to use `puts` to dynamically generate text files and HTML markup, doing so would not be very practical. In the example that follows, `puts` is used to render a web page to display the rainfall averages stored in a hash data structure. The HTML markup, however, is not easy to write or update as it is enclosed in quotation marks. Ruby is also used to output a lot of static content. An easier approach would be to keep the static textual content or markup as is and have special delimiters to insert the Ruby code that needs to be interpreted. This is the exact purpose of ERb.

```
page_title = "Rainfall Averages"
puts "<html>"
puts "<head>"
puts "<title>#{page_title}</title>"
puts "</head>"
puts "<body>"
rainfall =
    {
            "Jan - Mar" => "10mm",
```

```
            "Apr - Jun" => "20mm",
            "Jul - Sep" => "2mm",
            "Oct - Dec" => "6mm",
    }
puts "<h2>#{page_title}</h2>"
puts "<table border='1'>"
puts "<tr><td>Quarter</td><td>Rainfall</td></tr>"
rainfall.each do |key, value|
        puts "<tr><td>#{key}</td><td>#{value}</td></tr>"
end

puts "</table>"
puts "<hr>"
puts "Last updated: #{Time.now}"
puts "</body>"
puts "</html>"
```

ERb loads a file, outputs the text, and processes the Ruby code found within the <% and %> delimiters. The <%= and %> delimiters output an expression or variable. The following example generates a web page with a random message:

```
<% page_title = "Random Message" %>
<html>
<head>
<title><%=page_title%></title>
</head>
<body>
<h2><%=page_title%></h2>
<%
# Generate a random number between 1 and 3
rand_no = rand(3)
if rand_no == 0
%>
        Random Message 1 <br>
<%
elsif rand_no == 1
%>
        Random Message 2 <br>
```

```
<%
else
%>
        Random Message 3 <br>
<%
end
%>
<hr>
Last updated: <%=Time.now%>
</body>
</html>
```

ERb is run from the `erb` **command line utility:**

```
$ erb erbdemo.rb
```

The `erbdemo.rb` **file produces the following output:**

```
<html>
<head>
<title>Random Message</title>
</head>
<body>
<h2>Random Message</h2>

        Random Message 1 <br>

<hr>
Last updated: Thur Sep 21 12:12:04 E. Australian Standard Time 2006
</body>
</html>
```

We can now use ERb to simplify the rainfall averages example. I am sure you will agree that the HTML code is now easier to maintain and comprehend.

```
<% page_title = "Rainfall Averages" %>
<html>
<head>
        <title><%=page_title%></title>
</head>
```

```
<body>
<%
rainfall =
            {
            "Jan - Mar" => "10mm",
            "Apr - Jun" => "20mm",
            "Jul - Sep" => "2mm",
            "Oct - Dec" => "6mm"
            }
%>
<h2><%=page_title%></h2>
<table border="1">
<tr><td>Quarter</td><td>Rainfall</td></tr>
<%
rainfall.each do |key, value|
%>
    <tr><td><%=key%></td><td><%=value%></td></tr>
<%
end
%>
</table>
<hr>
Last updated: <%=Time.now%>
</body>
</html>
```

Using Webrick to Serve ERb Templates

ERb is a great command line utility for processing Ruby embedded within a text document. ERb, however, prints the output to the console. This might not be ideal as HTML is best viewed from within a popular web browser such as Firefox. The solution would be to serve the ERb templates via a lightweight http server such as Webrick. We first encountered Webrick in Chapter 1, "Getting Started," when it was used to serve your first Ruby on Rails application.

The following script saved with a `.rhtml` extension does some amazingly complex things in a few lines of code. A web server is set to run from port 3000, a mime type is created for `.rhtml` files, and then the directory which stores the .rhtml files is mounted. Once this script is run (`startwebrick.rb`), all the `.rhtml` files places in the mounted directory will be available for viewing from a web browser.

```
# Run a Webrick http server to serve Embedded Ruby files on port 3000
require 'webrick'
include WEBrick
# Create a new http server on port 3000
wb_server = HTTPServer.new(:Port => 3000)
# Associate the text/html mime type with .rhtml files
HTTPUtils::DefaultMimeTypes.store('rhtml', 'text/html')
# Not needed on Unix/Linux/ -  CGIHandler is only required on Windows.
wb_server.config.store( :CGIInterpreter, "#{HTTPServlet::CGIHandler::Ruby}")
# Mount the folder that contains the .rhtml files to be served
wb_server.mount('/', HTTPServlet::FileHandler, '\
RubyOnRailsPower\Chapter2\code\webrick\www')
# Shut down if an error is trapped
['TERM', 'INT'].each do |signal|
trap(signal){ wb_server.shutdown }
end
# Start the server
wb_server.start
```

Figure 2.2 shows the rainfall averages web page served by Webrick. The web browser sends a request to Webrick. Webrick receives the request and recognizes that a `.rhtml` file is required. Webrick retrieves the file, uses ERb to interpret the embedded Ruby code, and then sends the resulting HTML file back to the web browser. The web browser renders the HTML markup and the page is displayed.

Figure 2.2
Delivering dynamic ERb templates with Webrick.

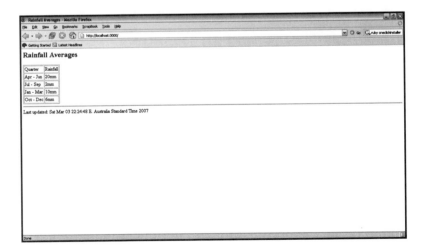

Conclusion

A lot of Ruby language syntax and concepts were covered in this chapter. Ruby is simple, powerful, and elegant and allows you to do more with less code. You have learned to use the Interactive Ruby shell (irb), run your Ruby code with the Ruby interpreter, write simple programs to perform mathematical calculations and process text, model your own objects, and finally serve dynamic web pages with embedded Ruby. These concepts will be extended and used throughout the rest of this book. The Rails framework is, after all, powered by the Ruby language. In the next chapter we will take a look at Ruby conventions used in the Rails framework.

Prototyping Database-Driven Applications with Rails

In Chapter 1, "Getting Started," the MVC architecture was introduced. We also explored the view and controller components as implemented by Rails. Our focus now turns to Active Record, the Rails component responsible for building models that interact with a database. This is designed to be a very practical chapter because Active Record is introduced in the context of prototyping a contact list, FAQ manager, and weblog. Although it may seem overly ambitious to create three database-driven applications in a single chapter, rest assured that this is all made possible by the powerful built-in functionality that Rails brings to web development.

In this chapter you'll learn how to:

* Design a MySQL database
* Use Active Record to scaffold a model to a database table
* Perform simple input validation
* Customize the code generated by a scaffold
* Create a contact list
* Create an FAQ manager
* Create a weblog

Creating a Contact List

Our journey begins with the need for a simple tool to manage the contact details of all your friends. You would like to store the data in a database and publish the list of contact details to a password-protected location on your web site. It would also be nice to be able to maintain the list via a web interface. A simple Create, Retrieve, Update, and Delete (CRUD) interface is all that is required.

> **Note**
>
> A MySQL database server is required. If you have not installed MySQL, please refer to Chapter 1.

Let's create a new Rails application called `contactlist`:

`$ rails contactlist` ✓

The `rails` **command will create a directory called** `contactlist` **with the skeleton code and structure that a Rails application requires.**

The `config/database.yml` **file stores the details required to access a database. The** `.yml` **extension belongs to a YAML file. YAML is a human-readable data format and stands for YAML Ain't Markup Language. This is great; we don't need to enter our database access details into an overly complex XML format. Open the** `config/database.yml` **file:**

```
development:
  adapter: mysql
  database: contactlist_development
  username: root
  password: your_password
  host: localhost
test:
  adapter: mysql
  database: contactlist_test
  username: root
  password: your_password
  host: localhost
production:
  adapter: mysql
  database: contactlist_production
  username: root
  password: your_password
  host: localhost
```

The `config/database.yml` **file stores details for a development, test, and production database. These databases will be used in the different environments that are required during a project's development and maintenance lifecycle. The adapter, database, username, password, and host details need to be entered for each environment. As we are using a MySQL database, the adapter is set to MySQL. The database name is simply the name of the Rails project followed by an underscore and the environment (development, test, or production); another convention to make** your life easier. If you are running the MySQL server on the same machine as the web server, then the host must be set to `localhost`, which is also the default. Enter the password to access your database server and save the `database.yml` file.

> ❄ **Tip**
>
> A space is required after the colon before you enter any of the settings. As an example, `password: your_password` is correct while `password:your_password` would cause a database access error. I have made this error many times.

We now need to create a database called `contactlist_development`—use your MySQL visual editor to create the database. The database requires a single table called contacts. The contacts table requires the following fields:

❄	`id`	This is a unique, auto-incrementing primary key.
❄	`firstname`	The `firstname` field stores a name or nickname.
❄	`lastname`	The `lastname` field stores the surname.
❄	`email`	The `email` field stores the email address.
❄	`mobile`	The `mobile` field stores the mobile phone number.
❄	`note`	The `note` field stores the arbitrary text/information.

Some table and field naming conventions to remember:

- ❄ Table names are plural. Tables contain multiple rows or items so this makes sense.
- ❄ Auto-incrementing primary key fields must be called `id`.

We can use `script/generate` to create a model. We will create a model called contact (the model name is the singular equivalent of the table name). We have a table called contacts, so the model is called contact.

```
$ ruby script/generate model contact
```

The following files are created:

```
exists   app/models/
exists   test/unit/
exists   test/fixtures/
create   app/models/contact.rb
create   test/unit/contact_test.rb
create   test/fixtures/contacts.yml
```

```
create   db/migrate
create   db/migrate/001_create_contacts.rb
```

Open the `db/migrate/001_create_contacts.rb` file. This file is a migration: we use it to create the contacts table. We could use an SQL script to create the table, but writing a migration is simpler, done in Ruby, and database neutral. We will learn all about migrations in Chapter 4, "Active Record." We don't need to specify the `id` field; the migration is smart enough to automatically create one for us. Create the contacts table and all the required fields:

```ruby
class CreateContacts < ActiveRecord::Migration
    def self.up
        create_table :contacts do |t|
            t.column :firstname, :string
            t.column :surname, :string
            t.column :email, :string
            t.column :mobile, :string
            t.column :note, :text
        end
    end
    def self.down
        drop_table :contacts
    end
end
```

Run the migration:

```
$ rake db:migrate
```

The following has been output to the console, and the contacts table is created. You can verify that the table exists with a visual editor for MySQL:

```
(in C:/rails/contactlist)
== CreateContacts: migrating =================================================
-- create_table(:contacts)
   -> 0.0940s
== CreateContacts: migrated (0.0940s) ========================================
```

Open the `app/models/contact.rb` file. A class called `Contact` has been created and inherits from `ActiveRecord::Base`:

```ruby
class Contact < ActiveRecord::Base
end
```

Create a controller called `contact`:

```
$ ruby script/generate controller contact
```
name ✓

The following files are created:

```
exists   app/controllers/
exists   app/helpers/
create   app/views/contact
exists   test/functional/
create   app/controllers/contact_controller.rb
create   test/functional/contact_controller_test.rb
create   app/helpers/contact_helper.rb
```

We need to link the `contact` controller to the `contact` model. The simplest way to do this is with a scaffold. With one line of code, we can enable a CRUD interface for the Contact List application. Open the `app/controllers/contact_controller.rb` file and enter **scaffold :contact.**

```
class ContactController < ApplicationController
     scaffold :contact
end
```

Start the built-in Webrick web server by typing the following at the command prompt:

```
$ ruby script/server
```

Open the http://localhost:3000/contact URL in a web browser. The Contact List application will be displayed (see Figure 3.1). The Listing contacts heading, a table with column heading for each field stored in the contacts table, and a link called New contact, which maps to the `/contact/new` action, is displayed.

We don't have any details in the `contactlist_development` database, so let's add some entries by clicking on the New contact link. The New contact form is displayed in Figure 3.2. The form contains input fields for you to enter the `firstname`, `lastname`, `email`, `mobile`, and `note` fields. Active Record was even smart enough to know that the `note` field required a multi-line text input box.

At this point you realize that a `homephone` field will be valuable as some of your friends either don't have a mobile phone or turn it off at night. So before you use the New contact form, you add this field to the contacts table (see Figure 3.3).

ut

require 'rake' —old rakefile

Figure 3.1
Displaying the Contact List
application.

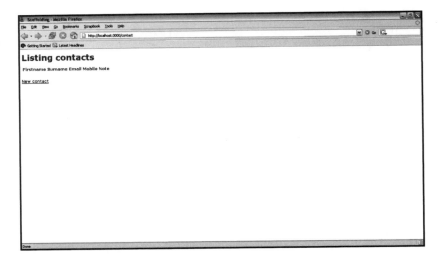

Figure 3.2
The New contact form.

Refresh the New contact form (http://localhost:3000/contact/new). Without a server restart, Active Record and the scaffolding has picked up the table changes. The homephone field is added to the form (see Figure 3.4). Add a contact and click on the Create button.

The http://localhost:3000/contact/list URL is displayed (see Figure 3.5). At the top of the page a confirmation message is present: "Contact was successfully created". The table now displays the contact details we have just entered. We also have links to show, edit, and delete the record. This is great because it provides a simple CRUD maintenance interface for our application. Give the interface a good test by creating, editing, and deleting records.

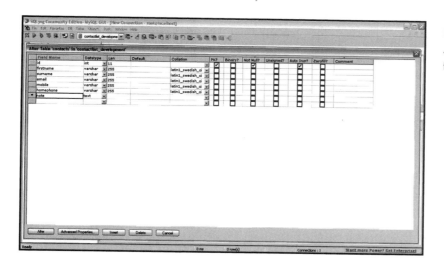

Figure 3.3
Adding the homephone
field to the contacts table.

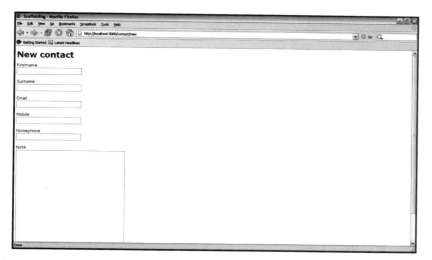

Figure 3.4
The homephone field is
added to the New contact
form.

There is no input field validation and you are able to add blank records to the contact list. This can easily be fixed. The enforcement of required fields is a business rule and should therefore be placed in the model (app/models/contact.rb). Here is the syntax to make the firstname field mandatory with validates_presence_of:

```
class Contact < ActiveRecord::Base
     validates_presence_of :firstname
end
```

Figure 3.5
Display CRUD interface.

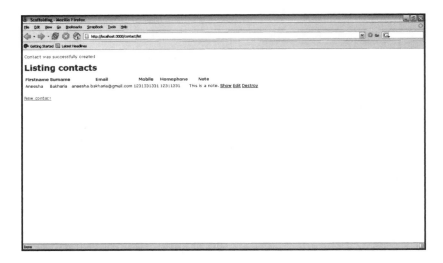

We could also ensure that multiple fields are validated by separating variable names with a comma:

```
class Contact < ActiveRecord::Base
     validates_presence_of :firstname, :surname, :email
end
```

> ※ **Note**
>
> Rails includes a comprehensive list of validation routines such as `validates_size_of`, `validates_numericality_of`, and `validates_format_of`. These will be covered Chapter 4, "Active Record."

When we try to add a contact with the `firstname` field blank we now get a validation error message. Rails even highlights the field that violates the validation rules. This is shown in Figure 3.6. It is amazing what we can achieve by adding a single line to our model.

Passing the contact model to the `scaffold` method in the `ContactController` was all we needed to create a CRUD for the contacts table. We have been able to deliver all of the required features in record time. The application is fully functioning, but we would like to make some cosmetic changes such as change the title to Contact List, add a border to the table that displays the contacts, and change "destroy" to "delete" (see Figure 3.7). The `scaffold` command uses internal Rails code to dynamically render the interface each time the application is called. We can, however, generate our own version of the `scaffold` controller and view files:

```
$ ruby script/generate scaffold contact contact
```

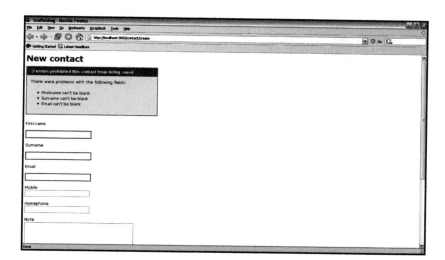

Figure 3.6
Oops! I have not filled out a mandatory field.

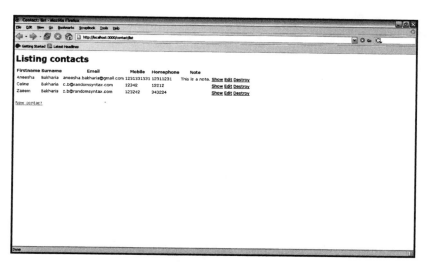

Figure 3.7
The Contact List application with a few contacts added.

The following is output to the console:

```
exists    app/controllers/
exists    app/helpers/
exists    app/views/contact
exists    test/functional/
dependency  model
```

```
exists      app/models/
exists      test/unit/
exists      test/fixtures/
identical      app/models/contact.rb
identical      test/unit/contact_test.rb
identical      test/fixtures/contacts.yml
create  app/views/contact/_form.rhtml
create  app/views/contact/list.rhtml
create  app/views/contact/show.rhtml
create  app/views/contact/new.rhtml
create  app/views/contact/edit.rhtml
overwrite app/controllers/contact_controller.rb? [Ynaq] Y
force  app/controllers/contact_controller.rb
overwrite test/functional/contact_controller_test.rb? [Ynaq] Y
force  test/functional/contact_controller_test.rb
identical  app/helpers/contact_helper.rb
create  app/views/layouts/contact.rhtml
create  public/stylesheets/scaffold.css
```

As you can see, `script/generate` is very smart about what it keeps identical, what it creates, and what needs to be overwritten. While running the `scaffold` command, we were asked whether the `app/controllers/contact_controller.rb` file could be overwritten. We replied Yes by typing Y at the command line. The `app/models/contact.rb` file has not been changed. Let's take a peek at the updated `app/controllers/contact_controller.rb` file:

```ruby
class ContactController < ApplicationController
  def index
    list
    render :action => 'list'
  end
  # GETs should be safe (see http://www.w3.org/2001/tag/doc/whenToUseGet.html)
  verify :method => :post, :only => [ :destroy, :create, :update ],
         :redirect_to => { :action => :list }
  def list
    @contact_pages, @contacts = paginate :contacts, :per_page => 10
  end
  def show
    @contact = Contact.find(params[:id])
```

```
    end
 def new
     @contact = Contact.new
    end
   def create
     @contact = Contact.new(params[:contact])
     if @contact.save
       flash[:notice] = 'Contact was successfully created.'
       redirect_to :action => 'list'
     else
       render :action => 'new'
     end
   end
 def edit
     @contact = Contact.find(params[:id])
   end
   def update
     @contact = Contact.find(params[:id])
     if @contact.update_attributes(params[:contact])
       flash[:notice] = 'Contact was successfully updated.'
       redirect_to :action => 'show', :id => @contact
     else
       render :action => 'edit'
     end
   end
   def destroy
     Contact.find(params[:id]).destroy
     redirect_to :action => 'list'
   end
end
```

The Contact **controller contains the** index, list, show, new, create, edit, update, **and** destroy **actions. Each action is a method—the** def **keyword is used to define methods. These actions are all required in the contact list CRUD. The** index **action calls the** list **action, which in turn, renders the** app/views/contact/list.rhtml **template. The** app/views/contact/list.rhtml **template is where we would like to make our alterations. The amended code, with a new heading, a border added to the table, and the** "destroy" **link changed to** "delete", **appears (see Figure 3.8):**

Figure 3.8
The Contact List application with a few amendments.

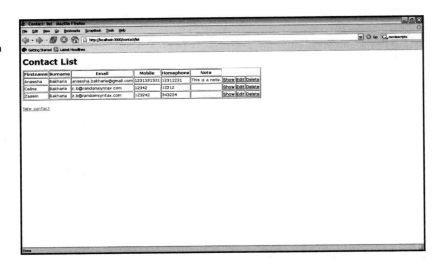

```
<h1>Contact List</h1>
<table>
  <tr>
  <% for column in Contact.content_columns %>
    <th><%= column.human_name %></th>
  <% end %>
  </tr>

<% for contact in @contacts %>
  <tr>
  <% for column in Contact.content_columns %>
    <td><%=h contact.send(column.name) %></td>
  <% end %>
    <td><%= link_to 'Show', :action => 'show', :id => contact %></td>
    <td><%= link_to 'Edit', :action => 'edit', :id => contact %></td>
    <td><%= link_to 'Delete', { :action => 'destroy', :id => contact },
            :confirm => 'Are you sure?', :post => true %></td>
  </tr>
<% end %>
</table>
<%= link_to 'Previous page', { :page => @contact_pages.current.previous } if
    @contact_pages.current.previous %>
```

```
<%= link_to 'Next page', { :page => @contact_pages.current.next } if
    @contact_pages.current.next %>
<br />
<%= link_to 'New contact', :action => 'new' %>
```

The table column names are dynamically generated—this is why we can add new fields to the database table and refresh the page for our changes to take effect. If more than 10 records are available, the result set will be paginated with Next and Previous links. You will notice that there are no opening and closing <html> tags. This is because the page layout has been abstracted. The `app/views/layouts/contact.rhtml` is used by all views rendered by the `Contact` controller:

```
<html>
<head>
  <title>Contact: <%= controller.action_name %></title>
  <%= stylesheet_link_tag 'scaffold' %>
</head>
<body>
<p style="color: green"><%= flash[:notice] %></p>
<%= yield  %>
</body>
</html>
```

Note

The `yield` variable contains the rendered content of the requested action. The `<%=` and `%>` delimiters are used to render this variable within the page layout.

The `list.rhtml`, `show.rhtml`, `new.rhtml`, `edit.rhtml`, and `_form.rhtml` templates contain the forms used in the CRUD and are stored in the `app/views/contact/`. Please explore the code in these files on your own.

Creating an FAQ Manager

We now turn our attention to a slightly more complex application: a Frequently Asked Questions (FAQ) Manager. The FAQ Manager will allow help desk support staff to maintain a categorized list of answers to commonly asked questions. The inclusion of categories means that our database will need two related tables.

After an initial scoping meeting with your client, you determine that the following functionality is required:

* A CRUD interface to maintain the questions and answers.
* Each question and answer must be associated with a category.
* A CRUD interface to maintain the categories.
* Wiki markup formatting support within the answers field.

The converting of wiki markup to HTML adds a nice touch to the FAQ Manager, but you have no idea how to make this happen and meet the project deadlines. A routine web search, however, reveals that Rails includes a helper method called Textilize. Table 3.1 shows a sampling of the markup support provided by Textilize. Textilize uses RedCloth, a library for Ruby. We will need to install RedCloth before we can use the Textilze() helper method within a view:

```
$ gem install RedCloth
```

Table 3.1 Formatting with RedCloth

Textile Markup	Rendered HTML
italic	*italic*
bold	**bold**
*italic and bold*	***italic and bold***
"A link":http://rubyonrails.com	A link

Create a database called faqmanager_development. The database requires two tables: faqs and categories. The faqs table requires id, question, answer, and category_id fields. The category_id field will relate an FAQ to a category. Related fields are named after the singular version of the table name and suffixed with _id. This is a Rails convention. The categories table requires an id and name field. Create a new Rails application called faqmanager:

```
$ rails faqmanager
```

The skeleton structure will be created. Don't forget to open the config/database.yml file and update the database settings.

Start the Webrick server:

```
$ ruby script/server
```

Generate the faq model:

```
$ ruby script/generate model faq
```

The following is output to the console:

```
exists   app/models/
exists   test/unit/
exists   test/fixtures/
create   app/models/faq.rb
create   test/unit/faq_test.rb
create   test/fixtures/faqs.yml
create   db/migrate
create   db/migrate/001_create_faqs.rb
```

Edit the db/migrate/001_create_faqs.rb **migration. We need to create a table with** question, answer, **and** category_id **fields:**

```ruby
class CreateFaqs < ActiveRecord::Migration
    def self.up
        create_table :faqs do |t|
            t.column :question, :string
            t.column :answer, :text
            t.column :category_id, :integer
        end
    end
    def self.down
        drop_table :faqs
    end
end
```

Generate the category **model:**

```
$ ruby script/generate model category
```

The following is output to the console:

```
exists   app/models/
exists   test/unit/
exists   test/fixtures/
create   app/models/category.rb
create   test/unit/category_test.rb
create   test/fixtures/categories.yml
exists   db/migrate
create   db/migrate/002_create_categories.rb
```

Edit the db/migrate/002_create_categories.rb **migration. We need to create a table with a** name **field:**

```
class CreateCategories < ActiveRecord::Migration
    def self.up
        create_table :categories do |t|
                t.column :name, :string
        end
    end
    def self.down
        drop_table :categories
    end
end
```

Run the migrations:

```
$ rake db:migrate
```

The following has been output to the console and the contacts table is created. You can verify that the table exists with a visual editor for MySQL:

```
(in C:/rails/faqmanager)
== CreateFaqs: migrating ===================================================
-- create_table(:faqs)
   -> 0.0930s
== CreateFaqs: migrated (0.0930s) ==========================================

== CreateCategories: migrating =============================================
-- create_table(:categories)
   -> 0.1090s
== CreateCategories: migrated (0.1090s) ====================================
```

In the faq **model, we ensure that the** question **field is mandatory. An** faq **belongs to a category. We can specify this relationship in the** app/models/faq.rb **file (**Faq **class):**

```
class Faq < ActiveRecord::Base
    belongs_to :category
    validates_presence_of :question
end
```

Within the category model, the name **field is required. A category has many faqs. We need to define a** has_many **relationship in the** app/models/category.rb **file (**Category **class).**

```
class Category < ActiveRecord::Base
     has_many :faqs
     validates_presence_of :name
end
```

We can now create controllers called faq and category:

```
$ ruby script/generate controller faq
$ ruby script/generate controller category
```

The interface for managing the FAQs is created by scaffolding for the faq model to the faq controller. You can test the interface from http://localhost:3000/faq (see Figure 3.9):

```
$ ruby script/generate scaffold faq faq
```

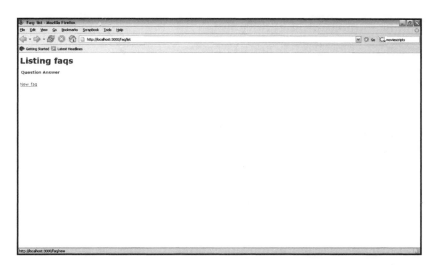

Figure 3.9
The FAQ manager.

We generate a scaffold to the maintain categories as well. You can view the Categories manager at http://localhost:3000/category (see Figure 3.10):

```
$ ruby script/generate scaffold category category
```

We have working add and edit forms, but they don't allow a user to specify a category for an FAQ. The add form must contain a drop-down box where a user can select an appropriate category. The edit form should display the selected option within the drop-down list. We need to retrieve a list of all categories and make this collection available to the edit and new views. Open the app/controllers/faq.rb file and add an @categories instance variable to the edit and new actions. The @categories instance variable must be set to Category.find_all.

Figure 3.10
Maintaining categories.

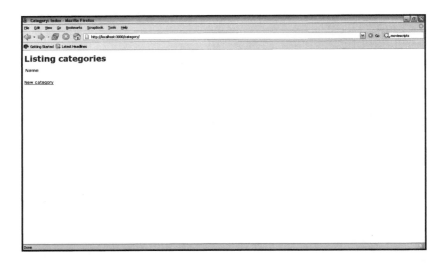

The `find_all` method simply returns all records within the `Category` model (i.e. categories table). Here are the amended methods:

```
def edit
      @faq = Faq.find(params[:id])
      @categories = Category.find_all
end
def new
      @faq = Faq.new
      @categories = Category.find_all
end
```

Both the new and edit views use a partial to render the form elements. This makes our life easy as we only need to add code to one file and have the categories drop-down list appear on both the new and edit forms. We use an `each do` loop to iterate over the categories collection and print `<option>` tags for each category. We also use an `if` statement to determine whether an option should be selected within the drop-down list when the edit form is loaded. The New faq form with a category drop-down list is displayed in Figure 3.11. Here is the source code listing for the `app/views/faq/_form.rhtml` partial.

```
<%= error_messages_for 'faq' %>
<!--[form:faq]-->
<p><label for="faq_question">Question</label><br/>
<%= text_field 'faq', 'question'  %></p>
<p><label for="faq_answer">Answer</label><br/>
```

```
<%= text_area 'faq', 'answer'  %></p>
<p><label for="faq_category">Category</label><br/>
  <select name="faq[category_id]">
    <% @categories.each do |category| %>
        <option value="<%= category.id %>"
          <%= ' selected' if category.id == @faq.category_id %>>
          <%= category.name %>
        </option>
    <% end %>
  </select>
</p>
<!--[eoform:faq]-->
```

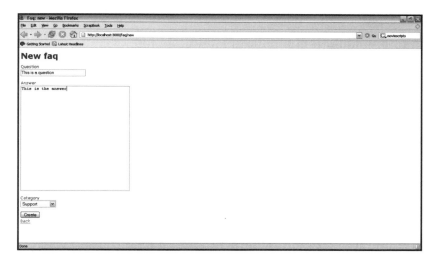

Figure 3.11
Specifying a category within the New faq form.

Finally, we need to spice up the FAQ listing. We want to display the FAQs sequentially, one below the other, and not in a table, so we open the `app/views/faq/list.rhtml` template and remove the table and the loop that renders the table column names. We display the question, answer, and category, each on a new line. The `Textilize()` helper method is used to parse the `answer` field and render textile markup as HTML. The category name is referenced using dot notation: `faq.category.name`. The Show, Edit, and Destroy links are positioned after the category name. We also include a link to the `Category` controller so that users can easily access the interface to maintain categories. Figure 3.12 displays the completed application.

The final code listing for the `app/views/faq/list.rhtml`:

```
<h1>FAQ Manager</h1>
<% for faq in @faqs %>
  <strong><%=faq.question %></strong><br>
  <%= textilize(faq.answer) %><br>
  Category: <%=faq.category.name %>
  (<%= link_to 'Show', :action => 'show', :id => faq.id %> |
  <%= link_to 'Edit', :action => 'edit', :id => faq.id %> |
  <%= link_to 'Destroy', { :action => 'destroy', :id => faq.id }, :confirm =>
'Are you sure?', :post => true %>)
  <hr>
<% end %>
<%= link_to 'Previous page', { :page => @faq_pages.current.previous } if
@faq_pages.current.previous %>
<%= link_to 'Next page', { :page => @faq_pages.current.next } if
@faq_pages.current.next %>
<br />
<%= link_to 'New faq', :action => 'new' %> |
<%= link_to 'Manage Categories', :action => 'list', :controller => 'category' %>
```

Figure 3.12
The FAQ manager in action.

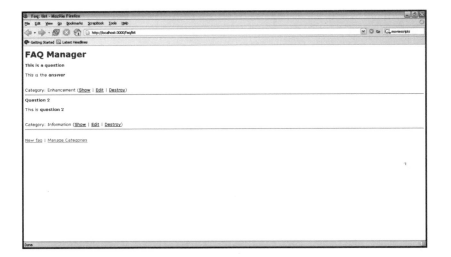

Creating a Weblog

I am sure that you either have a weblog or you subscribe to weblogs. A weblog is essentially a diary. You make entries, which are date stamped, and web site visitors can add comments. In this section, you are going to build a simple but fully functional weblog that is powered by Ruby on Rails. Here are the functional requirements:

- ❋ Display a list of entries in reverse chronological order.
- ❋ Add new posts with a form.
- ❋ Format posts with Textile markup.
- ❋ Allow visitors to add comments.

First create a new Rails application called weblog:

```
$ rails weblog
```

Start the Webrick web server:

```
$ ruby script/server
```

Open the `config/database.yml` **file and enter the password to access your local database server. Save the** `database.yml` **file.**

Create a database called `weblog_development`. **The** `weblog_development` **database requires two tables: posts and comments. The** `posts` **table will store each entry made to the weblog. The** `posts` **table has** `id`, `title`, `body`, **and** `created_at` **fields. The** `created_at` **field is a** `datetime` **data type in MySQL. The** `comments` **table requires** `id`, `body`, **and** `post_id` **fields. The** `post_id` **field relates the** `comments` **table to the** `posts` **table. A post can contain many comments.**

Create a model called `post`:

```
$ ruby script/generate model post
```

The following is output to the console:

```
exists   app/models/
exists   test/unit/
exists   test/fixtures/
create   app/models/post.rb
create   test/unit/post_test.rb
create   test/fixtures/posts.yml
create   db/migrate
create   db/migrate/001_create_posts.rb
```

Edit the `db/migrate/001_create_posts.rb` **migration. We need to create a table with** `question`, `answer`, **and** `category_id` **fields:**

```
class CreatePosts < ActiveRecord::Migration
    def self.up
        create_table :posts do |t|
            t.column :title, :string
            t.column :body, :text
            t.column :created_at, :datetime
        end
    end
    def self.down
        drop_table :posts
    end
end
```

Run the migration to create the `posts` **table:**

```
$ rake db:migrate
```

The following is output to the console:

```
(in C:/rails/weblog)
== CreatePosts: migrating =====================================================
-- create_table(:posts)
   -> 0.0930s
== CreatePosts: migrated (0.0930s) ============================================
```

Create a controller called `blog`:

```
$ ruby script/generate controller blog
```

The `title` **field of a post is mandatory, so we add this rule to the** `app/models/post.rb` **file:**

```
class Post < ActiveRecord::Base
    validates_presence_of :title
end
```

We are anxious to play with the weblog, so we scaffold the blog controller to the post model. This is achieved by passing `:post` **to the** `scaffold()` **method in the** `app/controllers/blog.rb`:

```
class BlogController < ApplicationController
    scaffold :post
end
```

Point your web browser to http://localhost:3000/blog. Figure 3.13 shows the weblog after two entries have been made. The entries are displayed in a table. This is not suitable because weblog entries are usually displayed one below the other. Also, the body field may be lengthy depending upon the nature of the post, so it makes sense for each post to be displayed separately.

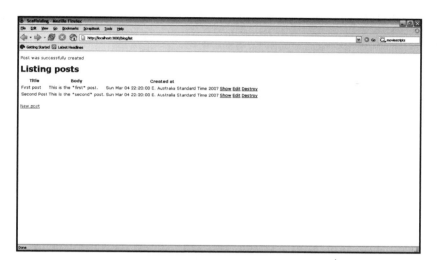

Figure 3.13
Weblog entries displayed in a table.

It is obvious that we need to customize the `view/blog/list.rhtml` file. We need to get Rails to generate the source code by typing the following at the command prompt:

```
$ ruby script/generate scaffold post blog
```

We remove the table, display each weblog entry individually, and use the `Textilize()` helper method to format the body:

```
<h1>My Weblog</h1>
<p><%= link_to 'New post', :action => 'new' %></p>
<% for post in @posts %>
<div>
<h2><%= link_to post.title, :action => 'show', :id => post %></h2>
<p><%=textilize(post.body) %></p>
<p><%=post.created_at.to_s() %>
(<%= link_to 'Edit', :action => 'edit', :id => post %> | <%= link_to 'Destroy',
{ :action => 'destroy', :id => post }, :confirm => 'Are you sure?',
:post => true %>)
</p>
</div>
```

```
<% end %>
</table>
<%= link_to 'Previous page', { :page => @post_pages.current.previous } if
@post_pages.current.previous %>
<%= link_to 'Next page', { :page => @post_pages.current.next } if
@post_pages.current.next %>
```

Figure 3.14
Displaying weblog entries in a list.

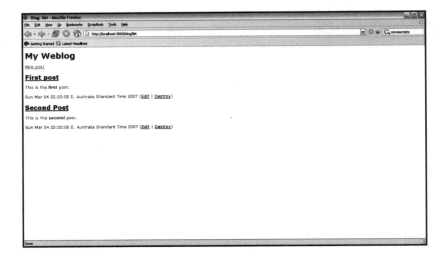

Figure 3.14 shows the new and improved weblog display. The entries, however, are displayed in order of posting (first to last). We would like to display the post in reverse chronological order (see Figure 3.15). We can do this by looping over post.reverse:

```
<h1>My Weblog</h1>
<p><%= link_to 'New post', :action => 'new' %></p>
<% for post in @posts.reverse %>
<div>
<h2><%= link_to post.title, :action => 'show', :id => post %></h2>
<p><%=textilize(post.body) %></p>
<p><%=post.created_at.to_s() %>
(<%= link_to 'Edit', :action => 'edit', :id => post %> | <%= link_to 'Destroy',
{ :action => 'destroy', :id => post }, :confirm => 'Are you sure?',
:post => true %>)
</p>
</div>
```

```
<% end %>
</table>
<%= link_to 'Previous page', { :page => @post_pages.current.previous } if
@post_pages.current.previous %>
<%= link_to 'Next page', { :page => @post_pages.current.next } if
@post_pages.current.next %>
```

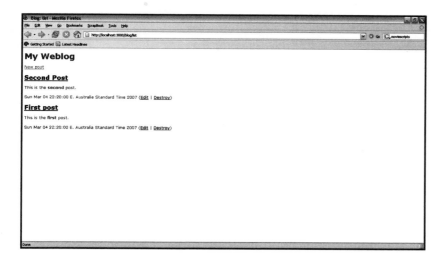

Figure 3.15
Displaying recent weblog
entries first.

We have formatted the display of a weblog post on the `list.rhtml` template. We would like this formatting to be used on the `show.rhtml` template as well. Rather than copying the code to the `show.rhtml` template, we create a partial that both `list.rhtml` and `show.rhtml` can reference. We are putting the Don't Repeat Yourself (DRY) principle into action. The name of a partial always begins with an underscore. We call our partial `_post.rhtml`. Here is the code:

```
<div>
<h2><%= link_to post.title, :action => 'show', :id => post %></h2>
<p><%=textilize(post.body) %></p>
<p><%=post.created_at.to_s() %>
(<%= link_to 'Edit', :action => 'edit', :id => post %> | <%= link_to 'Destroy',
{ :action => 'destroy', :id => post }, :confirm => 'Are you sure?',
:post => true %>)
</p>
</div>
```

We can now use the `render_partial` **helper in the** `list.rhtml` **template. We don't need to place this call within a loop because the** `render_partial` **helper is able to take a collection:**

```
<h1>My Weblog</h1>
<p><%= link_to 'New post', :action => 'new' %></p>
<%= render :partial => "post", :collection => @posts.reverse %>
<%= link_to 'Previous page', { :page => @post_pages.current.previous } if
@post_pages.current.previous %>
<%= link_to 'Next page', { :page => @post_pages.current.next } if
@post_pages.current.next %>
<br />
```

The `show.rhtml` **file is also simplified:**

```
<%= render :partial => "post", :object => @post  %>
<%= link_to 'Edit', :action => 'edit', :id => @post %> |
<%= link_to 'Back', :action => 'list' %>
```

We are able to post and display weblog entries, but we still need to include a commenting system. Let's generate a `comments` **model:**

```
$ ruby script/generate model comment
```

The following is output to the console:

```
      exists   app/models/
      exists   test/unit/
      exists   test/fixtures/
      create   app/models/comment.rb
      create   test/unit/comment_test.rb
      create   test/fixtures/comments.yml
      exists   db/migrate
      create   db/migrate/002_create_comments.rb
```

Edit the `db/migrate/002_create_comments.rb` **file and create the** `comments` **table:**

```
class CreateComments < ActiveRecord::Migration
    def self.up
        create_table :comments do |t|
            t.column :body, :text
            t.column :post_id, :integer
        end
```

```
        end

    def self.down
        drop_table :comments
    end
end
```

Run the migration to create the comments **table:**

```
$ rake db:migrate
```

The following is output to the console:

```
(in C:/rails/weblog)
== CreateComments: migrating ===============================================
-- create_table(:comments)
   -> 0.1090s
== CreateComments: migrated (0.1090s) ======================================
```

Add a belongs_to **reference to the** comments.rb **file:**

```
class Comment < ActiveRecord::Base
    belongs_to :post
end
```

Add a has_many **relationship to the** post.rb **file:**

```
class Post < ActiveRecord::Base
    validates_presence_of :title
    has_many :comments
end
```

We are now able to get all comments attached to a post with @post.comments, which is a collection that we can iterate over and access sub-fields such as comment.body. We will use this in the show.rhtml file to display the comments below the weblog entry. Finally, we include a form with a text area where a visitor can enter and submit a comment (see Figure 3.16). The comment is posted to the comment action. The form_tag, text_area, and submit_tag helpers are used to generate their HTML counterparts.

The code listing for the show.rhtml **file:**

```
<%= render :partial => "post", :object => @post  %>
<%= link_to 'Edit', :action => 'edit', :id => @post %> |
<%= link_to 'Back', :action => 'list' %>
```

```
<h2>Comments</h2>
<% for comment in @post.comments %>
<%= comment.body %>
<hr />
<% end %>
<%= form_tag :action => "comment", :id => @post %>
<%= text_area "comment", "body" %> <br />
<%= submit_tag "Comment!" %>
</form>
```

Figure 3.16
Adding comments to a weblog entry.

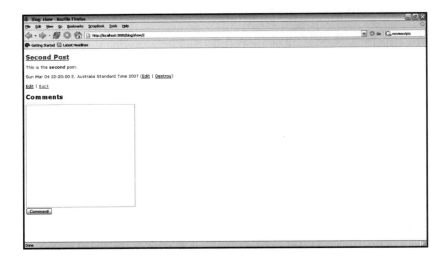

We are almost done, but we still need to build the comment action. The comment action (or comment method in blog_controller.rb) needs to add a comment to the database, provide the user with a confirmation message, and redirect to the show action. We are able to achieve all of this in three lines of code:

```
def comment
    Post.find(params[:id]).comments.create(params[:comment])
    flash[:notice] = "Your comment has been added!"
    redirect_to :action => "show", :id => params[:id]
end
```

Conclusion

In a single chapter we have built three applications: contact list, FAQ manager, and weblog. You were easily able to connect Rails to a database, create a model of a database, enforce input validation, and generate a CRUD interface to add, edit, delete, and display data. The concepts and philosophies behind the Ruby on Rails platform have certainly changed database-driven web development forever and for the better. Convention over configuration increases programmer productivity—this is a huge benefit. In the next chapter, we will delve into Active Record and increase the complexity of the applications that we will be developing.

Active Record

In this chapter, you'll discover why Active Record is a key component of the Rails framework. Active Record is an implementation of object-relational mapping (ORM). Active Record maps Ruby objects to the rows and columns in a database table, allowing us to easily insert, update, search, and delete data without needing to write queries. Active Record comes configured by default and is able to dynamically map table columns to object attributes. You don't need to write accessor methods for each column in a table. This chapter also covers migrations—a handy way to place a database schema under version control as well as create and alter database tables while you develop and enhance a web application. In this chapter you'll learn to:

* Create and modify database tables and columns with migrations.
* Use migrations to update and reverse changes to a database schema.
* Use Active Record models.
* Add data validation to Active Record models.
* Use the `find` method to search a database and return Active Record objects.
* Model one-to-one, one-to-many, and many-to-many relationships with Active Record.
* Use the `acts_as_list` and `acts_as_tree` Active Record extensions.
* Automatically insert and update timestamp fields.

Migrations

The process for designing a web application usually starts with a database and a few tables. Agile practices dictate that the database tables will change over time as requirements are gathered and implemented. As a developer, on numerous occasions a full database schema has been demanded of me, and although I was able to deliver a schema, it had no resemblance to that of the deployed product. It is simply impossible to design a completed database schema at the beginning of a project. Tables will be added, column names will change, and new relationships will be mapped as the product reaches a release milestone. Each increment in product version will have its share of database changes.

This raises an interesting question: How do we manage the changes that occur to the structure of the tables in a database? Remember that we need to deploy changes across our development, testing, and production environments. This problem gets compounded because we usually work in a team that is comprised of numerous other developers. Add to this the fact that your product may need to support multiple databases such as MySQL and Oracle. So, as developers, we need to realize that agile development practices need to be supported by agile database design techniques. Luckily, this is something Rails addresses (and provides a solution for) in the form of migrations. In the first instance, migrations remove the need to write database-specific scripts to create and modify tables. Migrations allow us to write Ruby code to create and modify a database. While this is important in itself, migrations also allow us to roll back or undo the changes that have been made to a database. Each change or addition is stored in a new migration file (version) and must contain code to undo the specified changes. At any time, we can update a database to the latest migration or revert to a previous migration.

A migration template is created when we use `script/generate` to create a model:

```
$ ruby script/generate model employee
```

The following directories and files are created:

```
exists   app/models/
exists   test/unit/
exists   test/fixtures/
create   app/models/employee.rb
create   test/unit/employee_test.rb
create   test/fixtures/employees.yml
create   db/migrate
create   db/migrate/001_create_employees.rb
```

Migrations are stored in the db/migrate directory. The filename for a migration follows a specific naming convention—a three-digit sequence number, the word `create`, and the plural name of the model (i.e., the table name) each separated by an underscore. The sequence number begins at 1, and Rails automatically increments the sequence number when a new migration is created.

A migration can also be generated manually:

```
$ ruby script/generate migration CreateEmployees
```

Open the `001_create_employees.rb` file. The template for the migration will be displayed:

```ruby
class CreateEmployees < ActiveRecord::Migration
  def self.up
    create_table :employees do |t|
      # t.column :name, :string
    end
  end
  def self.down
    drop_table :employees
  end
end
```

A migration is a subclass of `ActiveRecord:Migration`. A migration requires a `self.up` and `self.down` method. The `self.up` method needs to implement the code to add to or alter a database. The `self.down` must contain code to undo the changes made in the `self.up` method. As the `CreateEmployees` migration is created by the model generator, it already contains code to create and drop a table called employees. Within the `create table` code block, we need to add the columns or fields that we require. A commented out example to define a column is given (`# t.column :name, :string`) in the template. The employees table requires columns to store the `firstname`, `lastname`, `email`, `phoneext`, `department`, and `salary` of an employee. Let's add these to the migration:

```ruby
class CreateEmployees < ActiveRecord::Migration
  def self.up
    create_table :employees do |t|
      t.column :firstname, :string
      t.column :lasttname, :string
      t.column :email, :string
      t.column :phoneext, :string
      t.column :department, :string
      t.column :salary, :float
    end
```

```
  end
  def self.down
    drop_table :employees
  end
end
```

We need to specify the column name and the data type. Data types of `:binary`, `:boolean`, `:date`, `:datetime`, `:decimal`, `:float`, `:integer`, `:string`, `:text`, `:time`, and `:timestamp` are available. These data types provide a level of abstraction from the underlying database. Table 4.1 contains the optional parameters for columns creation. The `:string` type would create a column of type `varchar(255)` on a MySQL database but a type of `char varying(255)` on a Postgres database. The benefits are twofold. We can specify a column type with a simple declarative syntax (less to remember) and also apply migrations to a variety of databases, including MySQL, Oracle, Postgres, and SQLite.

Table 4.1   Optional Column Parameters

Option	Description
`:null => true or false`	Sets the columns to a null value
`:limit => size`	Sets the number of characters in a text column
`:default => value`	Sets the default value that must be assigned when a new record is created
`:precision` and `:scale`	Available for decimal columns. It is wise to specify `:precision` and `:scale` due to database incompatibilities. A precision of 5 and a scale of 0 store −99,999 to +99,999.

We can run the migration:

```
$ rake db:migrate
```

The table is created:

```
(in C:/rails/migrations)
== CreateEmployees: migrating =================================================
-- create_table(:employees)
   -> 0.1250s
== CreateEmployees: migrated (0.1250s) ========================================
```

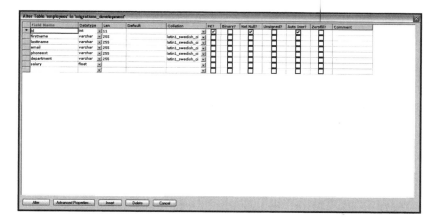

Figure 4.1
The Employees table.

Figure 4.1 shows the table that has been created. You'll notice that a primary key called id has been created automatically. This is useful because id is the assumed default for all primary keys in Rails. An additional table called schema_info has also been created. The schema_info table contains a single column called version, which will contain the version of the last applied migration (see Figure 4.2). Rails uses this information to determine the migration that needs to be applied or reverted.

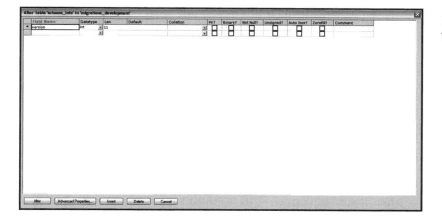

Figure 4.2
The schema_info table.

Adding and Removing Columns from a Table

The most common database alteration you will need to make is adding a column to an existing table. This too can be managed by a migration. The add_column method does exactly what its title suggests. The add_column method takes the name of the table that a column must be added to as its first parameter. The name of the field to be added and its data type must also be specified. We will add a column called `gender` to the employees table.

Generate a migration called `add_gender_column`:

```
$ ruby script/generate migration add_gender_column
      exists  db/migrate
      create  db/migrate/002_add_gender_column.rb
```

As you can see, the migration sequence is now at number 2. Open the `002_add_gender_column.rb`, **we will need to add code to the skeleton created by the** `script/generate` **command:**

```
class AddGenderColumn < ActiveRecord::Migration
  def self.up
  end
  def self.down
  end
end
```

Because this migration was not created by the `generate model` **command, we have empty** `self.up` **and** `self.down` **methods. We need to add code that will add a column in the** `self.up` **method and code to undo the action (remove the column) in the** `self.down` **method.**

```
class AddGenderColumn < ActiveRecord::Migration
  def self.up
    add_column :employees, :gender, :string
  end
  def self.down
    remove_column :employees, :gender
  end
end
```

Run the migration:

```
$ rake db:migrate
```

The field is added to the employees table:

```
(in C:/rails/migrations)
== AddGenderColumn: migrating =================================================
-- add_column(:employees, :gender, :string)
```

```
    -> 0.2970s
== AddGenderColumn: migrated (0.2970s) =======================================
```

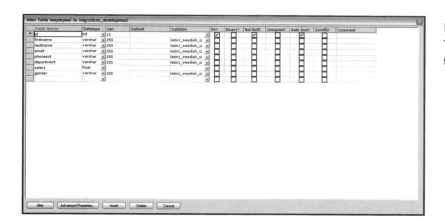

Figure 4.3
The gender field added to
the employees table.

We check the employees table (see Figure 4.3) just to make sure that the `gender` field has actually been added. At any time, we can revert back to version 1 of the migration:

```
$ rake db:migrate VERSION=1
```

The change made to the database by the `AddGenderColumn` **migration is reverted:**

```
(in C:/rails/migrations)
== AddGenderColumn: reverting ================================================
-- remove_column(:employees, :gender)
   -> 0.4690s
== AddGenderColumn: reverted (0.4690s) =======================================
```

Running `rake db:migrate` **again will return the database to the latest version:**

```
$ rake db:migrate
```

The `gender` **column is added again:**

```
(in C:/rails/migrations)
== AddGenderColumn: migrating ================================================
-- add_column(:employees, :gender, :string)
   -> 0.2810s
== AddGenderColumn: migrated (0.2810s) =======================================
```

Altering Columns in a Table

Terminology changes as a project progresses. It is wise to update the affected models, database tables, and column names. While this will involve some work, it will make debugging, product maintenance, and upgrades easier. Developers added to the project at a later date will be less confused and very grateful.

The `rename_column` method is used to change the name of a column. The `rename_column` method takes three parameters: the table name, the existing column name, and the new column name. In the example that follows we change the `lastname` column to `surname`:

```
class RenameColumn < ActiveRecord::Migration
  def self.up
      rename_column(employees, lastname, surname)
  end

  def self.down
      rename_column(employees, surname, lastname)
  end
end
```

The `rename_column` method only changes the name of a column. There may be occasions when you need to change the data type and other options such as the size or default value of a column. The `change_column` method enables you to alter the data type and allows various options to be set. The `change_column` method takes four parameters : the `table_name`, the `column_name`, the `data type`, and a hash of options.

In this example we change the `phoneext` field from a string to an integer:

```
class ChangeColumn < ActiveRecord::Migration
  def self.up
      change_column :employees, :phoneext, :integer
  end

  def self.down
      change_column :employees, :phoneext, :string
  end
end
```

Use the `change_column` method with great care. Although it may be possible to convert a field with 1 to an integer, it is not possible to convert the string One to an integer value—an exception will be thrown. It is best to review the data stored in a field prior to using the `change_column` method; you may need to programmatically massage the data into an acceptable format. In some cases it may be necessary to make a migration that can't be reversed:

```
class ChangeColumn < ActiveRecord::Migration
  def self.up
    change_column :employees, :phoneext, :integer
  end

  def self.down
    raise ActiveRecord::IrreversibleMigration
  end
end
```

Creating, Renaming, and Dropping Tables

The `create_table` method takes the name of the table and a hash of options as parameters. The `:force => true` option will drop or delete a table if it already exists. Use the `:force` option with care as data will be lost. Setting `:temporary => true` will create a temporary table. Temporary tables get deleted when an application is disconnected from a database.

The `rename_table` method is used to change the name of a table:

```
class RenameEmployees < ActiveRecord::Migration
  def self.up
    rename_table :employees, :workers
  end
  def self.down
    rename_table :workers, :employees
  end
end
```

Defining Indices

Fields that are regularly used as search criteria should be indexed to improve database performance. We can add and remove indices from within a migration. The `add_index` and `remove_index` methods take the name of the table and the name of a column. In this example we add an index to the `firstname` column:

```
class AddNameIndexToEmployees < ActiveRecord::Migration
  def self.up
    add_index :employees, :firstname
  end
```

```
def self.down
    remove_index :employees, :firstname
  end
end
```

 Tip

Watch the Migrations Screencast presented by David Heinemeier Hansson, the creator of the Rails framework, at http://www.rubyonrails.com/screencasts.

Working with Active Record Models

Active Record is undeniably both the simplest and most powerful implementation of object-relationship mapping (ORM). Active Record is able to map a class to a database table without requiring a programmer to enter any specific table column to object attributes mapping configuration details. Active Record comes configured by default—all you need to do is learn a few conventions:

* **Table names must be in plural form.** The table to store employee details is therefore called employees. The class that maps to the employees table, also known as a model, must have the singular name of the table (employee).

* **The unique primary key must be called id.** In fact, when we used the create_table method within a migration, we did not even need to specify a primary key because one called id was added automatically.

Active Record maps tables to classes, table rows to objects, and columns (or fields) to object attributes. Active Record includes methods to create, update, delete, and search for records. In the previous section we created a model called employee and used the CreateEmployees migration (001_create_employees.rb) to create an employees table with firstname, surname, email, gender, salary, phoneext, and department. All the examples of Active Record usage in this section will be illustrated from within the Rails console. The first thing we will do is get a list of columns within the employees table:

```
$ ruby script/console
Loading development environment.
>> Employee.column_names
```

```
=> ["id", "firstname", "lastname", "email", "phoneext", "department", "salary",
"gender"]
```

Now let's add a new record. We need to create a new `Employee` object, assign data to the object's attributes, and then call the `save` method to insert the record into the database table:

```
>> an_employee = Employee.new
=> #<Employee:0x396b538 @attributes={"department"=>nil, "phoneext"=>nil, "salary
"=>nil, "gender"=>nil, "lastname"=>nil, "firstname"=>nil, "email"=>nil}, @new_re
cord=true>
>> an_employee.firstname = "Aneesha"
=> "Aneesha"
>> an_employee.lastname = "Bakharia"
=> "Bakharia"
>> an_employee.email = "aneesha.bakharia@gmail.com"
=> "aneesha.bakharia@gmail.com"
>> an_employee.phoneext = 1234
=> 1234
>> an_employee.gender = "Female"
=> "Female"
>> an_employee.salary = 25000
=> 25000
>> an_employee.department = "IT"
=> "IT"
>> an_employee.save
=> true
```

After calling the `save` method, we check the database to make sure the record has been added (see Figure 4.4).

The `create` method is also very handy as it takes a hash of attributes and saves them to the database in a single call:

```
an_employee = Order.create(
:firstname => "Celine",
:lastname => "Bakharia",
:phoneext => "2345",
:department => "Marketing",
:email => "c@randomsyntax.com",
```

```
:salary => "23456",
:gender => "Female")
```

Figure 4.4
Making sure a new
employee has been added.

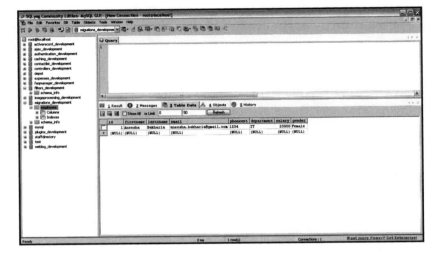

Multiple records can be inserted with the `create` method:

```
orders = Order.create(
[ { :firstname => "Celine",
:lastname => "Bakharia",
:phoneext => "2345",
:department => "Marketing",
:email => "c@randomsyntax.com",
:salary => "23456",
:gender => "Female"
},
{ :firstname => "Zaeem",
:lastname => "Bakharia",
:phoneext => "34567",
:department => "Sales",
:email => "z@randomsyntax.com",
:salary => "23456",
:gender => "Male"
} ] )
```

Each record in a database table has a unique primary key called id. The find method in its simplest form takes an id as a parameter and returns the table row as an object. The find method is very powerful and will be covered in detail in the section that follows. We will use find to retrieve the record with an id of 1, make it into an object, update the department attribute, and then save the record back to the database table:

```
>> an_employee = Employee.find(1)
=> #<Employee:0x3934858 @attributes={"department"=>"IT", "phoneext"=>"1234",
"salary"=>"25000", "gender"=>"Female", "lastname"=>nil, "firstname"=>"Aneesha",
"id
"=>"1", "email"=>"aneesha.bakharia@gmail.com"}>
>> an_employee.department = "Marketing"
=> "Marketing"
>> an_employee.save
=> true
```

The update method takes an id and a hash of values that need to be updated. The update method updates the data without the need to call the save method:

```
an_employee = Employee.update(3, :department => "Sales", :email =>
"sales@randomsyntax.com")
```

The delete method takes the id of the record that must be deleted as a parameter:

```
>> Employee.delete(2)
=> 1
```

The delete method can also be used to delete an array defining multiple records:

```
Employee.delete([5,7,9,10])
```

Using Active Record Without Rails

If you build database applications with Ruby that are not web-based, you'll be happy to know that Active Record can be used without Rails, even though it is a crucial component of Rails. In the example that follows, we connect to a database (with the establish_connection method), create a class for our model (the singular name of the table), search for the employee with an id of 1, and then update their firstname:

```
require "rubygems"
require_gem "activerecord"
ActiveRecord::Base.establish_connection(:adapter => "mysql",
:host => "localhost", :database => "testdb")
```

```
class Employee < ActiveRecord::Base
end
staff_member = Employee.find(1)
staff_member.firstname = "Aneesha"
staff_member.save
```

Retrieving Records with find

Each model inherits a method called `find`. The `find` method in its simplest form takes an `id` or an array of `ids` and returns the matching records as objects. When the `find` method is passed a `:conditions` hash, it becomes a powerful replacement for raw SQL. The first parameter the `find` method takes is either the `:first` or `:all` symbols. `:first` returns a single row, while `:all` returns multiple rows that match the specified criteria.

Anything passed to the `:conditions` symbol will be added to the SQL statement's where clause. The following search will produce `"Select * from Employees WHERE firstname='Aneesha' and lastname='Bakharia'"` as the query:

```
employees = Employee.find(:all,
:conditions => "firstname='Aneesha' and lastname='Bakharia'")
```

Note

The `find` method returns an empty array if no records match the search criteria.

Never reference variables directly when specifying `:conditions`. This leaves your application susceptible to SQL injection.

```
# Extremely bad practice
employees = Employee.find(:all,
:conditions => "firstname='#{firstname}' and lastname='#{lastname}'")
```

The safe alternative is to use a placeholder in the form of a question mark (?). Active Record escapes and quotes the inserted values for you. You then pass the matching variables as an array to the `:conditions` symbol. The above example could be re-written as follows:

```
employees = Employee.find(:all,
:conditions => "firstname= ? and lastname=?", firstname, lastname)
```

Sometimes keeping track of the order of placeholders can be tedious and error-prone. Luckily, we can also use `:symbols` to name placeholders:

```
employees = Employee.find(:all,
:conditions => "firstname= :firstname and lastname= :lastname",
{:firstname => firstname, :lastname => lastname})
```

We can even use the % wildcard character in a search:

```
employees = Employee.find(:all,
:conditions => ["lastname= ?", lastname +"%"])
```

The :order option allows us to determine the order of returned records:

```
employees = Employee.find(:all,
:conditions => "lastname='Bakharia'", :order => "lastname, firstname DESC")
```

Limiting the number of records returned with :limit:

```
employees = Employee.find(:all,
:conditions => "lastname='Bakharia'", :limit => 5)
```

The find method produces an SQL query that retrieves all columns in the table being queried (select *). If a table contains many fields, but you only need to utilize data from a few columns, improved performance will be accomplished if you only return the required columns in the query. The columns to be returned can be specified with :select. In this example only the lastname and firstname columns are returned:

```
employees = Employee.find(:all,
:conditions => "lastname='Bakharia'", :select => "firstname,lastname")
```

The :first symbol can be used to return the first matching record. Here are a few examples:

```
an_employee = Employee.find(:first)
an_employee = Employee.find(:first, :conditions => "firstname = 'Celine'")
```

Using find_by_sql

The find method serves us well but the need to utilize SQL is compelling under certain circumstances. You may need to optimize queries for performance, utilize SQL specific to a particular database (MySQL or Oracle), or create complex queries with Group By and Having clauses for reporting purposes. The find_by_sql takes an SQL query and returns an array of Active Record objects. The attributes of the returned Active Record objects correspond to the column names specified in the Select clause of the SQL query.

To illustrate the use of find_by_sql, we will create a table to store popular songs by genre. Each song will have a sales figure associated with it. A Group By query will be used to return the total sales per genre. The array of objects returned by `find_by_sql` will be passed to a view for display.

Create a model called song:

```
$ ruby script/generate model song
```

The migration (`006_create_songs.rb`) will create a table called songs. The songs table requires title, sales, and genre columns. We also use the migration to insert data into the table. The `Song.create` method can be used from within a migration and provides an efficient way to load sample data:

```ruby
class CreateSongs < ActiveRecord::Migration
  def self.up
    create_table :songs do |t|
      t.column :title, :string
      t.column :sales, :float
      t.column :genre, :string
    end
    Song.create :title => 'Song 1', :sales => 12308, :genre => 'Pop'
    Song.create :title => 'Song 2', :sales => 60000, :genre => 'Rock'
    Song.create :title => 'Song 3', :sales => 80000, :genre => 'Classical'
    Song.create :title => 'Song 4', :sales => 15000, :genre => 'Pop'
    Song.create :title => 'Song 5', :sales => 12000, :genre => 'Techno'
    Song.create :title => 'Song 6', :sales => 55000, :genre => 'Rap'
    Song.create :title => 'Song 7', :sales => 45000, :genre => 'Techno'
    Song.create :title => 'Song 8', :sales => 35000, :genre => 'Rap'
  end
  def self.down
    drop_table :songs
  end
end
```

Run the migration:

```
$ rake db:migrate
```

The songs table is created:

```
(in C:/rails/migrations)
== CreateSongs: migrating ===========================================================
-- create_table(:songs)
```

```
   -> 0.1100s
== CreateSongs: migrated (0.3910s) ========================================
```

Create a controller called song:

```
$ ruby script/generate controller song
```

Within the song **controller, we create an action called** report. **The** @report **object stores the results returned as arrays from the** find_by_sql **method. The query passed to the** find_by_sql **method uses a** Group By **clause to return the total sales for each musical genre:**

```
class SongController < ApplicationController
    def report
        @report = Song.find_by_sql("SELECT genre, sum(sales) AS total FROM
songs GROUP BY genre ORDER BY total DESC")
    end
end
```

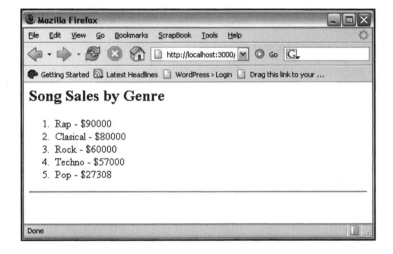

Figure 4.5
A report created with data from the find_by_sql method.

The app\views\song\report.rhtml **file loops over the** @report **object and prints out the total sales for each music genre (see Figure 4.5):**

```
<h2>Song Sales by Genre</h2>
<ol>
<% for item in @report %>
<li><%= item.genre %> - $<%= item.total %>
<% end %>
```

```
</ol>
<hr>
```

 Tip

You can use `find_by_sql` without a model. The `find_by_sql` method just executes SQL and returns a result set and does not need to interact with the methods of a model.

Dynamic Finders

Most of the time, you'll find yourself searching individual table columns for a specified value. Dynamic finders use pure Ruby magic to accomplish this task. We simply need to append the name of the field that must be searched to the `find_by_` method. The `find_by_` method returns a single record. The `find_all_by` method, as its name suggests, returns all records that match the criteria.

Search the `firstname` column for `"Aneesha"`:

```
an_employee = Employee.find_by_firstname("Aneesha")
```

Find all employees in the `"Marketing"` department:

```
employees = Employee.find_all_by_department("Marketing")
```

Behind the scenes `find_by_firstname("Aneesha")` is converted to:

```
find(:firstname,:conditions => ["firstname = ?", "Aneesha"])
```

Dynamic finders also support an optional hash just like the `find` method:

```
employees = Employee.find_all_by_department("Marketing", :limit => 10,
:conditions => "gender = 'Female'")
```

Dynamic finders can even be used to search multiple columns:

```
employees = Employee.find_by_firstname_and_lastname("Aneesha", "Bakharia")
```

Column Statistics—Average, Max, Min, Sum, and Count

The Active Record model object also wraps the aggregate functions available in common databases such as MySQL. Using these methods, we are able to determine the average, maximum, minimum, and total salary for an employee. We can also get a count of all records in the employees table:

```
average = Employee.average(:salary)
max = Employee.maximum(:salary)
min = Employee.minimum(:salary)
total = Employee.sum(:salary)
number = Employee.count
```

We can even get a count of a filtered result set:

```
custom_count1 = Employee.count "salary > 20000"
custom_count2 = Employee.count ["salary > ?", minimum_salary]
```

Validation

Display a form to a user and no matter how detailed and descriptive your instructions are, there will always be users who enter data that is invalid or in an incorrect format. Invalid data in a database is hard to process and unless you contact each user individually, you will be left with incomplete information. This is why validation is so important. The most sensible place to put our validation rules is within the model. The model interacts directly with the database table to insert new data as well as update existing data.

The employee model (app\models\employee.rb) currently has no validation and we are able to store an invalid email address and blank fields in the database:

```
$ ruby script/console
Loading development environment.
>> an_employee = Employee.new
=> #<Employee:0x39c47a0 @attributes={"department"=>nil, "phoneext"=>nil, "salary"=>nil, "gender"=>nil, "lastname"=>nil, "firstname"=>nil, "email"=>nil}, @new_record=true>
>> an_employee.firstname = "Aneesha"
=> "Aneesha"
>> an_employee.email = "somewhere"
=> "somewhere"
>> an_employee.lastname = ""
=> ""
>> an_employee.save
=> true
```

The following validation helpers are available for inclusion on a model:

* validates_acceptance_of
* validates_associated
* validates_confirmation_of
* validates_each
* validates_exclusion_of
* validates_format_of
* validates_inclusion_of
* validates_length_of
* validates_numericality_of
* validates_presence_of
* validates_size_of
* validates_uniqueness_of

We need to ensure that the firstname and lastname attributes are not blank, so we use the validates_presense_of helper. The salary needs to be a numeric value, so validates_numericality_of can be used to enforce this constraint. Finally, we use the validates_format_of helper to match the entered email address to a regular expression. A regular expression consists of a sequence of characters that define a pattern. The regular expression in the example that follows contains a sequence of characters that match a valid email address. Here is the updated employee model (app\models\employee.rb) file:

```
class Employee < ActiveRecord::Base
     validates_presence_of :firstname, :lastname
     validates_numericality_of :salary
     validates_format_of :email,
                    :with => /^([^@\s]+)@((?:[-a-z0-9]+\.)+[a-z]{2,})$/i
end
```

Validation will now be performed prior to data being saved. When a new Employee object has invalid data, it can't be saved:

```
$ ruby script/console
Loading development environment.
>> new_employee = Employee.new
=> #<Employee:0x39c2950 @attributes={"department"=>nil, "phoneext"=>nil, "salary
"=>nil, "gender"=>nil, "lastname"=>nil, "firstname"=>nil, "email"=>nil}, @new_re
```

```
cord=true>
>> new_employee.firstname = "Aneesha"
=> "Aneesha"
>> new_employee.lastname = ""
=> ""
>> new_employee.email = "nowhere"
=> "nowhere"
>> new_employee.save
=> false
```

An `error` object is added to the Active Record model when invalid data is encountered. We are able to access the list of errors:

```
>> new_employee.errors.each {|attribute, error| puts attribute + ": " + error}
salary: is not a number
lastname: can't be blank
email: is invalid
=> {"salary"=>["is not a number"], "lastname"=>["can't be blank"],
"email"=>["is invalid"]}
```

Within a Rails application, if validation fails on an Active Record object, the error object is populated with the validation error messages and the form is re-displayed. The `error_messages_for` helper is used within a view template to display validation errors:

```
<h1>New Employee</h1>
<%= start_form_tag :action => 'create' %>
<%= error_messages_for 'employee' %>
<p><label for="employee_firstname">Firstname</label>;
<%= text_field 'employee', 'firstname'%></p>
<p><label for="employee_lastname">Lastname</label>;
<%= text_field 'employee', 'lastname' %></p>
<p><label for="employee_email">Email</label>;
<%= text_field 'employee', 'email'%></p>
<%= submit_tag "Add" %>
<%= end_form_tag %>
<%= link_to 'Back', :action => 'list' %>
```

If we return to the contact list we developed in Chapter 3, "Prototyping Database-Driven Applications with Rails," we can analyze the interaction between the form to add a new contact (the view), the controller, and the model to get a better understanding of validation and the display of error messages. In the contact model (/app/models/contact.rb), we included a validates_presense_of helper to ensure that the firstname, surname, and email columns in the contacts database table are mandatory:

```
class Contact < ActiveRecord::Base
    validates_presence_of :firstname, :surname, :email
end
```

The _form.rhtml partial in the /app/views/contact/ folder, which is used by both new and edit forms, includes the error_messages_for helper. The error_messages_for helper takes the name of the model as a parameter:

```
<%= error_messages_for 'contact' %>
<!--[form:contact]-->
<p><label for="contact_firstname">Firstname</label><br/>
<%= text_field 'contact', 'firstname'  %></p
<p><label for="contact_surname">Surname</label><br/>
<%= text_field 'contact', 'surname'  %></p>
<p><label for="contact_email">Email</label><br/>
<%= text_field 'contact', 'email'  %></p>
<p><label for="contact_mobile">Mobile</label><br/>
<%= text_field 'contact', 'mobile'  %></p>
<p><label for="contact_homephone">Homephone</label><br/>
<%= text_field 'contact', 'homephone'  %></p>
<p><label for="contact_note">Note</label><br/>
<%= text_area 'contact', 'note'  %></p>
<!--[eoform:contact]-->
```

The form to insert a new contact (app/views/faq/new.rhtml) simply includes the _form.rhtml partial and posts the data entered by the user to the create action:

```
<h1>New contact</h1>

<% form_tag :action => 'create' do %>
  <%= render :partial => 'form' %>
  <%= submit_tag "Create" %>
<% end %>

<%= link_to 'Back', :action => 'list' %>
```

We can now take a look at an excerpt from the `contact_controller.rb` file to see how the `create` action determines whether a contact object is invalid (i.e., fails validation) and passes the `error` object to the `new.rhtml` template for display. A new object (`@contact`) is created by passing `params[:contact]` to the `Contact.new` method—this assigns all the input fields from the form to the appropriate attributes in the `@contact` object. The `@contact` object is then saved by calling the `save` method. Remember that if validation fails, the object will not be saved and that the `save` method will return a false result and set the `error` object. An `if` statement is used to check if the `@contact` object is saved (i.e., `@contact.save` returns a true value) and display the `list.rhtml` template. If the `@contact` object is not saved, the new contact form is displayed (`new.rhtml` template). The `@contact` object, which is passed to the template, has the form data entered by the user, so the data is preserved between redirects. Because validation has failed, the error object is also populated and will be displayed by the `error_messages_for` helper. Figure 4.6 illustrates the display of a validation error message on the new contact form.

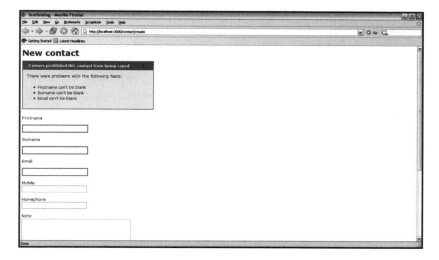

Figure 4.6
Validation error messages
in Rails.

```
class FaqController < ApplicationController

...

    def new
        @contact = Contact.new
    end
    def create
        @contact = Contact.new(params[:contact])
        if @contact.save
```

```
            flash[:notice] = 'Contact was successfully created.'
            redirect_to :action => 'list'
        else
            render :action => 'new'
        end
    end
...
end
```

Mapping Relationships with Active Record

Relational databases have multiple tables! We have thus far only looked at single table Active Record models—this is all about to change in this section. The employees table we created in the migrations section of this chapter had a column called department, in which we stored data like `"Marketing"`, `"IT"`, and `"Sales"`. Multiple employees belong to each department, so multiple records would store the name of the department. What happens when a department changes its name? We could write an update query across all records that match the department name. This would be terribly inefficient and is a classic example of why databases need to be normalized. The solution is to create a table that just stores the names of the departments and has a unique id for each department. The employees table then only needs to reference the foreign key of the department's table. We now only need to update a single record if a department name changes.

It would be nice if we could get the name of the department by simply typing:

```
department_name = employee.department.name
```

instead of:

```
department_id = employee.department_id
department = Department.find(department_id)
department_name = department.name
```

Guess what? You can!

Foreign key relationships are converted to object mappings by Active Record. Foreign keys must follow a naming convention—they are the lowercase version of the related table's model name (or the singular form of the table name) with _id added as a suffix. The foreign key that relates the employees table to the departments table is called department_id. A sample migration to illustrate the creation of a foreign key:

```ruby
class BuildProjectDb < ActiveRecord::Migration
  def self.up
    create_table :employees do |t|
        t.column :firstname, :string
        t.column :department_id, :integer
    end
    create_table :departments do |t|
        t.column :name, :string
    end
  end
  def self.down
    drop_table :employees
    drop_table :departments
  end
end
```

Active Record needs a little help in order to pick up the relationships between tables, so we annotate our models with declarations: has_one, has_many, belongs_to, and has_and_belongs_to_many (habtm).

As an example to illustrate the use of has_many and belongs_to, we will model a Project Task List Manager. In this application, each project has multiple tasks associated with it. The database contains a projects and a tasks table. The tasks table has a foreign_key called project_id.

A project is associated with a many tasks, so we add the has_many declaration to the project model:

```ruby
class Project < ActiveRecord::Base
    has_many :tasks
end
```

A task belongs_to a project:

```ruby
class Task < ActiveRecord::Base
    belongs_to :project
end
```

One-to-One Relationships

A one-to-one relationship occurs when a row in a table is associated with either one or zero records in another table via a foreign key. We have a table called users in our database. We want to store a photo for each user in the users table but decide to create a new photos table.

The main reason for adding the photos table rather than adding a photo column to the users table is because we need to add width and height columns to define the dimensions of the photo. The `photos` table contains the `filename`, `width`, `height`, and `user_id` columns. The `user_id` is the foreign key that relates the record back to the `users` table.

A user is associated with a single photo, so we add the `has_one` declaration to the user model:

```
class User < ActiveRecord::Base
    has_one :photo
end
```

A photo is attached to a user so, we add `belongs_to` to the photo model:

```
class Photo < ActiveRecord::Base
    belongs_to :user
end
```

Tip
As a rule of thumb, the table with the foreign key always gets the `belongs_to` declaration.

One-to-Many Relationships

A one-to-many association occurs when a row in a table is associated with multiple rows in another table. A book, for example, is made up of many chapters. The books table simply contains the name of the book. The chapters table contains the `book_id`, `name`, and `position` columns. The `book_id` field is the foreign key that associates a chapter with a book.

We add the `has_many` declaration to the Book model:

```
class Book < ActiveRecord::Base
    has_many :chapters
end
```

A chapter is attached to a book, so we add `belongs_to` to the chapter model:

```
class Chapter < ActiveRecord::Base
      belongs_to :book
end
```

Return the chapter that has an id of 1:

```
a_chapter = Chapter.find(1)
```

Get the id for the associated book:

```
a_chapter.book.id
```

Get the name of the associated book:

```
a_chapter.book.name
```

Create and save a new book:

```
a_chapter.book = Book.new(:name => "Power Rails")
a_chapter.save!
```

Get the id of the newly added book:

```
a_chapter.book.id
```

Get the name of the newly added book:

```
a_chapter.book.name
```

Finally, we can use the `create_modelname` **method to initialize and save a book:**

```
a_chapter.create_book(:name => "Rails Rulz")
```

Many-to-Many Relationships

Multiple records in a table are associated with multiple records in another table. We have a products table in our database. We wish to categorize the products. It is impossible to assign a product to a single category, so we need a way to associate multiple categories with a product. A product will be associated with multiple categories, and a category will be associated with multiple products.

There is a collection of items on each side of the relationship. A simple foreign key won't allow us to model this relationship—we need a join table. A join table contains two foreign keys. The name of the join table is the concatenation of the two related tables in alphabetical order. We use the plural table names as is. In our example, the join table will be called `categories_products`.

Many-to-many relationships are modeled with the `has_and_belongs_to_many` declaration. Both the product and the category models get the `has_and_belongs_to_many` declaration.

The product model:

```
class Product < ActiveRecord::Base
    has_and_belongs_to_many :categories
end
```

The category model:

```
class Category < ActiveRecord::Base
    has_and_belongs_to_many :products
end
```

Sorting with acts_as_list

In a list, the order is used to display the items. We also need to provide the user with the ability to re-order the items in list. The `acts_as_list` declaration adds a number of methods to facilitate the re-ordering of items. To illustrate the use of `acts_as_list`, we will build a handy Project Task List Manager. This little utility can be used to prioritize the tasks in a project.

We generate a migration called `build_project_db`:

```
$ ruby script/generate migration build_project_db
```

In the `build_project_db` migration we will create two tables: projects and tasks. We also insert initial project and task data. Instead of first creating a model and then editing the generated migration, we have chosen to design the database first. We can still work in an agile manner and use migrations to add/remove columns as needed:

```
class BuildProjectDb < ActiveRecord::Migration
  def self.up
    create_table :projects do |t|
        t.column :title, :string
    end
    vid_project = Project.create :title => 'Video Transcripts'
    create_table :tasks do |t|
        t.column :project_id, :integer
        t.column :title, :string
        t.column :position, :integer
    end
```

```
      Task.create :project_id => vid_project.id,
                  :title => 'Set up site',
                  :position => 1
      Task.create :project_id => vid_project.id,
                  :title => 'Learn Flex',
                  :position => 2
      Task.create :project_id => vid_project.id,
                  :title => 'Build a video annotation tool in Flex',
:position => 3
      Task.create :project_id => vid_project.id,
                  :title => 'Build backend with Rails',
                  :position => 4
      Task.create :project_id => vid_project.id,
                  :title => 'Design Interface',
                  :position => 5
  end
  def self.down
      drop_table :projects
      drop_table :tasks
  end
end
```

Now we generate models called project and task. We don't need to generate a migration file with the models, so we pass --skip-migration as a command line argument to the generator:

```
$ ruby script/generate model project --skip-migration
$ ruby script/generate model task --skip-migration
```

Add the has_many declaration to the project model. A project has_many tasks:

```
class Project < ActiveRecord::Base
    has_many :tasks, :order => "position"
end
```

Add the belongs_to declaration to the task model. A task belongs_to a project. The tasks within a project have a priority (i.e., an ordering). We specify the scope as :project because each project will have its own related task list:

```
class Task < ActiveRecord::Base
     belongs_to :project
     acts_as_list :scope => :project
end
```

Create the projects **and** tasks **tables:**

```
$ rake db:migrate
(in C:/rails/migrations)
== BuildProjectDb: migrating ================================================
-- create_table(:projects)
   -> 0.1090s
-- create_table(:tasks)
   -> 0.1570s
== BuildProjectDb: migrated (0.5310s) =======================================
```

A summary of methods added to a model with acts_as_list **added:**

- decrement_position
- first?
- higher_item
- in_list?
- increment_position
- insert_at
- last?
- lower_item
- move_higher
- move_lower
- move_to_bottom
- move_to_top
- remove_from_list

Create a controller called tasks. The index action displays the task list. Next to each task we provide links to re-order the items. The move **action responds to these requests to re-position a task and redirects back to display the task list (i.e.,** index **action):**

```
$ ruby script/generate controller tasks
class TasksController < ApplicationController
```

```
       def index
            @project = Project.find(1)
            @tasks = Task.find(:all, :conditions => ["project_id = %d", 1],
                             :order => "position")
       end
       def move
            if
["move_lower","move_higher","move_to_top","move_to_bottom"].include?
(params[:method]) \
                  and params[:task_id] =~ /^\d+$/
                  Task.find(params[:task_id]).send(params[:method])
            end
            redirect_to(:action => "index", :id => 1)
       end
end
```

The index.rhtml **(see Figure 4.7) allows the user to prioritize tasks:**

```
<h1>Project: <%= @project.title %></h1>
<h2>Tasks:</h2>
<ol>
<% for task in @tasks %>
<li>
<%= task.title %>
<% unless task.first? %>
<%= link_to "up", {:action => "move",:method => "move_higher",
                  :id => 1, :task_id => task.id } %>
<%= link_to "first", {:action => "move",:method => "move_to_top",
                     :id => 1, :task_id => task.id } %>
<% end %>
<% unless task.last? %>
<%= link_to "down", {:action => "move",:method => "move_lower",
                  :id => 1, :task_id => task.id  } %>
<%= link_to "last", {:action => "move",:method => "move_to_bottom",
                  :id => 1, :task_id => task.id } %>
<% end %>
</li>
<% end %>
</ol>
```

Note

The Up and First links are not shown for the first item in the list. The Down and Last links are not shown for the last item.

Figure 4.7
Providing the user with the ability to re-order a list.

Hierarchies with acts_as_tree

An organization chart, your family tree, and the sections in a book are all examples of hierarchical data. A single database table is used to store parent-child relationships. Each record has a field, called parent_id by convention, which relates the record to its parent. Hierarchical data is modeled with the acts_as_tree declaration.

The chapters, sections, and subsections in a book are an example of a hierarchy. We will create a sections table to store this hierarchy and use the acts_as_tree declaration to help us model the hierarchy so that we can access the hierarchical tree in an object-oriented manner (i.e., friendly Active Record manner).

We start by creating a model called section:

```
$ ruby script/generate model section
```

A migration was created when the model generator was run. We edit 008_create_sections.rb and create parent_id and title columns in the sections table. We use Section.create to insert example chapters and sections in the book. The root node (which just stores the title of the book) has a null parent_id:

```
class CreateSections < ActiveRecord::Migration
  def self.up
    create_table :sections do |t|
      t.column :parent_id, :integer
```

```
      t.column :title, :string
    end
    Section.create :title => 'Power Ruby on Rails'
    Section.create :parent_id => 1, :title => 'Chapter 1'
    Section.create :parent_id => 1, :title => 'Chapter 2'
    Section.create :parent_id => 3, :title => 'Chapter 2 - Section 1'
    Section.create :parent_id => 3, :title => 'Chapter 2 - Section 2'
    Section.create :parent_id => 3, :title => 'Chapter 2 - Section 3'
    Section.create :parent_id => 2, :title => 'Chapter 1 - Section 1'
  end
  def self.down
    drop_table :sections
  end
end
```

We use rake db:migrate **to create the sections table:**

```
$ rake db:migrate
(in C:/rails/migrations)
== CreateSections: migrating ===============================================
-- create_table(:sections)
   -> 0.1410s
== CreateSections: migrated (0.3280s) ======================================
```

We now add the acts_as_tree **declaration to the section model:**

```
class Section < ActiveRecord::Base
      acts_as_tree :order => "title"
end
```

Before we jump in and use the methods acts_as_tree **has added to our model in a controller, we will first give them a test within the Rails console:**

```
$ ruby script/console
Loading development environment.
```

We can use the find **method to return the root by searching for a record with a** parent_id **set to null:**

```
>> root = Section.find(:first, :conditions => "parent_id is null")
=> #<Section:0x395e090 @attributes={"title"=>"Power Ruby on Rails", "id"=>"1", "
parent_id"=>nil}>
```

A call to children gives us all the sub nodes below the root. This includes `"Chapter 1"` **and** `"Chapter 2"`:

```
>> root.children
=> [#<Section:0x3955b5c @attributes={"title"=>"Chapter 1", "id"=>"2", "parent_id
"=>"1"}>, #<Section:0x3955b20 @attributes={"title"=>"Chapter 2", "id"=>"3", "par
ent_id"=>"1"}>]
```

We now turn our attention to adding nodes to our tree. We add `"Chapter 3"`:

```
>> new_chapter = Section.create(:parent_id => 1, :title => "Chapter 3")
=> #<Section:0x3948204 @attributes={"title"=>"Chapter 3", "id"=>8, "parent_id"=>
1}, @new_record=false, @new_record_before_save=true, @errors=#<ActiveRecord::Err
ors:0x3945978 @base=#<Section:0x3948204 ...>, @errors={}>>
```

We can get the siblings or node at the same level as our newly added chapter. `"Chapter 1"` **and** `"Chapter 2"` **are at the same level as** `"Chapter 3"`:

```
>> new_chapter.siblings
=> [#<Section:0x3939948 @attributes={"title"=>"Chapter 1", "id"=>"2", "parent_id
"=>"1"}>, #<Section:0x39398e4 @attributes={"title"=>"Chapter 2", "id"=>"3", "par
ent_id"=>"1"}>]
```

We can use `children.create` **to create subsections for** `"Chapter 3"` **without specifying the** `parent_id`:

```
>> new_chapter.children.create(:title => "Chapter 3 - Section 1")
=> #<Section:0x3934e34 @attributes={"title"=>"Chapter 3 - Section 1", "id"=>9, "
parent_id"=>8}, @new_record=false, @new_record_before_save=true, @errors=#<Activ
eRecord::Errors:0x3934218 @base=#<Section:0x3934e34 ...>, @errors={}>>
>> new_chapter.children.create(:title => "Chapter 3 - Section 2")
=> #<Section:0x392bb2c @attributes={"title"=>"Chapter 3 - Section 2", "id"=>10,
"parent_id"=>8}, @new_record=false, @new_record_before_save=true, @errors=#<Acti
veRecord::Errors:0x392a2a4 @base=#<Section:0x392bb2c ...>, @errors={}>>
```

At any time, we can get the parent of a node:

```
>> new_chapter.parent
=> #<Section:0x393ba04 @attributes={"title"=>"Power Ruby on Rails", "id"=>"1", "
parent_id"=>nil}, @children=[#<Section:0x3939948 @attributes={"title"=>"Chapter
1", "id"=>"2", "parent_id"=>"1"}>, #<Section:0x39398e4 @attributes={"title"=>"Ch
```

```
apter 2", "id"=>"3", "parent_id"=>"1"}>, #<Section:0x39398a8 @attributes={"title
"=>"Chapter 3", "id"=>"8", "parent_id"=>"1"}>]>
```

Let's use `acts_as_tree` in a controller and render the tree in a view. We start by creating a controller called chapters:

```
$ ruby script/generate controller chapters
```

We create an action called `showtree` in the `chapters_controller.rb` file. We set `@root` to `Section.find_by_parent_id(nil)`. The `find_by_parent_id` method is a dynamic finder and is the equivalent of `Section.find(:first, :conditions => "parent_id is null")`:

```
class ChaptersController < ApplicationController
      def showtree
            @root = Section.find_by_parent_id(nil)
      end
end
```

The `showtree.rhtml` file simply uses a code block to print out the chapters in the book (see Figure 4.8):

```
<h2>Book Chapters for <%=@root.title %></h2>
<ul>
<% @root.children.each do |child| %>
<li><%= child.title %> (parent: <%= child.parent.title %>)
<% end %>
</ul>
<hr>
```

Figure 4.8
Displaying hierarchical data.

> **Tip**
>
> In Chapter 14, "Designing Rails Applications," we will build a threaded forum using `acts_as_nested_tree`.

Timestamping Records

Active Record has one more trick up its sleeve—the ability to timestamp fields that are called `created_at`, `created_on`, `updated_at`, and `updated_on`. Once these fields are detected, Active Record automatically adds a timestamp when the record is saved.

To illustrate the use of `created_at` and `updated_at`, we create an item model:

```
$ ruby script/generate model item
      exists   app/models/
      exists   test/unit/
      exists   test/fixtures/
      create   app/models/item.rb
      create   test/unit/item_test.rb
      create   test/fixtures/items.yml
      exists   db/migrate
      create   db/migrate/005_create_items.rb
```

Edit the `005_create_items.rb` migration file and add `created_at` and `updated_at` columns to the `items` table. The data type is set to `datetime`:

```ruby
class CreateItems < ActiveRecord::Migration
  def self.up
    create_table :items do |t|
      t.column :title, :string
      t.column :created_at, :datetime
      t.column :updated_at, :datetime
    end
  end

  def self.down
    drop_table :items
  end
end
```

Run the migration to create the items table:

```
$ rake db:migrate
(in C:/rails/migrations)
== CreateItems: migrating ================================================
-- create_table(:items)
   -> 0.1090s
== CreateItems: migrated (0.1090s) =======================================
```

Now we use the create method to insert a record directly into the items table:

```
$ ruby script/console
Loading development environment.
>> Item.create :title => "Item 1"
=> #<Item:0x39c2874 @attributes={"updated_at"=>Mon Jan 08 19:18:36 E. Australia
Standard Time 2007, "title"=>"Item 1", "id"=>1, "created_at"=>Mon Jan 08 19:18:3
6 E. Australia Standard Time 2007}, @new_record=false, @errors=#<ActiveRecord::E
rrors:0x396bac4 @base=#<Item:0x39c2874 ...>, @errors={}
```

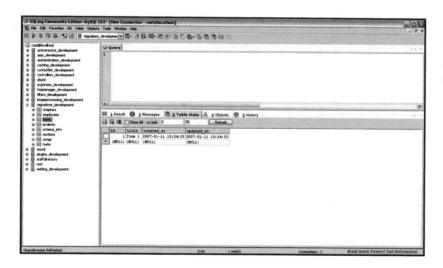

Figure 4.9
The timestamped created_at and updated_at fields.

The record that is saved back to the items table has the current time entered into the
created_at and updated_at fields (see Figure 4.9). If we update the record, only the
updated_at field will change. The timestamp is based on local time, but this can be configured
to Coordinated Universal Time (UTC) by editing the config/environment.rb file:

```
ActiveRecord::Base.default_timezone = :utc
```

Tip

It is convention to store `updated_on` and `created_on` columns as `Date` fields while `updated_at` and `created_at` **must be** `DateTime` **fields.**

We can disable timestamping on a per model basis:

```
class Item < ActiveRecord::Base
     self.record_timestamps = false
end
```

Automatic timestamping can be turned off on a per application basis by setting `ActiveRecord::Base.record_timestamps` to false in the `environment.rb` file:

```
ActiveRecord::Base.record_timestamps = false
```

Conclusion

Phew! We have covered a lot of ground and learned to use a crucial component of the Rails framework. Active Record greatly simplifies database access while still remaining extremely powerful. We looked at `find` as an alternative to writing SQL and modeled one-to-one, one-to-many, and many-to-many relationships. Out of the box, the default Active Record settings were able to serve us well. As you proceed to future chapters, take a moment to recap the Active Record naming conventions:

* Primary keys must be called `id`.
* Table names must be in plural (e.g. employees).
* Model names must be singular (e.g. employee).
* Foreign keys must take the name of their related table's class name and have `_id` as a suffix (e.g. `department_id`).
* Table columns that need to be timestamped must be called `created_at`, `created_on`, `updated_at`, **or** `updated_on`.

5 } Action Controller

This is the second chapter dedicated to the MVC paradigm, and it covers Action Controller—the component responsible for controllers in Rails. Action Controller implements functionality that is crucial to the underpinning architecture of any web application. Key to Action Controller's success is its tight integration with Action View. From within a controller, where all our application's business logic must be placed, we are able to persist data across requests, redirect incoming requests, retrieve posted form data, and customize template rendering. Finally, we will cover the concepts behind creating new routing rules for URLs within your Rails application.

In this chapter you'll learn to:

* Process forms
* Retrieve environment variables
* Use the `render` method to display templates
* Redirect requests
* Use cookies and sessions
* Use a temporary session-based storage area known as the flash to share messages between requests
* Understand and customize routing rules

Processing Form Elements

Rails, acting as a framework, wires everything together in a cohesive and transparent manner. In previous chapters we have used the `script/generate scaffold` command to output all the required controllers, actions, and views to deliver CRUDS for our Active Record models. The forms to insert and edit a model were automatically tied to a controller's action. It is useful to understand how forms elements are constructed, posted to a controller's action, retrieved in an action, and passed to a view. In this section we will build an example form and process the form elements with a simple action.

We start by generating a `formprocessor` controller:

```
$ ruby script/generate controller formprocessor
```

The following is output to the console:

```
exists app/controllers/
exists app/helpers/
create app/views/formprocessor
exists test/functional/
create app/controllers/formprocessor_controller.rb
create test/functional/formprocessor_controller_test.rb
create app/helpers/formprocessor_helper.rb
```

The `app\views\formprocessor\showform.rhtml` file will be rendered by an action called `showform`. An action is simply a method within a controller's class. The `showform.rhtml` template uses helpers to generate form elements. The `start_form_tag` helper renders an opening HTML form tag (`<form>`). We specify that the `show_formdata` action must be used to process the form. The `end_form_tag` helper closes the form with a `</form>` tag. The form also uses the `text_field_tag` (text input field), `select_tag` (drop down select box), `check_box_tag` (checkbox), and `submit_tag` (submit button) helpers to insert form elements. Figure 5.1 shows the form displayed in a browser.

```
<h2>A Simple Form</h2>
<%= start_form_tag(:action => "show_formdata") %>
<p>Text Field:
<%= text_field_tag("name","Aneesha") %></p>
<p>Drop-down Selection Box:
<% languages = ["Ruby", "Java", "C#"].map do |lang|
"<option>#{lang}</option>"
end.to_s %>
<%= select_tag("prog_languages[]", languages, :multiple => "true") %></p>
<p>Checkboxes:
<%= check_box_tag("operating_systems[]","Windows") %> Windows
<%= check_box_tag("operating_systems[]","Linux") %> Linux
<%= check_box_tag("operating_systems[]","Mac") %> Mac
</p>
```

```
<%= submit_tag("Submit Form") %>
<%= end_form_tag %>
```

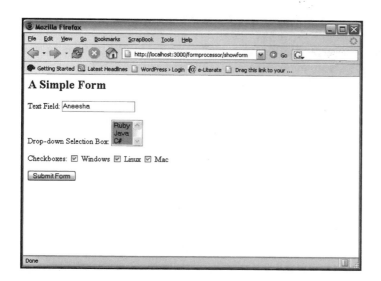

Figure 5.1
A simple form created with helpers.

The generated HTML source code when the showform action is rendered:

```
<h2>A Simple Form</h2>
<form action="/formprocessor/show_formdata" method="post">
<p>Text Field:
<input id="name" name="name" type="text" value="Aneesha" /></p>
<p>Drop-down Selection Box:
<select id="prog_languages[]" multiple="multiple" name="prog_languages[]">
<option>Ruby</option>
<option>Java</option>
<option>C#</option>
</select></p>
<p>Checkboxes:
<input id="operating_systems[]" name="operating_systems[]" type="checkbox"
value="Windows" /> Windows
<input id="operating_systems[]" name="operating_systems[]" type="checkbox"
value="Linux" /> Linux
<input id="operating_systems[]" name="operating_systems[]" type="checkbox"
value="Mac" /> Mac
```

```
</p>
<input name="commit" type="submit" value="Submit Form" />
</form>
```

The `formprocessor` **controller (**`formprocessor_controller.rb` **file) has two actions. The** `showform` **action displays the form shown in Figure 5.1. The** `show_formdata` **action retrieves the posted form data and stores the data in** `instance` **variables. These** `instance` **variables can be accessed within the** `show_formdata.rhtml` **template. This means that we can use** `show_formdata.rhtml` **to display the contents of the posted form. Posted form data is stored within the** `params` **hash. We can access each form element as either a string or symbol or key from the** `params` **hash:**

```
class FormprocessorController < ApplicationController
    def showform
    end

    def show_formdata
        @name = params[:name]
        @prog_languages = params[:prog_languages] || []
        @operating_systems = params[:operating_systems] || []
    end
end
```

The `@name` **variable is set by retrieving the** `:name` **symbol from the** `params` **hash. The** `:name` **symbol contains the data entered into the** `name` **input field. The** `prog_languages` **drop-down select box contains multiple elements, but because it is stored as an array with the** `params` **hash, we can still just reference it as** `params[:prog_languages]`. **The checkboxes used to specify an operating system are also stored as an array as multiple checkboxes could be checked.**

Here is an example `params` **hash:**

```
{
"prog_languages"=>["Ruby", "Java", "C#"],
"operating_systems"=>["Windows", "Linux", "Mac"]
}
```

Finally, we create a template (`show_formdata.rhtml`**) to display the posted form data. The** `@name`, `@prog_languages`, **and** `@operating_systems` **variables are available for use within the template. The** `@name` **variable can simply be displayed by using the** `<%=` **and** `%>` **delimiters.**

Because the `@prog_languages` and `@operating_systems` variables are arrays, we need to use a `join` method to display their contents as a comma delimited list:

```
<h2>Display Posted Form Data</h2>
Name: <%= @name %> <br />
Programming Languages: <%= @prog_languages.join(", ") %> <br />
Operating Systems: <%= @operating_systems.join(", ") %> <br />
<p>
YAML Output from Debug: <br />
<%= debug(params) %>
</p>
```

Note

The `debug` method displays the `params` hash in YAML, which is completely human readable. This is a simple way to display and analyze posted form data. The name of the executed controller and action are also displayed.

Retrieving Environment Variables

The request object also holds numerous variables related to the request and the server processing the request. These variables are known as environment variables. All server-side platforms used for web development (including JSP, Servlets, ASP.NET, PHP, and ColdFusion) provide access to these variables via a request object. Table 5.1 contains a list of useful environment variables.

Table 5.1   Environment Variables

Variable	Description
REQUEST_URI	The full request URL
SERVER_NAME	The domain name or IP address of the server
SERVER_PROTOCOL	Name and revision of the request protocol
SERVER_PORT	The port the request was made on
REQUEST_METHOD	The type of request made. This could be either GET or POST
PATH_INFO	The virtual path of the file or script being requested
PATH_TRANSLATED	The physical location or mapping of the virtual path
QUERY_STRING	Variables (key-value pairs) that follow the ? in the URL
REMOTE_HOST	Domain name of the computer making the request
REMOTE_ADDR	IP address of the computer making the request

Variable	Description
CONTENT_TYPE	The type of data attached to the POST request
CONTENT_LENGTH	The size of data sent with the request
HTTP_ACCEPT	Content or mime-types supported by the web browser making the request
HTTP_USER_AGENT	The web browser making the request

Create a controller called `environmentvariables`:

```
$ ruby script/generate controller environmentvariables
```

Within the `app/views/environmentvariables/index.rhtml` **template, we can now access a range of environment variables including** `request.env["REQUEST_METHOD"]` **and** `request.env["REMOTE_ADDR"]`:

```
<h2>Displaying Environment Variables</h2>
REQUEST_URI: <%= request.env["REQUEST_URI"] %> <br />
SERVER_NAME: <%= request.env["SERVER_NAME"] %> <br />
SERVER_PROTOCOL: <%= request.env["SERVER_PROTOCOL"] %> <br />
SERVER_PORT: <%= request.env["SERVER_PORT"] %> <br />
REQUEST_METHOD: <%= request.env["REQUEST_METHOD"] %> <br />
PATH_INFO: <%= request.env["PATH_INFO"] %> <br />
PATH_TRANSLATED: <%= request.env["PATH_TRANSLATED"] %> <br />
SCRIPT_NAME: <%= request.env["SCRIPT_NAME"] %> <br />
QUERY_STRING: <%= request.env["QUERY_STRING"] %> <br />
REMOTE_HOST: <%= request.env["REMOTE_HOST"] %> <br />
REMOTE_ADDR: <%= request.env["REMOTE_ADDR"] %> <br />
CONTENT_TYPE: <%= request.env["CONTENT_TYPE"] %> <br />
CONTENT_LENGTH: <%= request.env["CONTENT_LENGTH"] %> <br />
HTTP_ACCEPT: <%= request.env["HTTP_ACCEPT"] %> <br />
HTTP_USER_AGENT: <%= request.env["HTTP_USER_AGENT"] %> <br />
```

Figure 5.2 displays the rendered web page. You are probably thinking that a template error should be produced instead because we have not created an index action within the `environmentvariables` controller. We don't need to specify an index action unless we need to include additional business logic. If no action is specified in the URL path and no index action is present in the controller, the `index.rhtml` template will be displayed automatically.

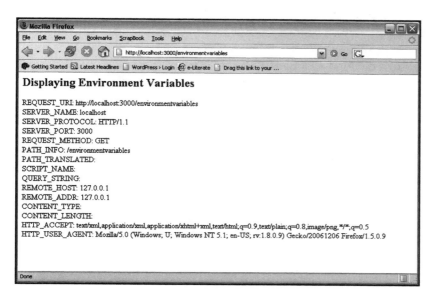

Figure 5.2
Retrieving and displaying
environment variables in a
template.

Exploring the Render Method

This section looks at how web pages are generated—a process known as *rendering* in Rails. Once an action has run, Rails looks for and renders a `.rhtml` template with the same name as the action. This is very powerful and saves us from having to map actions to templates manually. In most cases, this default behavior is exactly what we require, but once you start building applications, you will encounter situations where you need to customize the mapping of actions to templates. The `render` method in the `ActionController::Base` class allows us to specify an alternate template.

The following controller has two methods: `index` and `show_cities`. The `index` action calls the `show_cities` action by passing `'show_cities'` as the `:action` to the `render` method:

```
class SampleController < ApplicationController
    def index
        @cities = ['Brisbane', 'Sydney', 'Cairns']
        render :action => 'show_cities'
    end
    def show_cities
        @cities = ['Perth', 'Gold Coast', 'Melbourne']
    end
end
```

If the show_cities action is called, the show_cities method will be executed and then the show_cities.rhtml template will be rendered. If the index action is called, the @cities instance variable will be set, and once all code in the method is run, the show_cities.rhtml template will be rendered. Even though we are passing the :action to render, the show_cities action is not executed. The render method, as its name suggests, only renders a template. This means that if the template references any variables, these will need to be set in the current action. As you can see, we set the @cities variable in both the index and show_cities actions.

Note

The template specified by the render method is only generated once all code in the action is run. The render method is only allowed to be called once within an action. Calling render multiple times will produce an error.

If you really wanted to both call an action and render a template, we could do this as follows:

```
class SampleController < ApplicationController
    def index
        show_cities and render :action => 'show_cities'
    end
    def show_cities
        @cities = ['Perth', 'Gold Coast', 'Melbourne']
    end
end
```

Sometimes we just need to send some text to a browser and don't actually need a full template. The render method in its simplest form is able to just take a string as a parameter and send the string as text to a browser:

```
class TextController < ApplicationController
  ' def display_text
        render(:text => "Hey - Rails is cool!")
    end
end
```

We can also pass the absolute path and filename of the template file to the render method. The file extension must be included. If the template file is in the default location, set the optional :use_full_path parameter to true. We use the :locals hash to set variables that can be accessed within the specified template:

```
render(:file =>path, [ :use_full_path =>true|false ], [ :locals =>hash ])
```

The `:template` parameter allows us to specify a template from another controller. The action and the controller names must be separated with a forward slash (/):

```
class SampleController < ApplicationController
    def index
        render(:template => "controller/sample_action")
    end
end
```

Using an Action to Generate Files

Instead of rendering a template after an action is run, we can also send a binary stream to a web browser. A binary stream could be a file or an image—you must, however, specify an appropriate mime or content type and content disposition. The web browser uses the content type and content disposition to determine whether to display the data inline, launch an application, or ask the user to save the file. The `send_data` method takes the binary stream as the first parameter. The :filename, :type, and :disposition must also be specified. The `:filename` is the name that the file will be saved as when it is downloaded by a user. The `:type` is the mime-type or content type of the binary data stream. The default content type is `application/octet-stream`. The `:disposition` setting allows us to determine whether the data should be displayed inline or saved/downloaded.

Here is an example of using the `send_data` method to retrieve an image stored as binary data (blob) within a database field and render the image as a png image format:

```
def render_pic
    @pic = Pic.find(params[:id])
    send_data(@pic.data,
                :filename => @pic.name,
                :type => @pic.content_type,
                :disposition => "inline")
end
```

The `send_file` method is also useful. With the `send_file` method, we can specify a file to be sent to a browser. This is handy if we want to hide the file location of a file, password protect files, or only allow access to logged in users:

```
send_file('/path/to.jpeg', :type => 'image/jpeg', :disposition => 'inline')
```

Redirection

The `redirect_to` method is located within the `ActionController::Base` class. The `redirect_to` method performs HTTP redirection. You are able to redirect a request to an external URL or to a controller and action within your current application. With `redirect_to`, we can redirect a request to another action within the currently called controller, an action in another controller, and even external URL. Redirecting to an external web site is easy because we only need to pass a URL to the `redirect_to` method. More complex internal site redirects require a hash with an optional controller, action, and id keys.

> **Note**
>
> Actions with a call to `redirect_to` don't need a `.rhtml` template because the body of the HTTP redirect is not displayed within a browser.

In this example, various calls to `redirect_to` are made to illustrate the use of the optional `:action`, `:controller`, and `:id` settings:

```ruby
class RedirectionController < ApplicationController
    def rubyonrails_site
        # Redirect to an external URL
        redirect_to "http://www.rubyonrails.org/"
    end
    def checkout
        # Redirect to the goto_checkout action in the current controller
        redirect_to :action => 'goto_checkout'
    end
    def index
        # Redirect to the show_book action in the book controller
        redirect_to :controller => 'book', :action => 'show_book'
    end
    def reserve_book
        # Redirect to the request_book action and pass the id
        redirect_to :action => 'request_book', :id => params[:id]
    end
    def buy_book
        # Redirect to the purchase_book action and pass the id
        redirect_to :action => 'purchase_book', :id => 234563
```

```
    end
end
```

You'll notice that in some of the actions we neglected to specify a controller and an action. If no controller is specified, the current controller is assumed. If no action is specified, the index action will be run.

 Warning

Execution does not stop when a redirect_to is encountered. Rails still runs the code placed after a redirect_to. Don't place any code that may be harmful or dangerous after a redirect_to call, as it won't be ignored.

Cookies

Rails includes a cookie object, which encapsulates the HTTP cookie protocol. Cookies were introduced as a solution to the statelessness of the HTTP protocol. Cookies store data within a client's browser. Cookies can be accessed between HTTP requests. The cookie object returns a hash of key/value pairs.

Setting a cookie called my_name:

```
cookies[:my_name] = "Aneesha"
```

Retrieving a cookie called my_name:

```
my_name = cookies[:my_name]
```

Even though a cookie key/value pair is set in code, the data will only be saved as a cookie in a user's browser once the request is completed. In the following example, we use both the redirect_to and render methods covered in previous sections. We set a cookie, then redirect to an action that will retrieve and display the value stored in the cookie:

```
class CookiecutterController < ApplicationController
    def set_cookie
        cookies[:my_name] = "Aneesha"
        redirect_to :action => "show_cookie"
    end
    def show_cookie
        my_name = cookies[:my_name]
        render(:text => "Hello #{my_name}!")
```

```
      end
end
```

> **Tip**
>
> Cookies are only useful for storing string data, and are only able to store four kilobytes of data. Use sessions, covered in the next section, to store objects and structured data.

Cookies expire and are deleted once the current web browser is closed. We can, however, manually set the expiration date. In the following example, the cookie will expire after 24 hours:

```
cookies[:my_name] = { :value => 'Aneesha', :expires => Time.now + 24.hour}
```

We can also delete cookies from within our code:

```
cookies.delete :my_name
```

There are optional parameters we could include in the `cookies` hash. The `:domain` and `:path` options determine the domains and paths within an application that can read and update a cookie. Setting `:secure` to true will only allow cookies to be accessed over HTTPS or secure encrypted connections.

Sessions

Cookies would be much more useful if we could store structured data and data that exceeded the four kilobyte limit. Sessions were introduced to address these limitations. A session only stores a unique id as a cookie. The unique id (_session_id) is used to identify the user and associates the user with data stored on the server. A session is a hash and is able to store multiple key/value pairs. Because the data is stored on the server, structured data and serializable objects are able to be stored.

Storing a key/value pair in the session hash:

```
session[:username] = "Aneesha"
```

Retrieving a key/value pair from the session hash:

```
@username = session[:username]
```

If you are running more than one Rails application on a server, you should customize the session_key. The session_options are set in the config/environment.rb file:

```
ActionController::Base.session_options[:session_key] = 'your_app_name'
```

Session data by default is stored locally in a flat file known as `PStore`. PStore, however, does not scale very well and can't be shared across multiple servers in a clustered environment. We can, however, store sessions within the current Rails applications database using `ActiveRecordStore`.

The session storage option is set by the `session_store` attribute of `ActiveRecord::Base`:

```
config.action_controller.session_store = CGI::Session::PStore
```

We need to change the `session_storage` option to `:active_record_store` to enable database storage:

```
config.action_controller.session_store = :active_record_store
```

There is a Rake command to run a migration to create a `sessions` table:

```
$ rake db:sessions:create
```

The sessions table has an index on the `session_id` field. There is also a timestamped `updated_at` field.

Using the Flash

The *flash* is a temporary storage area where data can be preserved between action calls (requests) and redirects. We can store key/value pairs in the flash—it is just a hash stored within the current session. The flash is handy when you need to inform the user of the outcome of the last action or display an error message. Values stored in the *hash* are only available to the next request and then deleted.

Storing data in the flash:

```
flash[:info] = "The entry has successfully been added."
```

We are able to store multiple key/value pairs in the flash:

```
flash[:info] = "The entry has successfully been added."
flash[:error] = "An error has occurred."
```

The flash can be accessed from within a template:

```
<div id="info">
    <%= @flash[:info] %>
</div>
```

We can use an `if` statement to check whether a key/value pair exists in the hash and then display the `div` tag:

```
<% if @flash[:info] %>
    <div id="info">
        <%= @flash[:info] %>
    </div>
<% end %>
```

It is also possible to set a key/value pair and only make it available to the current request (not save it as a session):

```
flash.now[:info] = "Just for this request"
```

The `keep` method allows us to store a key/value pair for an additional request:

```
flash.keep(:info)
```

If no parameters are passed to the `keep` method, all key/values pairs in the flash will be preserved for another request:

```
flash.keep()
```

Routing

In Chapter 3, "Prototyping Database-Driven Applications with Rails," we made an FAQ Manager. The FAQ Manager was primarily built using the `scaffold` command. While testing the application, you would have noticed that typing **http://localhost:3000/faq** as the URL loaded the `index` action of the `faq` controller. The `index` action displayed all the FAQs. They were displayed with links to show, edit, and delete individual FAQs. We were also able to add a new FAQ. The edit form is shown in Figure 5.3. You'll notice that the URL to display the edit form is **http://localhost:3000/faq/edit/1**. Rails is able to parse the URL and map the request to the appropriate controller and action as well as assign a value to the `:id`. The URL to show an FAQ is **http://localhost:3000/faq/show/1**. Again, Rails is able to route this request to the `show` controller. This raises some interesting questions. Where does this routing occur? How can we create custom routing rules?

Rails provides intelligent defaults in relation to routing requests to controllers and actions without requiring you to author complex XML configuration files. This does not mean that you can't easily change the default configuration settings. Routing is a classic example of the flexibility provided by Rails. The `config/routes.rb` file contains the URL routing rules. The code that Rails generates comes with two rules. The first rule handles the requests for a Web Service Description Language (WSDL) file. You'll learn more about WSDL in Chapter 7, "Web Services and RESTful Applications." The second routing rule is responsible for mapping **http://localhost:3000/faq/edit/1** to the `edit` action of the `faq` controller:

Figure 5.3
A simple form created with helpers.

```
ActionController::Routing::Routes.draw do |map|
    map.connect ':controller/service.wsdl', :action => 'wsdl'
    map.connect ':controller/:action/:id'
end
```

Each `map.connect` declaration is responsible for a routing rule. The first match is used and, if no match occurs, a routing error will be produced. The pattern matching `':controller/:action/:id'` matches URLs with three components separated by a forward slash (/). The components preceded with a : (i.e., symbols in Ruby) are added as keys to the `params` hash.

The `params` hash produced for http://localhost:3000/faq/edit/1:

```
@params = { :controller => 'faq', :action => 'edit', :id => 1 }
```

Additional parameters accepted by `map.connect`:

```
:defaults => { :name => "value", ... }
```

This allows us to set any default values. As an example, we could specify the default action to be index and the :id to be nil.

```
defaults => { :action => "index", :id => nil }
```

This matches a URL component to a regular expression. This can be very powerful and we will use this to help us match dates in a URL.

```
:requirements => { :name =>/regularexpression/, ...}
```

We can specify the request type under which a route will be matched by using :conditions. This is very handy because we could map the same URL to different actions based upon whether a get or post request was made. Here is an example:

```
ActionController::Routing::Routes.draw do |map|
    map.connect 'faq/destroy',
        :conditions => { :method => :get },
        :controller => "faq",
        :action => "show"
    map.connect 'faq/destroy',
        :conditions => { :method => :post },
        :controller => "faq",
        :action => "destroy"
end
```

Creating a Date-Based Routing Rule for a Weblog

The following map.connect rule allows http://localhost:3000/article/2007/12/8 to be used to display all the articles published on the 8th of December 2007. Regular expressions are used to match the year, month, and day and to add the key/value pairs to the params hash. We also set defaults if the day and month are missing:

```
map.connect "article/:year/:month/:day",
    :controller => "article",
    :action => "show",
    :requirements => { :year => /(19|20)\d\d/,
    :month => /[01]?\d/,
    :day => /[0-3]?\d/},
    :day => nil,
    :month => nil
```

Changing an Application's Default Page

You probably have noticed that even though we have built numerous sample applications, the default mapping of the domain (http://localhost:3000) has still been pointing to the "Welcome to Rails" page, which is located in the public/index.html (see Figure 5.4). The public/index.html page can be customized, but it is still going to be a static page. In most cases, a static home page is inappropriate—we are, after all, building dynamic database-driven applications. Routing comes to the rescue and allows us to map the home page to any controller and action within our application.

Figure 5.4
The Welcome to Rails starting page.

The public/index.html must be removed. Due to the inbuilt Rails routing rule, if the public/index.html file is found, it will always be displayed no matter what other mappings are specified.

We add a mapping to the config/routes.rb file that displays the homepage action of the welcome controller when only the domain is called from within a browser (http:// http://localhost:3000/):

```
ActionController::Routing::Routes.draw do |map|
    map.connect '', :controller => "welcome", :action => "homepage"
    map.connect ':controller/service.wsdl', :action => 'wsdl'
    map.connect ':controller/:action/:id'
end
```

The first `map.connect` call we make in the `config/routes.rb` file has a blank initial argument. In this rule, no path is specified and the call will match all the URLs where only the domain has been specified (i.e., blank URLs). We are then able to set the controller and its actions that must be called when a pathless URL has been specified.

Using the Rails Console to Test Routing Rules

Routing rules can be tested from within the Rails console. In some cases this is easier than testing the routing rules in a web browser. Run the Rails console for any Rails application:

```
$ ruby script/console
Loading development environment.
```

Create an instance of `ActionController::Routing::Routes`. The `RouteSet` is quite complex—the full result produced is not listed:

```
>> r = ActionController::Routing::Routes
=> #<ActionController::Routing::RouteSet:0x323c794
@builder=#<ActionController::
Routing::RouteBuilder:0x3ac8f0c @optional_separators=["/"], @separators=["/",
";
```

Use `puts` to list the routing rules for the current application. Three items are listed for each rule: the HTTP request to respond to, the format to match, and optional parameters:

```
>> puts r.routes
ANY /:controller/service.wsdl/ {:action=>"wsdl"}
ANY /:controller/:action/:id.:format/ {}
ANY /:controller/:action/:id/ {}
=> nil
```

We can now use the `recognize` method to check whether a path is valid:

```
>> r.recognize_path "/faq"
=> {:controller=>"faq", :action=>"index"}
```

We could also generate a path to access a controller:

```
>> r.generate :controller => :faq
=> "/faq"
```

If routing rules are changed, you will need to reload the `config/routes.rb` file. This can be done within the console:

```
>> load "config/routes.rb"
=> []
```

Conclusion

This chapter covered the essential elements that make up Action Controller. You learned to utilize methods to help customize template rendering, redirect incoming requests, use the flash to communicate between requests, and customize URL routing. You also learned how to process posted forms and use the `params` hash. Action Controller is only one half of Action Pack—Action View will be covered in depth in the chapter that follows.

6 } Action View

In the last two chapters we covered Active Record and Action Controller. We now turn our attention to Action View—the remaining component of the Model View Controller (MVC) paradigm. The View is responsible for rendering the data for display or interaction. Examples include records retrieved from a database displayed in a tabular manner within a web page or a form where a user can edit the data already stored in a database table. Key Rails concepts such as helpers, layouts, and partials will also be covered.

In this chapter you'll learn to:

* Create templates using Embedded Ruby (ERb)
* Use helper methods
* Share layouts across templates
* Use partials to share code across templates
* Use helpers to create forms
* Use helpers to associate form fields with a model

Embedded Ruby (ERb) and Templates

Action View is the Rails component responsible for rendering a view that is associated with a controller's action. A controller can have multiple actions (also known as methods), each of which is automatically mapped to render a view with the same name. A view is also known as a template or a template file. Actions automatically map to .rhtml templates, which are contained within the app/views folder. A .rhtml template renders HTML and can contain Ruby code. Embedded Ruby (ERb) allows Ruby code to be interpreted when it is placed in a text file. We first encountered ERb in Chapter 2, "Ruby Essentials."

A folder that corresponds to the name of each controller is created in the app/views folder. If we created a simple Rails application that has an admin and a user controller, the templates for the admin controller will be found in the `app/views/admin` folder. The templates for the user controller will be located in the `app/views/user` folder.

We are not restricted to using the automatic mapping of actions to `.rhtml` templates with the same name. The `render` method could be used to call another action, redirect to another controller's action, or call a template file that is located elsewhere:

```
render(:action => action_name') # render template from another action
render(:template => 'controller/name') # render the template of an action from
another controller
render(:file => 'folder_name/template') # render template from another folder
```

The rendered view does not have to be HTML. The generated view could also be XML, PDF, or RJS (Rails JavaScript). We will cover the generation of these different types of views throughout the book:

* XML generation is covered in Chapter 7, "Web Services and RESTful Applications."
* RJS generation is covered in Chapter 8, "AJAX and Rails."
* PDF generation is covered in Chapter 10, "Rails Plug-Ins."

Within a `.rhtml` file the `<%=` and `%>` delimiters are used to evaluate an expression, convert the result to a string (using a `to_s` method), and insert the result with the generated HTML file.

Displaying the current time:

```
<%= Time.now %>
```

The `<%` and `%>` delimiters can be used to insert arbitrary Ruby code. In the following example, a variable called `page_title` is set and then printed out in two places using the `<%=` and `%>` delimiters. The rainfall data is stored in a hash and output using a code block:

```
<% page_title = "Rainfall Averages" %>
<html>
<head>
    <title><%=page_title%></title>
</head>
<body>
<%
rainfall =
        {
      "Jan - Mar" => "10mm",
      "Apr - Jun" => "20mm",
      "Jul - Sep" => "2mm",
```

```
          "Oct - Dec" => "6mm"
            }
%>
<h2><%=page_title%></h2>
<table border="1">
<tr><td>Quarter</td><td>Rainfall</td></tr>
<%
rainfall.each do |key, value|
%>
    <tr><td><%=key%></td><td><%=value%></td></tr>
<%
end
%>
</table>
<hr>
Last updated: <%=Time.now%>
</body>
</html>
```

A newline character is included for each <% and %> delimiter pair. If this extra whitespace prevents you from debugging the generated HTML or causes an increase in bandwidth/download file size, the <% and -%> delimiters should be used. Here is an example that does not produce a newline character:

```
<% the_time = Time.now -%>
<%=the_time %>
```

Passing Objects and Variables to a Template

A view is able to access instance variables set in the action from which it was called. In the example that follows, an instance variable called the_time is set in the telltime action within the timefunctions controller.

The timefunctions_controller.rb file in the app/controllers folder:

```
class TimeFunctionsController < ApplicationController
    def telltime
        @the_time = Time.Now
    end
end
```

The `telltime.rhtml` file in the `app/views/timefunctions` folder:

```
<html>
<head>
    <title><%=the_time%></title>
</head>
<body>
<h2><%=the_time%></h2>
</body>
</html>
```

We also have access to posted form data, the session, and request and response objects:

```
<html>
<head>
    <title>Objects available to a View</title>
</head>
<body>
<h2>Session</h2> <%= debug(session) %>
<h2>Params</h2> <%= debug(params) %>
<h2>Response</h2> <%= debug(response) %>
</body>
</html>
```

> ❋ **Note**
>
> The debug method serializes objects to YAML and HTML escapes the output, making it easier to read the contents of an object you wish to review.

Creating Helpers

Even though business logic is placed in the controller, you will require Ruby code to help you format output for display. Rather than place this code directly within the view, Rails allows helper modules to be accessed from within a `.rhtml` template. Helpers promote code reuse because they can be shared across views. Helpers are also easier to test. You will really appreciate helpers when you need to work with an interface designer. A view file that does not have complex embedded Ruby is easier for an interface designer to work with.

A helper is a module, and a module in Ruby is simply a collection of functions. Each controller has its own helper module. All of the actions and views associated with a controller have access to its helper module. When `script/generate` is run, the helper module for a controller is created and named according to the Rails convention. A controller called FAQController has a helper module called FAQHelper that is stored in the `app/helpers/faq_helper.rb` file.

Here we made a FAQHelper (`app/helpers/faq_helper.rb`) with a `page_title` method:

```
module FAQHelper
    def page_title
        @page_title || "Frequently Asked Questions - FAQ"
    end
end
```

We can now call this method from an `.rhtml` template:

```
<html>
<head>
    <title><%= page_title %></title>
</head>
<body>
<h2><%= page_title %></</h2>
</body>
</html>
```

Sharing Helpers

The `application_helper.rb` helper module is available to views throughout your entire application. The `application_helper.rb` file is located within the `app/helpers` folder. We are also able to include helper modules from other controllers. In this example, the `TimeFunctions` controller is able to call methods from the `DateFunctions` controller:

```
class TimeFunctionsController < ApplicationController
    helper :datefunctions
end
```

Rails Inbuilt Helpers

Rails includes numerous helpers to assist with formatting. Let's explore a sampling.

Convert a file size from bytes to kilobytes:

```
<%= number_to_human_size(888_000) %> # 886.1 KB
```

Convert a decimal number to a percentage:

```
<%= number_to_percentage(52.22222222, :precision => 1) %> # 62.2%
```

As you can see, the inbuilt Rails helpers can be called from within the <%= and %> delimiters.

It is not advisable to display data entered by a user without first escaping any HTML code that could potentially break the layout of a web page. The html_escape helper, as its name suggests, escapes HTML markup. This means that some text will be displayed instead of **some text**. In this example, the first_name field is escaped with the shorthand syntax for calling html_escape:

```
The value of first_name is <%= h(params[:first_name]) %>
```

The sanitize helper leaves formatting intact but removes <form> and <script> tags because these may introduce security concerns. OnClick events as well as links that call JavaScript functions (<a href="Javascript:alert()">A Javascript link</a>) are also removed.

```
The value of form_text is <%= sanitize(params[:form_text]) %>
```

The auto_link helper makes all URLs and e-mail links clickable. We can also specify the href option that needs to be inserted. The following example changes the target of link to "_blank":

```
auto_link(form_text, :all, :target => '_blank')
```

The strip_links method removes all <a href> tags:

```
strip_links(form_text)
```

The simple_format method converts line breaks (\n) to <br \> tags and surrounds paragraphs with <p> and </p> tag pairs.

```
Simple_format(form_text)
```

The truncate helper only displays the specified number of characters and replaces the last three characters in the sequence with the truncate_string (" . . . ") if the text is longer than specified.

```
truncate(form_text, length = 15, truncate_string = "...")
```

There are also Rails helpers to support textile and markdown formatting. We used the textilize helper in Chapter 3 to mark up our blog posts. RedCloth must be installed to use the textilize helper. BlueCloth is required by the markdown helper.

```
textilize(form_text)
markdown(form_text)
```

Creating Links

In this section, we will be using helpers from the `ActionView::Helpers::UrlHelper` modules. The `link_to` helper inserts links to actions in a controller. This example will render a link called `"Add an FAQ"` that, when clicked, will send a `Get` request to the `add_faq` action:

```
<%= link_to "Add FAQ", :action => "add_faq" %>
```

The first parameter passed to `link_to` contains the text inserted between the `<a href>` and `</a>` tag pairs. The `:action` parameter is a hash, and it specifies the link's target. Here we call the `delete` action and pass the `id` of the object that must be deleted.

```
<%= link_to "Delete FAQ", { :action => "delete", :id => @faq} %>
```

There is an optional third parameter, which is also a hash and sets the HTML attributes. Here a `class` from a style sheet is specified:

```
<%=
link_to "Delete FAQ ", { :action => "delete", :id => @faq},
{ :class  => "faqlink" }
%>
```

To make sure that the user really wants to delete a record, we can display a JavaScript prompt:

```
<%=
link_to "Delete FAQ ", { :action => "delete", :id => @faq},
{
    :class  => "faqlink",
    :confirm => "Are you sure you want to delete this record?"
}
%>
```

❄ **Tip**

We can also use the `link_to` method to insert absolute URLs:

```
<%= link_to("Google", "http://www.google.com") %>
```

The `button_to` helper takes the same parameters as the `link_to` helper and inserts a button and a form.

In the example that follows, a `mailto` link will be inserted by the `mail_to` helper. A `mailto` link opens your mail client if it is an installed application, such as Eudora or Microsoft Outlook.

The `encode` **parameter uses JavaScript to make the link harder to be mined by e-mail address harvesters.**

```
<%= mail_to("superiorsupport@randomsyntax.com", "Get some help",
:subject => "Support request",
:encode => "javascript")
%>
```

 Tip

Use the `:replace_at` and `:replace_dot` options to replace @ and dots in the specified e-mail address. E-mail harvesters are getting smarter, so this is unlikely to work.

The `image_tag` **helper inserts images. The first parameter passed to the** `image_tag` **method is the path to the image. If the path does not begin with a** `/`**, it is assumed to be in the** `/images` **directory.**

The `image_tag` **helper can be used to create** `<img>` **tags. The image size may be specified using a single** `:size` **parameter (of the form width×height) or by explicitly giving the width and height as separate parameters. The** `size` **option can be used to specify both the width and the height of the image, or we could set these options separately.**

```
<%= image_tag("/images/rails.png", :size => "200x200") %>
<%= image_tag("/images/train.gif", :width => "200", :height => "230") %>
```

 Tip

It is an accessibility requirement to include alternate text for an image. You should always set the `alt` parameter, but if you don't, Rails will use the filename as the `alt` attribute.

In this example, we use an icon to delete a record by passing `image_tag` to the `link_helper`:

```
<%= link_to(
image_tag("deleteicon.gif", :size => "45x20"),
{ :controller => "managefaq",
:action => "delete",
:id => @faq},
{ :confirm => "Are you sure you want to delete this FAQ?" })
%>
```

Layouts

Page elements, such as a header, footer, and sidebar, are usually shared across an entire application or a subset of pages. When the `script/generate` is run, a layout file is also created and placed in the `app/views/layouts` folder. Each call to an action in a controller renders two templates—the template associated with the action and the layout file for the controller. The rendered output of the called action is actually passed to the layout as `:layout`. The `yield` method is used to insert the action's rendered content into the template.

An example `admin.rhtml` layout in `app/views/layouts`:

```
<html>
<head>
<title>Controller name: <%= controller.action_name %></title>
</head>
<body>
<%= yield :layout %>
</body>
</html>
```

This template is rendered by the sayhello action:

```
<h1>Say Hello</h1>
```

The output displayed in the browser includes the rendered layout:

```
<html>
<head>
<title>Form: sayhello</title>
</head>
<body>
<h1>Say Hello</h1>
</body>
</html>
```

Note

Instance variables available to an action's template are also available within the layout.

Including Template-Specific Content in a Layout

Templates can inject their own content into a layout. This is handy if you need to include specific HTML elements (such as a sidebar), stylesheets, or JavaScript for certain templates. The `content_for` **block stores the content in a symbol. Ruby code can be placed in the** `content_for` **block—just use normal ERb:**

```
<h1>Template with Sidebar</h1>
<% content_for(:sidebar) do %>
It is <%= Time.Now %>
<% end %>
```

If `:sidebar` **has been set, its content will be injected into the layout by** `yield :sidebar`:

```
<html>
<body>
<%= yield :sidebar %>
</body>
</html>
```

Including Scripts and Style Sheets in a Layout

The `AssetTagHelper` (`ActionView::Helpers::AssetTagHelper`) **module has a few methods that will come in handy when building layouts. The** `AssetTagHelper` **includes helpers to link to style sheets and JavaScript code.**

The `javascript_include_tag` **method inserts** `<script>` **tags for each JavaScript filename passed to the method in a comma separated list. The JavaScript files must be placed in the** `public/javascripts` **folder. If the** `:defaults` **parameter is passed to the** `javascript_include_tag`, **the JavaScript files for the Prototype and Scriptaculous libraries** (`prototype.js`, `effects.js`, `dragdrop.js`, **and** `controls.js`) **as well as** `application.js` **will be rendered.**

The `stylesheet_link_tag` **is used to output a** `<style>` **tag and reference the style sheets passed as a list to the helper.**

```
<%= stylesheet_link_tag("faq,admin"%>
```

> ❄ **Tip**
>
> Static content need not reside within your current application, or even on the same server. Sometimes it makes more sense to have a dedicated server to handle static content. The `asset_host` variable can be used to set the path to a static content or media server:
>
> ```
> ActionController::Base.asset_host = "http://www.randomsyntax.com/
> staticmedia"
> ```

Partials

A partial can best be described as a sub-template. A *partial* is a snippet of HTML markup and Ruby code that can be called from other templates. Objects can be passed to partials, making them very powerful. The name of a `.rhtml` template file that is a partial must be prefixed with an underscore. The naming convention is used to make it easy to differentiate partials and normal template files.

We use the `render_partial` helper in the `list.rhtml` template. Objects are passed to the partial via the `:object` attribute.

```
<h1>My Weblog</h1>
<p><%= link_to 'New post', :action => 'new' %></p>
<%= render (:partial => "post", :object => @posts.id) %>
```

We name our partial `_post.rhtml` and place it in the `app/views/blog` folder. The partial can access the properties of the object that has been passed to it. Here is the code:

```
<div>
<h2><%= link_to post.title, :action => 'show', :id => post %></h2>
<p><%=textilize(post.body) %></p>
<p><%=post.created_at.to_s() %> </p>
</div>
```

Partials and Collections

In the following template we use a `for` loop to iterate over all posts in our blog in reverse order:

```
<h1>My Weblog</h1>
<p><%= link_to 'New post', :action => 'new' %></p>
<% for post in @posts.reverse %>
<div>
<h2><%= link_to post.title, :action => 'show', :id => post %></h2>
<p><%=textilize(post.body) %></p>
<p><%=post.created_at.to_s() %>
(<%= link_to 'Edit', :action => 'edit', :id => post %> | <%= link_to 'Destroy',
{ :action => 'destroy', :id => post }, :confirm => 'Are you sure?', :post =>
true %>)
</p>
</div>
<% end %>
```

The HTML used to display the blog post needs to be used in the `show.rhtml` template as well. The `show.rhtml` file will have additional functionality to allow comments to be added to the blog. Instead of copying the code to display a post, we create a partial called `_post.rhtml`:

```
<div>
<h2><%= link_to post.title, :action => 'show', :id => post %></h2>
<p><%=textilize(post.body) %></p>
<p><%=post.created_at.to_s() %> </p>
</div>
```

The `show.rhtml` can simply call the `_post.rhtml` partial:

```
<%= render :partial => "post", :object => @post  %>
<%= link_to 'Edit', :action => 'edit', :id => @post %> |
<%= link_to 'Back', :action => 'list' %>
```

The `list.rhtml` file that displays all posts also gets drastically simplified. We don't need to place the partial within a loop because the `render` helper is able to take a collection:

```
<h1>My Weblog</h1>
<p><%= link_to 'New post', :action => 'new' %></p>
<%= render :partial => "post", :collection => @posts.reverse %>
```

The `:spacer_template` parameter allows us to specify a template after each iteration of the collection:

```
<h1>My Weblog</h1>
<p><%= link_to 'New post', :action => 'new' %></p>
<%= render :partial => "post", :collection => @posts.reverse, :spacer_template
=> "hrdivider" %>
```

> **※ Tip**
>
> Partials can be referenced by path. This makes it easy to share partials across controllers. It is a convention to place shared partials in a folder called `shared`.
>
> ```
> <%= render(:partial => "shared/post" , :object => @post) %>
> ```

Using Helpers to Create Forms

Forms allow users to enter and edit data. Rails has a unique way of mapping form elements to `ActiveRecord` model objects—making it very simple to build database-enabled web applications. Let's take a look at an insert FAQ form (`new.rhtml`) generated by `script/generate` **scaffold. The** `new.rhtml` **form allows users to enter a new FAQ that will be mapped to an** `faq` `ActiveRecord` **object and saved to the database.**

```
<h1>New faq</h1>
<%= start_form_tag :action => 'create' %>
  <%= render :partial => 'form' %>
  <%= submit_tag "Create" %>
<%= end_form_tag %>
<%= link_to 'Back', :action => 'list' %>
```

The `start_form_tag` **helper inserts the opening** `<form>` **tag and posts the form to the** `create` **action. The** `end_form_tag` **closes the form with the** `</form>` **tag. The** `submit_tag` **helper inserts a Submit button and names it Create. The** `link_to` **helper that we covered earlier in this chapter provides a link to the** `list` **action, which will render** `list.rhtml` **and display all the FAQs.**

The form elements are actually going to be the same across the Edit and New forms, so these elements have actually been extracted and placed within a partial called `_form.rthml`. **The automated scaffold generator is indeed smart. Let's take a peek into the** `_form.rhtml` **form:**

```
<%= error_messages_for 'faq' %>
<!--[form:faq]-->
<p><label for="faq_question">Question</label><br/>
<%= text_field 'faq', 'question'  %></p>
<p><label for="faq_answer">Answer</label><br/>
<%= text_area 'faq', 'answer'  %></p>
<p><label for="faq_category">Category</label><br/>
  <select name="faq[category_id]">
   <% @categories.each do |category| %>
      <option value="<%= category.id %>"
        <%= ' selected' if category.id == @faq.category_id %>>
        <%= category.name %>
      </option>
   <% end %>
  </select>
</p>
<!--[eoform:faq]-->
```

The `text_field` helper renders a text entry input box. It takes the name of the Active Record model and the attributes or properties that the form fields maps to. The `text_area` helper takes the same parameters. Table 6.1 lists the helpers used in the form, and shows the HTML that has been rendered. Here is what the rendered HTML source looks like:

```html
<h1>New faq</h1>
<form action="/faq/create" method="post">
<!--[form:faq]-->
<p><label for="faq_question">Question</label><br/>
<input id="faq_question" name="faq[question]" size="30" type="text" /></p>
<p><label for="faq_answer">Answer</label><br/>
<textarea cols="40" id="faq_answer" name="faq[answer]" rows="20">
</textarea></p>
<p><label for="faq_category">Category</label><br/>
  <select name="faq[category_id]">

        <option value="1">
          Databases
        </option>

        <option value="2">
          Forums
        </option>

        <option value="3">
          General
        </option>

        <option value="4">
          Intranet
        </option>
  </select>
</p>
<!--[eoform:faq]-->
<input name="commit" type="submit" value="Create" />
</form>
<a href="/faq/list">Back</a>
```

Table 6.1 Rendered Form Elements

Helper	Rendered HTML Tag
`<%= start_form_tag :action => 'create' %>`	`<form action="/faq/create" method="post">`
`<%= text_field 'faq', 'question' %>`	`<input id="faq_question" name="faq [question]" size="30" type="text" />`
`<%= text_area 'faq', 'answer' %>`	`<textarea cols="40" id="faq_answer" name="faq [answer]" rows="20"></textarea>`
`<%= submit_tag "Create" %>`	`<input name="commit" type="submit" value="Create" />`
`<%= end_form_tag %>`	`</form>`

In Table 6.1 you can clearly see how Rails makes use of the `id` and `name` elements of HTML form elements. The model name (`faq`), an underscore, and the model attribute name (`question`) are assigned to the `id`. The `name` attribute is set to the *modelname[modelattribute]* (faq [question]). Posted form data is stored in the `params` hash. Simple values are just stored as a scalar in the hash. If braces (`[]`) are present, Rails assumes that the fields are part of a structured data set and stored in a hash. The string inside the braces (`question`) is the key in the hash.

> ❈ **Note**
>
> The `form_tag` Helper is a block.
>
> In versions of Rails prior to 1.2, you might have noticed that the `form_tag` was not a code block and the HTML tag to close a form (`</form>`) had to be used:
>
> ```
> <%= form_tag :action => :edit  %>
> </form>
> ```
>
> In Rails 1.2, the `form_tag` is a proper block and the `end_form_tag` can be used to close the form:
>
> ```
> <%= form_tag :action => :edit %>
> <%= end_form_tag %>
> ```

Select Boxes

The `select` helper renders a select box. The `choices` parameter must contain a collection of items that must be displayed as options within the select box—arrays, hashes, and database records are all acceptable.

```
form.select(:attribute, choices, options, html_options)
```

In this example, the cities in Australia are displayed in a select box:

```
<% form_for :vacation do |form| %>
<%= form.select(:city, %w{ Brisbane Sydney Melbourne Perth}) %>
<% end %>
```

The following HTML is generated:

```
<select id="vacation_city" name="vacation[city]" >
<option value="Brisbane" selected="selected" >Brisbane</option>
<option value="Sydney" >Sydney</option>
<option value="Melbourne" >Melbourne</option>
<option value="Perth" >Perth</option>
</select>
```

We can also set the option values to an `id`:

```
<%= form.select(:id,
[
    ['Brisbane', 1],
    ['Sydney', 2],
    ['Melbourne', 3],
    ['Perth', 4],
])
%>
```

This will produce the following HTML:

```
<select id="vacation_id" name="vacation[id]" >
<option value="1" >Brisbane</option>
<option value="2" >Sydney</option>
<option value="3" >Melbourne</option>
<option value="4" selected="selected" >Perth</option>
</select>
```

Date and Time Fields

The `ActionView::Helpers::DateHelper` module has helpers to render a set of data and time select boxes. The `datetime_select` helper takes an Active model object as the first parameter and the `datetime` field as the second. An optional `start_year` parameter can also be specified:

```
datetime_select("blogpost", "updated_on")
datetime_select("blogpost", "created_on", :start_year => 2005)
If the time select boxes are not required, use the date_select helper:
date_select("blogpost", "updated_on")
date_select("blogpost", "updated_on", :start_year => 2005)
date_select("blogpost ", "created_on", :order => [:day, :month, :year])
```

Modeless Forms

Not all forms need to be associated with a model. The helpers from `FormTagHelper` only require a field name instead of a model object. In this example, we create a form to convert a Fahrenheit temperature to degrees Celcius.

```
<% form_tag :action => 'convert_temp' do %>
Enter Fahrenheit Temperature: <%= text_field_tag :temperature %>
<%= submit_tag "Convert to Celcius" %>
<% end %>
```

After the form is submitted, the field will be stored in the `params` hash. These are the available form field helpers found in the `FormTagHelper` module:

- ❋ `form_tag`
- ❋ `text_area_tag`
- ❋ `text_field_tag`
- ❋ `hidden_field_tag`
- ❋ `password_field_tag`
- ❋ `radio_button_tag`
- ❋ `select_tag`
- ❋ `check_box_tag`
- ❋ `file_field_tag`
- ❋ `submit_tag`

Conclusion

This chapter served to reinforce the role of the View in the MVC paradigm that Rails advocates and embraces. Helpers, partials, and layouts all play a crucial role in enforcing the Don't Repeat Yourself (DRY) principle. A few new Embedded Ruby (ERb) tips and tricks were also covered. We also used helpers to design forms that allow data to be inserted into a model or to edit the data stored in a model. The Fahrenheit to Celcius temperature converter was an example of a form not associated with a model.

7 } Web Services and RESTful Applications

Flickr, Google, YouTube, Amazon, Basecamp, Backpack, and Yahoo all expose their services via an API. Web services allow us to utilize the data and functionality made available by these companies in our own applications. Data is usually encoded into an XML format, so we will first cover working with XML in Ruby. REST, SOAP, and XML-RPC will be covered. We will also expose an API for a Rails application via REST and an Action Webservice (AWS) for use by the rest of the world.

In this chapter you'll learn to:

* ❋ Validate, parse, and generate XML
* ❋ Use REST, SOAP, WSDL, and XML-RPC
* ❋ Use the Flickr API via XML-RPC and REST
* ❋ REST-enable a Rails application
* ❋ Expose a web service API in Rails

Working with XML

XML certainly does not provide a lightweight way to transfer data, though it has been embraced as an industry standard. Ruby programmers have a preference for JSON and YAML because those formats are human readable and easily editable. We still need to interact with the rest of the world, so this section is dedicated to using Ruby to validate, parse, and generate XML.

Validating XML

Don't ever assume that an XML packet is valid or well formed. Sometimes a matching opening or closing tag may be missing. This could occur in an XML file you have generated or even a reliable XML feed that your Web application relies on. Using REXML, we are able to detect a `ParseException` and provide an appropriate error message. REXML throws a parse exception if it encounters invalid XML. We also use the Ruby rescue code block, first introduced in

Chapter 2, "Ruby Essentials." In the example that follows, a / is missing from the closing
<person> tag.

```
require 'rexml/document'
xml = "<xml><person>Aneesha<person>"
begin
    REXML::Document.new(xml)
rescue REXML::ParseException
    puts "An error has occurred - Invalid XML"
end
```

Note

REXML brings XML processing to Ruby. REXML allows us to manipulate XML using code blocks, which
really makes dealing with XML a pleasure in Ruby. REXML is written by Sean Russell.

Parsing an XML Document

There are two ways to manipulate XML: DOM (Document Object Model) and SAX (Simple API
for XML). DOM loads the entire XML file into a nested tree of objects. Depending upon the
size of the XML file, this can store lots of objects in memory. SAX uses the `StreamParser` class
and parses and processes an XML packet at the same time. Only one XML node is loaded into
memory at a time. SAX is the preferred method for processing large XML files.

We need to use the REXML `Document` class (`REXML::Document`) to process an XML packet via
the DOM method. The methods of `Document` and `Element` classes allow us to access the XML
tree data. We use `Document.root` to get the document's root element (`<orders>`) and then
call each element to iterate over the child nodes (`<order>` elements). Here is an example:

```
require 'rexml/document'
xml = %{
<orders>
<order>
<id>100192</id>
<date>05/11/2006</date>
<client>Aneesha Bakharia</client>
<items>
<item description="Pink Champagne" qty="1" />
<item description="Ruby Gems" qty="4" />
</items>
</order>
<order>
<id>100194</id>
```

```
<date>05/11/2006</date>
<client>Celine Bakharia</client>
<items>
<item description="Chocolate Cake" qty="2" />
</items>
</order>
</orders>
}
order_objs = REXML::Document.new(xml)
order_objs.root.each_element do |order|
      order.each_element do |node|
            if node.has_elements?
                  node.each_element do |child|
                        puts "#{child.name}: #{child.attributes['description']}
                               (Qty: #{child.attributes['qty']})"
                  end
            else
                  puts "#{node.name}: #{node.text}"
            end
      end
end
```

The following is output when the `xmlparse.rb` script is run:

```
$ ruby xmlparse.rb
id: 100192
date: 05/11/2006
client: Aneesha Bakharia
item: Pink Champagne (Qty: 1)
item: Ruby Gems (Qty: 4)
id: 100194
date: 05/11/2006
client: Celine Bakharia
item: Chocolate Cake (Qty: 2)
```

Generating XML

Generating XML was always a tedious task until I discovered Rails and Builder, an extremely lightweight and intuitive XML generator. The usefulness of Builder can best be explained with examples. We first need to install Builder:

```
$ gem install builder
```

We can play with Builder using irb, the interactive Ruby shell:

```
$ irb --simple-prompt
>> require 'builder'
```

We create an object called `xml` by calling the `XmlMarkup` method. We set `:target` to stdout. This will print the output to the console. We also set `:indent` to 1, which will output the XML nodes by one space.

```
>> xml = Builder::XmlMarkup.new(:target => $stdout, :indent => 1)
```

We call the `instruct` method to output the XML declaration:

```
>> xml.instruct!
=> <?xml version="1.0" encoding="UTF-8"?>
```

We can generate an XML comment:

```
>> xml.comment! "This is a comment"
=> <!-- This is a comment -->
```

Element nodes also are very simple:

```
>> xml.xmlnode "Text in xmlnode"
=> <xmlnode> Text in xmlnode </xmlnode>
```

We can add an attribute to a node:

```
>> xml.xmlnode ("Text in xmlnode", "type" => "test")
<xmlnode type="test"> Text in xmlnode </ xmlnode >
```

We can even place nodes within other nodes to create a hierarchy:

```
>> xml.event {
    xml.date "2006/11/22"
    xml.title "01"
    xml.duration "2 days"
}
=> <event>
    <date>2006>date>
    <title>01>title>
    <duration>01>duration>
<event>
```

As you can see, Builder makes generating valid XML a trivial task. In the next example we convert a hash to an XML packet:

```
require 'builder'
media = {
  'dialup' => 'dialup.wmv', 'broadband' => 'broad.wmv',
  'download' => 'download.wmv'
}
xml = Builder::XmlMarkup.new( :target => $stdout, :indent => 2 )
xml.instruct! :xml, :version => "1.1", :encoding => "utf-8"
xml.media do
    media.each do | name, filename |
        xml.media( filename, :item => name )
    end
end
```

The following XML packet is output to the console:

```
<?xml version="1.1" encoding="utf-8"?>
<media>
    <media item="dialup">dialup.wmv</media>
    <media item="download">download.wmv</media>
    <media item="broadband">broad.wmv</media>
</media>
```

Using Web Services

A web service runs on top of the HTTP protocol. A request (usually in the form of an XML packet) is sent to a web service, which in turns returns a response as an XML packet. Essentially, a web service provides a way for distributed systems to talk to each other (request services) over HTTP. None of the unfriendly XML gets shown to the user; instead, the returned XML is parsed, and the information is processed and presented in a user-friendly way to the user. The user need not even know that a web service has been accessed. There are three types of web services: REST-style services, XML-Remote Procedure Calls (RPC), and SOAP (Simple Object Access Protocol).

REST-Style Web Services

REST-style web services are the easiest to understand and use. REST is an acronym for Representational State Transfer. REST web services are simply HTTP GET and POST requests. A URL path maps to a service that returns an XML document. HTTP GET requests are used to retrieve data, while POST requests modify or delete data. The XML returned by RESTful web services is usually easy to read and parse with REXML: RDF, RSS, Atom, and proprietary XML formats. The emergence of REST has challenged mainstream web service standards such as SOAP. Web services were getting too complex, and REST, which Rails embraces, makes everything agile.

Because REST does not dictate a specific XML format, you will need to become proficient with REXML and parsing XML. This is the only downside to embracing REST.

Using the Flickr REST API

Flickr, a popular photo sharing site, provides an API via REST, XML-RPC, and SOAP. It is not uncommon to find popular sites supporting all three types of web services. Flickr's API is comprehensively documented at http://www.flickr.com/services/api/. An api_key is required to access the API. You will need to register as a developer to receive the api_key.

We are going to search for photos with a specific tag. The tag search is documented at http://www.flickr.com/services/api/flickr.photos.search.html. We need to pass the api_key, the tags, and the number of images that must be returned per page (per_page) in a URL. We will be passing the type of license, which is optional, because we want only images under the Creative Commons license returned. Information on the licensing options is found at http://www.flickr.com/services/api/flickr.photos.licenses.getInfo.html.

We can test our search from within a web browser. Please note that you will need to insert your own api_key in the following URL:

http://www.flickr.com/services/rest/?api_key=xxxcxx&

```
method=flickr.photos.search&
tags=flower&license=4&
per_page=5
```

The following XML is returned:

```
<?xml version="1.0" encoding="utf-8" ?>
<rsp stat="ok">
<photos page="1" pages="4195" perpage="5" total="20974">
    <photo id="318298688" owner="28481088@N00" secret="d545531b06"
            server="125" farm="1" title="Tulip shadow" ispublic="1"
            isfriend="0" isfamily="0" />
    <photo id="318296448" owner="28481088@N00" secret="b1f47266ee"
            server="141" farm="1" title="Tulips on blue 2" ispublic="1"
            isfriend="0" isfamily="0" />
    <photo id="318296449" owner="28481088@N00" secret="938e6a0ccb"
            server="135" farm="1" title="Tulips on blue 3" ispublic="1"
            isfriend="0" isfamily="0" />
    <photo id="318296447" owner="28481088@N00" secret="a4531cdb8a"
            server="142" farm="1" title="Tulips on blue 1" ispublic="1"
            isfriend="0" isfamily="0" />
```

```
       <photo id="318296444" owner="28481088@N00" secret="804cccf873"
              server="133" farm="1" title="Tulip on the window" ispublic="1"
              isfriend="0" isfamily="0" />
</photos>
</rsp>
```

Each photo has a unique ID, but we will need to look up how to construct the URL to each image so that we can display the photos on our own web page. This information can be found at http://www.flickr.com/services/api/misc.urls.html. The URL takes the following format:

http://static.flickr.com/{server-id}/{id}_{secret}.jpg

We can easily pass the returned XML and construct this URL for each image that needs to be displayed. Let's try to retrieve the first image in our web browser by typing:

http://static.flickr.com/125/318298688_d545531b06.jpg

The image loads in a web browser. We now move on to getting a Rails application to access the Flickr REST API. We start by creating a Flickr controller (`flickr_controller.rb`) with a `flickrsearch` action. The `flickrsearch` action dynamically constructs the REST URL, uses the `Net::HTTP.get()` method to call the Flickr server, and finally parses the returned XML with REXML. The parsed XML document is assigned to `@photos`, which we can access in `flickrsearch.rhtml`:

```
class FlickrController < ApplicationController
def flickrsearch
     tags = CGI.escape("flowers")
     flickr_API_key = "xxxxxxx"
     url = "http://www.flickr.com/services/rest/?api_key=#{flickr_API_key}&
           method=flickr.photos.search&
           tags=#{tags}&
           license=4&
           per_page=10"
     result = Net::HTTP.get(URI(url))
     @photos = REXML::Document.new result
end
end
```

In the view (`flickrsearch.rhtml`), we can parse the XML and output the images:

```
<%
@photos.root.each_element do |photo|
```

```
    photo.each_element do |node|
          image_url = "http://static.flickr.com/
                        #{node.attributes["server"]}/
                        #{node.attributes["id"]}_#
                        {node.attributes["secret"]}.jpg"
%>
<p>

    <%= image_tag(image_url, :border => "0", :height => "100") %><br>
    <%= node.attributes["title"] %>
</p>
<%

      end
end
%>
```

XML-RPC

XML - Remote Procedure Calls (RPC) is language independent and firewall friendly because it relies on the HTTP protocol. XML-RPC is an early ancestor of SOAP. An XML-RPC request is a specially formatted HTTP POST request: The name of the remote method and the parameters it requires are encoded as XML. The XML-RPC response contains serialized data structures. XML-RPC is available from a specific URL known as an end point URL.

Using the Flickr XML-RPC API

Information on XML-RPC Flickr services can be found at http://www.flickr.com/services/api/request.xmlrpc.html. The Flickr XML-RPC end point URL is http://api.flickr.com/services/xmlrpc/.

The following is a sample request to the flickr.test.echo service:

```
<methodCall>
    <methodName>flickr.test.echo</methodName>
    <params>
        <param>
            <value>
                <struct>
                    <member>
                        <name>name</name>
                        <value><string>value</string></value>
                    </member>
                    <member>
```

```
            <name>name2</name>
            <value><string>value2</string></value>
        </member>
      </struct>
    </value>
  </param>
 </params>
</methodCall>
```

In the following example we embed a Ruby XML-RPC client as an action within a controller. We make an XML-RPC call to the `flickr.interestingness.getList` service, which returns a list of interesting photos. We require only five images per page (so we set the `per_page` parameter to 5):

```
class FlickrController < ApplicationController
    def flickrxmlrpc
        flickruri = "http://www.flickr.com/services/xmlrpc/"
        server = XMLRPC::Client.new2(flickruri)
        flickr_API_key = "xxxxxxx"
        parameters = {:api_key => flickr_API_key, :per_page => "5"}
        result = server.call("flickr.interestingness.getList",
                parameters)
        @photos = REXML::Document.new result
    end
end
```

We use simple XML parsing in the view (flickrxmlrpc.rhtml) to display the images:

```
<%
@photos.root.each_element do |pic|
image_url = "http://static.flickr.com/#{ pic.attributes["server"]}/
#{ pic.attributes["id"]}_#{ pic.attributes["secret"]}.jpg"
%>
<%= image_tag(image_url, :border => "0", :height => "100") %><br>
<%= pic.attributes["title"] %>
<br>
<% end %>
```

SOAP

The Simple Object Access Protocol (SOAP) is a descendant of XML-RPC, but it certainly is more complex. SOAP involves encoding a method call into XML and sending the XML to a server, which in turn returns data structures serialized into XML. It sounds similar to XML-RPC, but the XML encoding is more elaborate.

In order to make a successful SOAP request, you need the web service end point URL, the namespace used by the web service, the name of the method you are calling, and the parameters you need to pass the method. In Ruby, we need to create a new instance of the `SOAP::RPC::Driver` and then use `add_method` to attach the method we need to call from the SOAP service. In the example that follows we need to access the Stockquote web service. The `getQuote()` method must be passed the symbol of a business—a stockquote for the business will be returned:

```
require 'soap/rpc/driver'
soapdriver = SOAP::RPC::Driver.new('http://services.xmethods.net/soap/',
                                    'urn:xmethods-delayed-quotes')
soapdriver.add_method('getQuote', 'symbol')
puts 'Stock price: %.2f' % soapdriver.getQuote('BBBB')
```

Using a WSDL File to Make SOAP Calls Easier

The Web Service Definition Language (WSDL) makes it easier to work with SOAP calls by loading the signature of all available method calls. This means that we don't need to read a SOAP call manually to determine which methods we need to use and what parameters are required.

We no longer need to use the `add` method to define the `getQuote` method, and the code is reduced to:

```
require 'soap/wsdlDriver'
wsdl = 'http://services.xmethods.net/soap/urn:xmethods-delayed-quotes.wsdl'
soapdriver = SOAP::WSDLDriverFactory.new(wsdl).create_rpc_driver
puts "Stock price: %.2f" % soapdriver.getQuote('BBBB')
```

Searching Google with WSDL

The Google search API is exposed via WSDL: http://api.google.com/GoogleSearch.wsdl (see Figure 7.1). You will need a developer API to access the service. We will create an action called `search` within a controller that calls the `doGoogleSearch()` method (see Figure 7.2):

```
class GoogleController < ApplicationController
    def search
        api_key = 'xxxxxxx'
        @searchquery = 'Ruby on Rails'
```

```
      XSD::Charset.encoding = 'UTF8'
      wsdlfile = "http://api.google.com/GoogleSearch.wsdl"
      driver = SOAP::WSDLDriverFactory.new(wsdlfile).create_rpc_driver
      @result = driver.doGoogleSearch(api_key, @searchquery, 0, 5, false, '',
false, '', '', '')
    end
end
```

Figure 7.1
The Google Search API
exposed via WSDL.

Figure 7.2
The doGoogleSearch()
method.

In the `search.rhtml` **template we display the five search results (see Figure 7.3):**

```
<p>
<strong>You searched for:</strong> <%= @searchquery %><br/>
<strong>Results Found:</strong> <%= @result.estimatedTotalResultsCount %>
</p>
<% @result.resultElements.each do |res| %>
<strong>Title:</strong> <%= res["title"] %><br/>
<strong>Summary:</strong> <%= res.snippet %><br/>
<strong>Link:</strong> <a href="<%= res["URL"] %>"><%= res["URL"] %></a>
<hr/>
<% end %>
```

Figure 7.3
Calling the
doGoogleSearch()
method via WSDL.

Building RESTful Web Services with Rails

REST-based web services deliver custom XML formats via an HTTP request (URL). It is very easy to map a URL to a controller and an action in Rails. We can get an action to render an XML document; this is known as an RXML template. RXML templates have a `.rxml` extension. When RXML templates are delivered, we need to turn off the rendering of layouts. Here is an example controller in which we render a layout for all actions except `restrequest`:

```
class RestController < ApplicationController
    layout "application", :except => [:restrequest]
    def restrequest
        @australiancities = ["Brisbane","Sydney","Perth"]
    end
end
```

The code for the `restrequest.rxml` view template is as follows:

```
xml.instruct! :xml, :version=>"1.0", :encoding=>"UTF-8"
      xml.australiancities do
            counter = 0
            @ australiancities.each do |city|
            counter = counter + 1
            xml.name(city, :id => counter)
      end
end
```

In an RXML template we can access the `Builder` class that is packaged with Rails. I am sure you will agree that the `Builder` class makes XML generation a trivial task. We can view the generated XML at http://localhost:3000/rest/restrequest.

> ❋ **Note**
>
> When an action is called, Action Pack looks for a matching RHTML template. If one is not found, it then looks for an RXML template. There is no need to map the action to the RXML template manually. This is another really useful Rails feature.

Converting an Active Record Model to XML

The `to_xml` method is extremely powerful and easy to use. We can convert a set of records (usually returned by using the `find` method) to XML with the `to_xml` method. In the code that follows, the `find` method returns all records in the employees table (i.e., the Employee model) and then renders the records to XML (see Figure 7.4):

```
class EmployeesController < ApplicationController
    def list
      @employees = Employee.find :all
      render :xml => @employees.to_xml
    end
end
```

Using the scaffold_resource Generator

There is more to being REST-enabled than simply generating XML. We need to be able to respond to HTTP GET requests for data retrieval as well as POST requests for the modification and deletion of data. We have used the `scaffold` command to generate a CRUD interface, we will now use the `scaffold_resource` command to REST-enable an application. The `scaffold_resource` **command takes the name of the model that we need to generate a REST interface for as its first argument. We then pass the name and data type of each field that is part of the model as arguments. The name of the field and the data type are separated by a colon (:). The data types are the same data types available for use within a migration.**

Figure 7.4
Active Record models converted to XML.

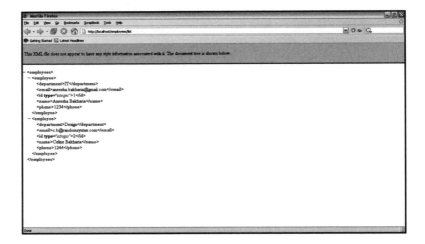

We are going to create an application to log bugs and expose its API via REST. The model name is `bug` and the bugs table will contain a title and a description field:

```
$ ruby script/generate scaffold_resource bug title:string
description:text
```

The scaffold_resource generator produces the `bugs` controller, related views, and a migration based upon the fields and data types we passed the `scaffold_resource` command:

```
      exists  app/models/
      exists  app/controllers/
      exists  app/helpers/
      create  app/views/bugs
      exists  test/functional/
      exists  test/unit/
      create  app/views/bugs/index.rhtml
      create  app/views/bugs/show.rhtml
      create  app/views/bugs/new.rhtml
      create  app/views/bugs/edit.rhtml
      create  app/views/layouts/bugs.rhtml
      create  public/stylesheets/scaffold.css
```

```
create  app/models/bug.rb
create  app/controllers/bugs_controller.rb
create  test/functional/bugs_controller_test.rb
create  app/helpers/bugs_helper.rb
create  test/unit/bug_test.rb
create  test/fixtures/bugs.yml
create  db/migrate
create  db/migrate/001_create_bugs.rb
 route  map.resources :bugs
```

The last thing the scaffold_resource generator does is modify the config/routes.rb file.
The map.resources :bugs command is added to the config/routes.rb file. This is
a very powerful command because it adds seven routes and four route helpers to the
BugsController. Table 7.1 lists the newly available routes.

The modified config/routes.rb file:

```
ActionController::Routing::Routes.draw do |map|
    map.resources :bugs
    map.connect ':controller/service.wsdl', :action => 'wsdl'
    map.connect ':controller/:action/:id.:format'
    map.connect ':controller/:action/:id'
end
```

Table 7.1   REST Routes and Helpers

HTTP Method	URL	Action	Helper
GET	/bugs	index	bugs_url
POST	/bugs	create	bugs_url
GET	/bugs/new	new	new_bugs_url
GET	/bugs/1	show	bugs_url(:id => 1)
PUT	/bugs/1	update	bugs_url(:id => 1)
GET	/bugs/1;edit	edit	edit_bugs_url(:id => 1)
DELETE	/bugs/1	destroy	bugs_url(:id => 1)

The scaffold_resource command has created a migration to create the bugs table and the
required fields (db/migrate/001_create_bugs.rb):

```
class CreateBugs < ActiveRecord::Migration
    def self.up
```

```
    create_table :bugs do |t|
        t.column :title, :string
        t.column :description, :text
    end
  end
  def self.down
      drop_table :bugs
  end
end
```

We can now run the migration:

```
$ rake db:migrate
```

The bugs table is created:

```
== CreateBugs: migrating ======================================================
-- create_table(:bugs)
   -> 0.2190s
== CreateBugs: migrated (0.2190s) =============================================
```

We can now run the Webrick web server and take a closer look at the application in action:

```
$ ruby script/server
```

We can access the application from http://localhost:3000/bugs . A link is displayed to add a new bug (see Figure 7.5). Click on the New bug link.

Figure 7.5
The Bugs application.

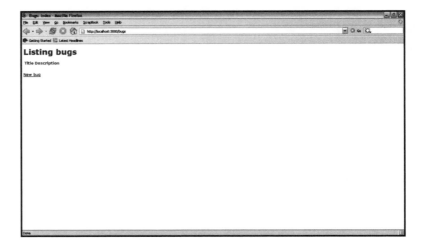

The form to add a new bug is located at http://localhost:3000/bugs/new. We are able to enter a title and description for the bug (see Figure 7.6). Click on the Create button.

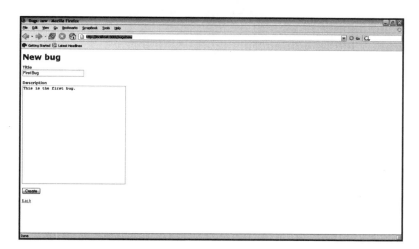

Figure 7.6
Adding a new bug.

The http://localhost:3000/bugs/1 URL is displayed (see Figure 7.7). This URL displays the bug report that has an `id` equal to 1.

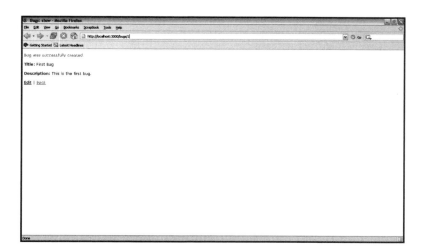

Figure 7.7
Using an id to display
a bug.

This is great, but it looks like a normal CRUD interface. How do we access the API to add, modify, and retrieve bugs via REST? Go to http://localhost:3000/bugs/1.xml (see Figure 7.8).

Figure 7.8
Using an id to display a bug
XML packet.

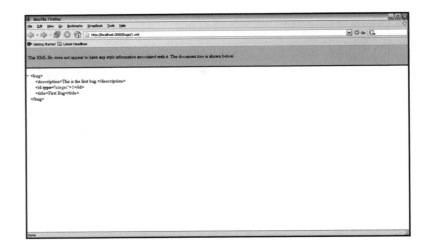

Go to http://localhost:3000/bugs and add a few more bug reports (see Figure 7.9). Show, Edit, and Destroy links are now shown for each bug.

Figure 7.9
A CRUD interface for the
Bugs application.

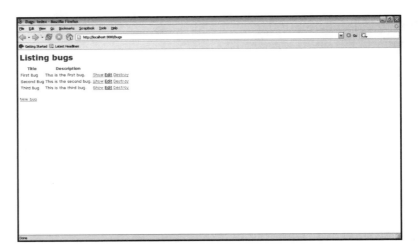

We can now retrieve all the bugs as an XML packet from http://localhost:3000/bugs.xml URL (see Figure 7.10).

The `BugsController` has seven actions: `index`, `show`, `new`, `edit`, `create`, `update`, and `delete`. The `index`, `show`, `new`, and `edit` actions respond to HTTP `GET` requests. The `create`, `update`, and `delete` actions respond to HTTP `POST` requests. A comment is included above each action to show you the URLs that access either the HTML or XML versions. The `respond_to` **code block determines the type of response that should be returned, in this case, either the** `.rhtml` **template or the XML packet. The** `to_xml` **method is used to convert the records returned by the** `find` **method to XML. Here is the generated controller code (**`app/controllers/bugs_controller.rb`**):**

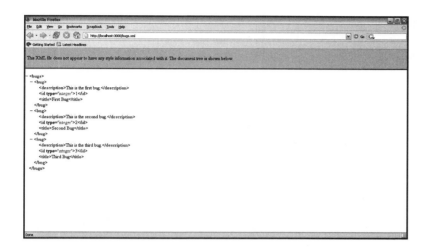

Figure 7.10
Displaying all bugs in an XML packet.

```ruby
class BugsController < ApplicationController
  # GET /bugs
  # GET /bugs.xml
  def index
    @bugs = Bug.find(:all)

    respond_to do |format|
      format.html # index.rhtml
      format.xml  { render :xml => @bugs.to_xml }
    end
  end

  # GET /bugs/1
  # GET /bugs/1.xml
  def show
    @bug = Bug.find(params[:id])

    respond_to do |format|
      format.html # show.rhtml
```

```ruby
      format.xml  { render :xml => @bug.to_xml }
   end
end


# GET /bugs/new
def new
  @bug = Bug.new
end

# GET /bugs/1;edit
def edit
  @bug = Bug.find(params[:id])
end

# POST /bugs
# POST /bugs.xml
def create
  @bug = Bug.new(params[:bug])

  respond_to do |format|
    if @bug.save
      flash[:notice] = 'Bug was successfully created.'
      format.html { redirect_to bug_url(@bug) }
      format.xml  { head :created, :location => bug_url(@bug) }
    else
      format.html { render :action => "new" }
      format.xml  { render :xml => @bug.errors.to_xml }
    end
  end
end


# PUT /bugs/1
# PUT /bugs/1.xml
def update
  @bug = Bug.find(params[:id])

  respond_to do |format|
```

```
      if @bug.update_attributes(params[:bug])
        flash[:notice] = 'Bug was successfully updated.'
        format.html { redirect_to bug_url(@bug) }
        format.xml  { head :ok }
      else
        format.html { render :action => "edit" }
        format.xml  { render :xml => @bug.errors.to_xml }
      end
    end
  end

  # DELETE /bugs/1
  # DELETE /bugs/1.xml
  def destroy
    @bug = Bug.find(params[:id])
    @bug.destroy

    respond_to do |format|
      format.html { redirect_to bugs_url }
      format.xml  { head :ok }
    end
  end
end
```

The `index.rhtml` **template, which corresponds to the** `index` **action, uses helper methods to display links to the** `show`, `edit`, **and** `destroy` **actions. These helpers were created by the inclusion of the** `map.resources :bugs` **command in the** `config/routes.rb` **file. The** `index` **action is accessed via http://localhost:3000/bugs:**

```
<h1>Listing bugs</h1>
<table>
  <tr>
    <th>Title</th>
    <th>Description</th>
  </tr>
<% for bug in @bugs %>
  <tr>
    <td><%=h bug.title %></td>
```

```
    <td><%=h bug.description %></td>
    <td><%= link_to 'Show', bug_path(bug) %></td>
    <td><%= link_to 'Edit', edit_bug_path(bug) %></td>
    <td><%= link_to 'Destroy', bug_path(bug),
            :confirm => 'Are you sure?', :method => :delete %>
    </td>
  </tr>
<% end %>
</table>
<br />
<%= link_to 'New bug', new_bug_path %>
```

The `new.rhtml` **template accessed via http://localhost:3000/bugs/new:**

```
<h1>New bug</h1>
<%= error_messages_for :bug %>
<% form_for(:bug, :url => bugs_path) do |f| %>
  <p>
    <b>Title</b><br />
    <%= f.text_field :title %>
  </p>
  <p>
    <b>Description</b><br />
    <%= f.text_area :description %>
  </p>
  <p>
    <%= submit_tag "Create" %>
  </p>
<% end %>
<%= link_to 'Back', bugs_path %>
```

The `show.rhtml` **template accessed via http://localhost:3000/bugs/1:**

```
<p>
  <b>Title:</b>
  <%=h @bug.title %>
</p>
<p>
  <b>Description:</b>
```

```
    <%=h @bug.description %>
</p>
<%= link_to 'Edit', edit_bug_path(@bug) %> |
<%= link_to 'Back', bugs_path %>
```

The `edit.rhtml` **template accessed via http://localhost:3000/bugs/1;edit:**

```
<h1>Editing bug</h1>
<%= error_messages_for :bug %>
<% form_for(:bug, :url => bug_path(@bug), :html => { :method => :put }) do |f| %>
  <p>
    <b>Title</b><br />
    <%= f.text_field :title %>
  </p>
  <p>
    <b>Description</b><br />
    <%= f.text_area :description %>
  </p>
  <p>
    <%= submit_tag "Update" %>
  </p>
<% end %>
<%= link_to 'Show', bug_path(@bug) %> |
<%= link_to 'Back', bugs_path %>
```

Using ActionWebService to Expose SOAP and XML-RPC Web Services

ActionWebService (AWS) is the Rails component responsible for SOAP and XML-RPC web services. AWS binds SOAP and XML-RPC methods to controllers in a Rails application. AWS does a lot of hard work for you behind the scenes. It parses an XML request and constructs the WSDL and XML response. All you need to worry about is the functionality you need to expose via an API.

Make sure you have the latest version of AWS:

```
$ gem install actionwebservice
```

AWS includes a script to generate the required files:

```
$ script/generate web_service WebServiceName Method1 Method2
```

Let's create a web service with a method called `sayhello`, **which takes a single string** `firstname` **parameter:**

```
$ script/generate web_service greetings sayhello
```

An `apis` **folder is added to the** `/app` **folder. The** `app/apis/greetings_api.rb` **and the** `app/controllers/greetings_controller.rb` **files are also created:**

```
create  app/apis/
exists  app/controllers/
exists  test/functional/
create  app/apis/greetings_api.rb
create  app/controllers/greetings_controller.rb
create  test/functional/greetings_api_test.rb
```

View the `app/apis/greetings_api.rb` .**This file includes the** `sayhello` **method. We need to define the data types that the method expects and returns:**

```
class GreetingsApi < ActionWebService::API::Base
    api_method :sayhello,
          :expects => [{:firstname => :string}],
          :returns => [{:greeting => :string}]
end
```

> ❄ **Note**
>
> We need to type the parameters our methods require and the values they return because Ruby is a loosely typed language (see Table 7.2). Other languages that we use to call our web service may be written in strongly typed languages such as Java and C#. The :expects and :returns hashes serve this purpose. AWS will raise an error if :expects is not specified. If :returns is not set, nothing will be returned.

Now we edit the `GreetingsController` **with the methods defined in our API. The GreetingsAPI maps to actions in the** `GreetingsController`, **which is stored in the** `app/controllers/greetings_controller.rb` **file:**

```
class GreetingsController < ApplicationController
    wsdl_service_name 'Greetings'
    def sayhello(firstname)
        "Hello #{ firstname }"
    end
end
```

Table 7.2   Action WebService (AWS) Data Types

:bool	Boolean
:int	Integer
:string	String
:base64	Binary Base-64 encoded data
:float	Floating-point number
:time	Timestamp
:datetime	Date and timestamp
:date	Date

View http://localhost:3000/greetings/wsdl in a web browser (see Figure 7.11). You will see that AWS has generated a WSDL file. This is an example of a direct-dispatching web service. Congratulations: You have exposed your first API.

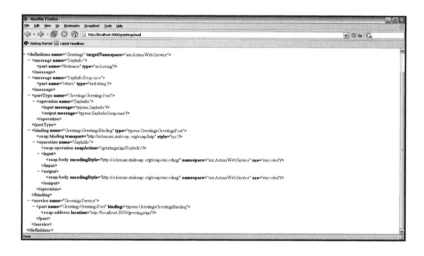

Figure 7.11
Viewing a Rails-generated WSDL file.

http://localhost:3000/greetings/api is the end point URL that you need to provide to SOAP clients. You may recall that we required the namespace as well when we made a SOAP request to get stock quotes. The namespace that AWS uses is urn:ActionWebService. AWS also generates an XML-RPC version accessible from http://localhost:3000/greetings/api.

Here is an XML-RPC client in Ruby to test the web service:

```
require 'xmlrpc/client'
xmlserver = XMLRPC::Client.new2("http://localhost:3000/greetings/api")
result = server.call("sayhello", "Celine")
puts result
```

This is a SOAP client in Ruby to test the web service:

```ruby
require 'soap/wsdlDriver'
wsdl = "http://localhost:3000/greeting/wsdl"
soapdriver = SOAP::WSDLDriverFactory.new(wsdl).create_rpc_driver
puts "Greeting: #{soapdriver.sayhello('Celine')}"
```

Rails automatically maps the API to the controller and sets the dispatching mode to :direct. There are three dispatching modes: :direct, :delegated, and :layered. The dispatching mode maps methods in your API to actions in controllers. The greetings API example used the AWS default of :direct. When :direct dispatching is used, you are allowed only to map an API to a single controller. Depending upon the complexity of your API and application, a single controller may just not be enough.

The :delegated and :layered dispatching modes use the same code. Web service methods are defined in a model and the model is associated with the API, which can then access methods from various controllers. The only difference between :layered and :delegated dispatching is the end point URL to access the web service. A separate URL is required to access each method with :delegated dispatching. :layered dispatching mode, on the other hand, has a single entry point URL and lets AWS do the routing. Of course, if you use WSDL, there is no difference between :layered and :delegated.

Here is an example of a :layered controller:

```ruby
class LayeredExampleController < ApplicationController
    web_service_dispatching_mode :layered
    web_service_scaffold :invoke
    web_service :book, BookService.new
    web_service :magazine, MagazineService.new
end
```

The code for the book searching service (app/apis/book_service.rb) is as follows:

```ruby
class BookService < ActionWebService::Base
    web_service_api BookApi
    def find_all_books
        Book.find(:all).map{ |book| book.id }
    end
    def find_book_by_id(id)
        Book.find(id)
    end
end
```

Conclusion

This chapter covered a lot of ground in terms of web services. First we looked at validating, parsing, and generating XML. We were then able to cover examples using each of the three types of web services, including using both XML-RPC and REST to access the Flickr API. We also learned to generate XML views (RXML templates), convert a collection of Active Record objects to XML (using the `to_xml` method), and use the `scaffold_resource` command to generate a CRUD interface that can also be accessed in a RESTful manner. Finally, we used Action WebService to expose an API in a Rails application.

8 } AJAX and Rails

AJAX is a buzz word that deserves most of the hype that has been thrust upon it. AJAX is an acronym for Asynchronous JavaScript and XML, and it is of interest to developers because it allows data to be transferred to and from a web server without a full page request. AJAX also caused a resurgence in the popularity of JavaScript. This propelled the development of enhanced effects and drag-and-drop techniques initially not thought possible with JavaScript. Ruby on Rails treats AJAX like a first class citizen. With Rails you are able to implement complex AJAX-enabled interfaces without writing heaps of JavaScript—all functionality is available either as a Ruby helper method or a Rails JavaScript (RJS) template.

In this chapter you'll learn to use:

* ❋ The `XMLHttpRequest` object
* ❋ The Prototype JavaScript library
* ❋ The Scriptaculous JavaScript library
* ❋ Rails AJAX Helpers
* ❋ Rails JavaScript (RJS) templates

What Is AJAX Anyway?

In 2004, Google introduced Google Maps and Google Suggest, two products that would trigger a web application renaissance and mark the beginning of Web 2.0. I remember the first time I played with Google Maps. I really did not think it would be possible to smoothly scroll and zoom in and out of maps using JavaScript (see Figure 8.1). How could new map data be sent to a web browser and rendered without the need for a page refresh? Google Suggest was even able to predict what I was searching for after I entered only a few characters of my search query (see Figure 8.2). Toward the end of 2004, tutorials for creating auto-completing text input fields and displaying search results without reloading a web page started to emerge. In all these tutorials, the XMLHttpRequest object was the key cross-browser ingredient. The AJAX acronym was first used in February 2005 by Jesse Games Garrett in his ground-breaking article entitled "Ajax: A New Approach to Web Applications." AJAX stands for Asynchronous JavaScript and XML.

Figure 8.1
Google Maps—is this really using JavaScript?

Figure 8.2
Google AutoSuggest—search suggestions before you finish typing?

The XMLHttpRequest Object

The XMLHttpRequest object was first introduced by Microsoft in Internet Explorer 5 way back in the 1990s, but it didn't become mainstream until 2004, when support was incorporated into the Mozilla and Safari web browsers. The XMLHttpRequest object is available to JavaScript and, as its name indicates, allows HTTP requests to be sent to a web server and the HTML or XML text returned to be processed. Rails and the JavaScript frameworks it includes do a lot of the hard work of wiring and responding to XMLHttpRequest object calls. So why bother learning about the XMLHttpRequest object? The answer is simple: Every developer needs to understand the fundamental concepts behind a technology. A working knowledge of how the XMLHttpRequest object works will help you push the boundaries of what is possible in a web browser, and it will also help you debug your applications. Rails does an awesome job of making AJAX easy to implement, but depending upon what you are trying to implement, you will encounter JavaScript errors along the way. Not knowing much about the fundamentals won't help you overcome hurdles.

Unfortunately, Internet Explorer does not share the same syntax as Mozilla-based browsers and Safari. This means that we need to write code to support two types of browsers. In Safari and Mozilla we just need to call the XMLHttpRequest() constructor:

```
var in_page_request = new XMLHttpRequest();
```

Internet Explorer's implementation is an ActiveX control, so we'll need to create an ActiveXObject instance:

```
var in_page_request = new ActiveXObject("Microsoft.XMLHTTP");
```

We can use the following code to ensure the XMLHttpRequest() object is cross-browser compatible:

```
in_page_request = null;
// code for Mozilla, Safari and FireFox
if (window.XMLHttpRequest)
{
        in_page_request = new XMLHttpRequest();
}
// code for Internet Explorer
else if (window.ActiveXObject)
{
        in_page_request = new ActiveXObject("Microsoft.XMLHTTP");
}
```

Table 8.1 lists the XMLHttpRequest object's methods. The open() and send() methods will be used the most. In the open() method, you specify whether you would like to send the request via POST or GET and set the URL for the server-side script that will process the request. Use GET if you are passing a few parameters in querystring of the URL and primarily retrieving data. The POST method should be used if you are sending data that could possibly exceed 512 bytes.

Table 8.1 XMLHttpRequest Object Methods

Method	Description
abort()	Aborts the current request
getAllResponseHeaders()	Returns the header labels and values
getResponseHeader("header_name")	Returns the value for a given header label
open("method", "url", "asynchronous_flag", "username", "password")	Sets the HTTP request method (GET or POST) and URL
send(data_to_send)	Sends data to the URL specified in open()

> **Note**
>
> Methods and functions in JavaScript require parentheses, e.g., open(), while parentheses in Ruby are optional.

The third parameter passed to open() is a Boolean value (i.e., either true or false) that dictates if the request should be handled asynchronously. Setting this flag to true means that the script does not stop and wait for a response once send() is triggered—this is an asynchronous call. This is useful because it allows the user to continue interacting with the web page. It also means that we can trigger multiple AJAX calls. It is not a good idea to set this flag to false because the network may hang while the browser continues to wait for a response.

Table 8.2 lists all the properties associated with the XMLHttpRequest object. The onreadyStateChange property is used to specify the JavaScript function that must be executed when a change in state occurs. The readystate property contains the current state. When a state change occurs (such as when onreadyStateChange is triggered), we can read the readystate property to determine the current state. When the send() method is called, readystate will be set to loading (1). When the server responds to the HTTP request, readystate will change to loaded (2) and the onreadystatechange event will be triggered.

The data that is sent back to the browser can be obtained from either the responseText or responseXML property. Use the responseText property if plain text or HTML is returned. The responseXML property returns an XML Document Object Structure (DOM) that you will need to traverse. A status code of 200 is returned if the request has been successful.

Table 8.2 XMLHttpRequest Object Properties

Property	Description
onreadystatechange	Used to specify an event handler that responds to a state change
readystate	Status flags:
	0 - uninitialized
	1 - loading
	2 - loaded
	3 - interactive
	4 - complete
responseText	Data returned as a string
responseXML	XML data returned as a DOM structure
status	Code returned by the HTTP server:
	404 - Page not found
	200 - Success
statusText	Label for the status code

In the example that follows, a link click triggers an asynchronous request for a text file, which when loaded is displayed with a `div` tag:

```
<html>
<head>
<title>XMLHttpRequest Object Example</title>
<script type="text/javascript">
var in_page_request

function loadText(url)
{
    in_page_request = null
    // code for Mozilla, Safari and FireFox
    if (window.XMLHttpRequest)
    {
        in_page_request = new XMLHttpRequest()
    }
    // code for Internet Explorer
    else if (window.ActiveXObject)
```

```
        {
                in_page_request = new ActiveXObject("Microsoft.XMLHTTP")
        }
        if (in_page_request != null)
        {
                in_page_request.onreadystatechange = process_Request
                in_page_request.open("GET",url,true)
                in_page_request.send(null)
        }
        else
        {
                alert("Oops - Your browser does not support AJAX!")
        }
}
function process_Request()
{
        if (in_page_request.readyState == 4) // if readyState is loaded
        {
                if (in_page_request.status == 200) // if status is OK
                {
document.getElementById('txt_display').innerHTML=in_page_request.responseText
                }
                else
                {
                        alert("Error retrieving data:" + status.statusText)
                        //display label associated with status code
                }
        }
}
</script>
</head>
<body>
        <h2>Playing with the XMLHttpRequest Object</h2>
        <div id="txt_display" style="border:1px solid
black;height:40;width:300"></div><br />
        <a onClick="loadText('text.txt')">Get Text via XMLHttpRequest Object</a>
```

❀ ❀ ❀

```
</body>
</html>
```

JavaScript Frameworks Packaged with Rails

AJAX frameworks essentially seek to simplify the use of the `XMLHttpRequest` object. The year 2005 saw the emergence of many AJAX- and JavaScript-related frameworks. It certainly felt like a new AJAX framework was beta released every week. Two popular and feature-rich frameworks are Prototype and Scriptaculous. Luckily, both Prototype and Scriptaculous are baked right into your favorite web application framework (see Figure 8.3).

Figure 8.3
Rails includes Prototype and Scriptaculous.

PROTOTYPE

Prototype is the creation of Sam Stephenson and was designed to ease object-oriented programming in JavaScript. There are many similarities between Ruby's built-in classes and the functionality provided by the library. Essentially, with Prototype you write less JavaScript code but are able to implement much more functionality. Prototype can be downloaded from http://www.prototypejs.org and is a single JavaScript file that is approximately 70KB.

Prototype has an incredibly powerful `Ajax.Updater` class. With an `Ajax.Updater` object we can issue an `XMLHttpRequest` and update the contents of a `div` element in a single line of code. The `loadText` function from the example in the previous section is replaced, and we don't need any other functions. The `prototype.js` file needs to be included. The `loadText()` function takes a single parameter, the URL of the page to call. Within the function we set a parameter that will be included as a querystring appended to the URL. We can then create a new instance of the `Ajax.Updater` object. The first argument is the ID of the `div` that will be updated. The second argument is the URL. Within the { and } curly braces, the HTTP method and querystring parameters are set. Remember that the HTTP method can be set to `GET` or `POST`.

```
<html>
<head>
<title>Prototype: Using the Ajax.Updater Class</title>
```

```
<script src="prototype.js" language="JavaScript" type="text/javascript">
</script>
<script>
function loadText(url)
{
    var pars = 'someParameter=12345232';
    var in_page_request = new Ajax.Updater( 'placeholder', url,
                          { method: 'get', parameters: pars });
}
</script>
</head>
<body>
<h2>Prototype: Using the Ajax.Updater Class</h2>
<div id="placeholder" style="border:1px solid black;height:40;width:300">
</div>
<br />
<input type="button" value="Trigger the Ajax.Updater object"
onclick="loadText('text.txt')">
</body>
</html>
```

Prototype includes numerous utility functions to help reduce programmer keystrokes. I wish all frameworks were this programmer friendly. The $()$ function is the equivalent of the `document.getElementById()` function of the DOM, but much shorter. $()$ will come in handy when you do many DOM manipulations. So if we wanted to retrieve the contents of a `div` tag, we would just need to write:

```
var d = $('myDiv');
alert(d.innerHTML);
```

If we used the default DOM syntax:

```
var d = document.getElementById('myDiv');
alert(d.innerHTML);
```

There is also a `$F()` method that replaces `document.form` when retrieving the contents of a form element:

```
<html>
<head>
<title>Using the $F() method</title>
```

```
<script src="prototype.js"></script>
<script>
function GetUsername()
{
        var username = $F('username');
        alert("The username is: " + username);
}
</script>
</head>
<body>
<h2>Using the $F() method</h2>
<form>
Username: <input type="text" id="username" value="aneesha"><br>
<input type="button" value="Display Username" onclick="GetUsername();"><br>
</form>
</body>
</html>
```

SCRIPTACULOUS

Scriptaculous (see Figure 8.4) adds effects, sortable lists, drag-and-drop, and controls to the mix. The controls available include sliders, in-place text editors, and auto-complete text input fields. Scriptaculous brings an amazing range of features to your web applications. It is obvious that a lot of thought has gone into the framework. Scriptaculous is built on top of Prototype and was created by Thomas Fuchs.

Figure 8.4
The ultra-cool
script.aculo.us domain.

Before I encountered Scriptaculous, I thought that I would need to write a lot of JavaScript code to allow users to be able to reorder items in a list in a drag-and-drop manner. I was very wrong. The `<ul>` and `<li>` tags are used to render a list in HTML. We need to give the list a unique ID. We then need to pass this unique ID to the `Sortable.create()` method, which does all the hard work.

```html
<html>
<head>
  <title>Scriptaculous Sortables Demo</title>
  <script src="prototype.js" type="text/javascript"></script>
  <script src="scriptaculous.js" type="text/javascript"></script>
</head>
<body>

<h2>Scriptaculous Sortables Demo</h2>
<ul id="testlist">
<li id="item_1">Item one</li>
<li id="item_1">Item two</li>
<li id="item_1">Item three</li>
</ul>

<p id="testlist_serialize">(waiting for onChange event)</p>

<script type="text/javascript">
// <![CDATA[
Sortable.create('testlist',
{ghosting:true,constraint:false,hoverclass:'over',
onChange:function(element)
{$('testlist_serialize').innerHTML = Sortable.serialize(element.parentNode)
}});
// ]]>
</script>

</body>
</html>
```

> ❋ **Tip**
>
> Don't forget to include `prototype.js` when you are using Scriptaculous.

Effects provide a great way to attract the attention of a user when an interface change is occurring or data has been updated after an AJAX request. Scriptaculous has a variety of effects available, such as Highlight, BlindUp, BlindDown, SlideUp, and SlideDown. An example of using a link to trigger these effects is seen here:

```
<html>
<head>
<title>Effects with Scriptaculous</title>
<script src="prototype.js" type="text/javascript"></script>
<script src="scriptaculous.js" type="text/javascript"></script>
<style type="text/css" media="screen">
      #example{ background-color: #888; }
</style>
</head>
<body>
<h1>Effects with Scriptaculous</h1>
<a href="#"
onclick="new Effect.Highlight('example',{duration:1.5});
return false;">Highlight</a> |
<a href="#"
onclick="new Effect.BlindUp('example',{duration:1.5});
return false;">BlindUp</a> |
<a href="#"
onclick="new Effect.BlindDown('example',{duration:1.5});
return false;">BlindDown</a> |
<a href="#"
onclick="new Effect.SlideUp('example',{duration:1.5});
return false;">SlideUp</a> |
<a href="#"
onclick="new Effect.SlideDown('example',{duration:1.5});
return false;">SlideDown</a>
<div id="example">
<div style="overflow:hidden">
This is a paragraph. This is a paragraph. This is a paragraph. This is a
paragraph. This is a paragraph. This is a paragraph. This is a paragraph. This
is a paragraph. This is a paragraph. This is a paragraph. This is a paragraph.
This is a paragraph. This is a paragraph. This is a paragraph. This is a
paragraph. This is a paragraph. This is a paragraph. This is a paragraph. This
is a paragraph. This is a paragraph. This is a paragraph.
```

```
</div>
</div>
</body>
</html>
```

The following code snippet inserts an `InPlaceEditor` control (see Figure 8.5). The `InPlaceEditor` replaces text onscreen with a text input field, an OK button, and a cancel link to revert to displaying the text. The `InPlaceEditor` provides a nice way to make content editable without refreshing the web page. The OK button posts data back to a server-side script.

```
<h1 id="ContentToEdit">To be edited</h1>
<script>
new Ajax.InPlaceEditor($(ContentToEdit), 'text.txt', {
        submitOnBlur: true, okButton: true, cancelLink: true,
        ajaxOptions: {method: 'get'}
        });
</script>
```

Figure 8.5
The InPlaceEditor
in action.

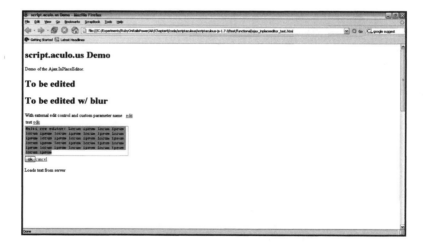

The `Ajax.Autocompleter()` method is used to create an autocompleter control. We first need an input box and a `div`. When the user enters text, the text is sent to a server. The server returns possible matches, and this is displayed in the `div`. The `Ajax.Autocompleter()` method takes four parameters. The first two parameters set the input field and the `div` tag. The third parameter specifies the server-side script that will return the suggestions. Finally, we can pass a series of parameters that will be appended to the querystring.

```
Autocompleter: <input id="ac1" type="text" name="ac1"/>
<div id="ac1update"
style="display:none;border:1px solid black;background-color:white;">
</div>
<script type="text/javascript" language="javascript">
// <![CDATA[
     new Ajax.Autocompleter('ac1',
                            'ac1update',
                            'autocomplete_result.html',
                            {parameters:'a=b&b=c'}
                           );
// ]]>
</script>
```

Rails JavaScript Helpers

We now turn our focus to adding server-side support to AJAX powered web interfaces. We'll be using Ruby on Rails to respond to AJAX calls. Rails will save data from `InPlaceEditors`, **send back suggestions for display in autocompletion controls, and update the order of list items after they have been dragged to a new position. As always, wiring up Rails and AJAX is a delight. We won't need to write any JavaScript. It is true that AJAX support in Rails relies on the Prototype and Scriptaculous libraries, but Rails includes helper tags that allow us to include these libraries in** `.rhtml` **templates.**

THE JAVASCRIPT_INCLUDE_TAG HELPER

The `javascript_include_tag` **is used to include the appropriate JavaScript library files from the** `public/javascript` **folder. The** `javascript_include_tag` **provides an alternative to using the standard HTML** <script> **tags to include the required libraries. The** `javascript_include_tag` **must be placed within the opening and closing** <head> **tags. Figure 8.6 displays the rendered output of using the** `javascript_include_tag` **with the** `defaults` **parameter.**

```
<html>
<head>
<title> javascript_include_tag  demo</title>
<%= javascript_include_tag :defaults %>
</head>
<body>
</body>
</html>
```

Figure 8.6
Viewing the output of the javascript_include_tag.

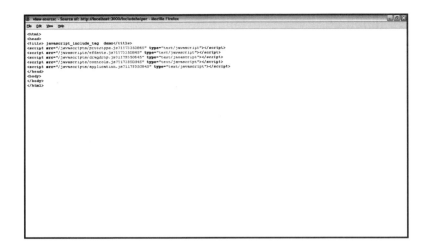

⁂ **Note**

Place JavaScript code that you would like included across your application in the `application.js` file. If `defaults` is specified and you have an `application.js` file, it will be included.

We could also choose to include only the `prototype.js` file:

```
<%= javascript_include_tag "prototype" %>
```

Multiple scripts can be included:

```
<%= javascript_include_tag "prototype,controls,effects,draganddrop" %>
```

You can even add your own JavaScript files. Place the `.js` **files in the** `public/javascripts` **folder and pass the files to the** `javascript_include_tag` **as a comma-delimited list. Don't include the** `.js` **extension:**

```
<%= javascript_include_tag "script1,script2,script3" %>
```

THE LINK_TO_REMOTE HELPER

The `link_to_remote` **helper inserts a link, wires the link up to a Rails action, and specifies the** `div` **where the returned text or HTML markup will be displayed. This is a pretty awesome helper. Here is the syntax:**

```
<%= link_to_remote( "Get the Time",

                    :update => "time_div",
```

```
                    :url =>{ :action => :tell_time }

                )

%>
```

Let's create a very simple example in which a user clicks a link to get the current time. We will first need a controller:

```
$ ruby script/generate controller linktoremote
```

Open the generated `linktoremote_controller.rb` file and add the `index` method:

```
class LinktoremoteController < ApplicationController
      def index
      end
end
```

Create an `index.rhtml` file and save it to the `app\views\linktoremote` folder. Enter the HTML markup for the "Get the Time" example. Don't forget to use the `javascript_include_tag` helper to insert the required JavaScript files—in this example we only need the `prototype.js` file. Include a `div` and set its id to `time_div`. Finally, we will add a `link_to_remote` helper. The `update` argument is set to the id of the `div` that will display the time. The `tell_time` action is wired up to handle the call.

```
<html>
<head>
<title>Get the Time</title>
<%= javascript_include_tag "prototype" %>
</head>
<body>
<h1>Get the Time</h1>
<div id="time_div">
</div>
<%= link_to_remote( "Get the Time",
                    :update => "time_div",
                    :url =>{ :action => :tell_time }
                )
%>
</body>
</html>
```

In the `linktoremote_controller.rb` file we add a `tell_time` method that simply returns the current time. In Ruby we can use the `now` method of the `DateTime` object to get the current time.

```
class LinktoremoteController < ApplicationController
     def index
     end
     def tell_time
            render_text "The time is: " + DateTime.now.to_s + "<br>"
     end
end
```

Figure 8.7 shows the "Tell Time" example in action. Let's take a peek at the source code that is generated. As you can see, the `link_to_remote` tag has inserted the required JavaScript code. You should not be surprised to see that the `Ajax.Updater` object from Prototype is being used to do all the hard work. Here is a listing of the resulting HTML and JavaScript code:

```
<html>
<head>
<title>Get the Time</title>
<script src="/javascripts/prototype.js?1160183870" type="text/javascript">
</script>
</head>
<body>
<h1>Get the Time</h1>
<div id="time_div">
</div>
<a href="#" onclick="new Ajax.Updater('time_div',
'/ajaxhelper/tell_time',
{asynchronous:true, evalScripts:true}); return false;">
Get the Time
</a>
</body>
</html>
```

It may not always be practical to replace the contents of a `div`. There are times when it would be beneficial to insert the new content above or below the current content. The `link_to_remote` tag includes an update option to allow insertion above or below the existing content in a `div`. The position option could be set to `before`, `top`, `bottom`, or `after`:

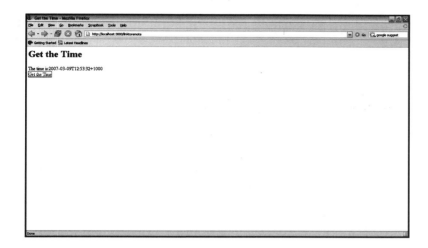

Figure 8.7
Using the
link_to_remote helper.

```
<%= link_to_remote( "Get the Time",
                    :update => "time_div",
                    :url =>{ :action => :tell_time },
                    :position => "after"                )
%>
```

DYNAMICALLY ADDING FORM ELEMENTS

We can also use the `link_to_remote` helper to add HTML markup to a web page. A practical application would be providing a user with a link to add more input boxes to a form dynamically (see Figure 8.8). This can easily be achieved by calling an action that renders a `.rhtml` template or just some HTML markup. Setting `:position` to `after` will append the rendered content to the existing content in the `div`.

Create a new controller called `formelements`:

```
$ ruby script/generate controller formelements
```

Add `index` and `add_form_element` methods to the `formelements _controller.rb` file. The `add_form_element` method only needs to output an `<input>` tag.

```
class FormelementsController < ApplicationController
    def index
    end
    def add_form_element
        render :text => '<br/><input type="text"><br/>'
    end
end
```

Finally, we create the `index.rhtml` file and place it in the `/views/formelements` folder. The `index.rhtml` file contains a form. The input boxes are placed with a `div` tag. Below the `div` tag we place the `link_to_remote` tag that will call the `add_form_element` method:

```
<html>
<head>
<title>Add form elements</title>
<%= javascript_include_tag "prototype" %>
</head>
<body>
<h1>Add form elements</h1>
<form>
<div id="inputs_div">
<input type="text">
</div>
<%= link_to_remote( "Add input box",
                    :update => "inputs_div",
                    :url =>{ :action => :add_form_element },
                    :position => "after"
)
%>
</form>
</body>
</html>
```

Figure 8.8
Dynamically adding form fields to a form.

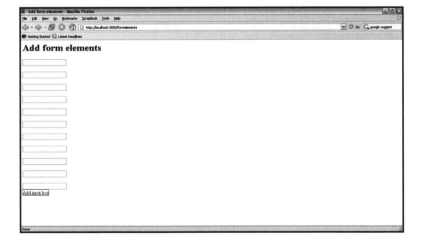

THE FORM_REMOTE_TAG HELPER

With the `form_remote_tag` helper, a Rails application can easily be AJAX enhanced. Simply replace the `form_tag` with the `form_remote_tag` when you need to post all the data entered into a form to an action and update the contents of a `div`.

```
<%= form_remote_tag(:url => { :action => "ask_dr_rails" },
                    :update => "dr_rails_reply",
                    :position => :top
)
%>
```

The `form_remote_tag` takes the following parameters:

❀   The URL is used to specify the Rails action.

❀   The `update` parameter sets the `div` tag that must be changed with the data that is returned.

❀   The `last` parameter allows you to specify how content gets inserted into the `div`.

We are now going to use the `form_remote_tag` to create an online psychiatrist called Dr. Rails. Dr. Rails will be on call 24-7 as long as your web server stays up. Dr. Rails will be able to hold a conversation with you. You just need to enter your problem in a text field and hit the Ask Dr. Rails button. The `form_remote_tag` will post your question to Dr. Rails (actually a Rails method called `ask_dr_rails()`). Dr. Rails will use some nifty Ruby code to try and hold an intelligent conversation with you (see Figure 8.9).

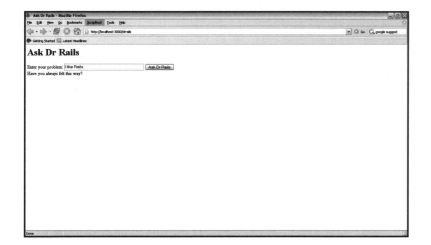

Figure 8.9
Chatting with Dr. Rails.

Let's create a `drrails` controller:

```
$ ruby script/generate controller drrails
```

To make Dr. Rails appear to be smart, we randomly select from a set of phrases such as "Tell me more?" or "Have you always felt this way?". Add the following code to the controller:

```ruby
class DrrailsController < ApplicationController
    def index
    end
    def ask_dr_rails
        randno = rand(3)
        if randno == 0
            render_text "Tell me more?"
        elsif randno == 1
            render_text "Have you always felt this way?"
        else
            problem_field = params[:problem_field]
            problem_field= problem_field.sub("I","You")
            problem_field= problem_field.sub(" am "," are ")
            problem_field= problem_field.sub(" my "," you ")
            render_text problem_field
        end
    end
end
```

Create an `index.rhtml` file and save it to the `app/views/drrails` folder. The template needs to contain:

- **An input box for a user to enter a problem**
- **A submit button**
- **A `div` tag called `dr_rails_reply`**

```html
<html>
<head>
<title>Ask Dr Rails</title>
<%= javascript_include_tag :defaults %>
</head>
<body>
<h1>Ask Dr Rails</h1>
<%= form_remote_tag(
        :url => { :action => "ask_dr_rails" },
```

```
            :update => "dr_rails_reply",
            :html => { :id => 'dr_rails_form' }
) %>
Enter your problem:
<%= text_field_tag 'problem_field', nil, :size => 40 %>
<%= submit_tag 'Ask Dr Rails' %>
<br>
<div id="dr_rails_reply"></div>
<%= end_form_tag %>
</body>
</html>
```

THE TEXT_FIELD_WITH_AUTO_COMPLETE HELPER

When a user enters data into a text field, we can match the characters he has entered with the data stored in a database and offer a list of possible suggestions. Rather than enter the whole word or phrase, the user can simply scroll through the list and select one of the selected items. The `text_field_with_auto_complete` helper makes wiring up auto-completion to an Active Record model a trivial task.

We will illustrate the use of `text_field_with_auto_complete` helper. The example that follows tries to match the characters entered to a database table that contains a list of Australian cities (see Figure 8.10).

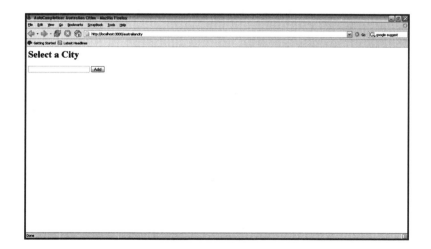

Figure 8.10
The AustralianCities table.

Generate a model called `australiancity`:

```
$ ruby script/generate model australiancity
```

The following will be output to the console:

```
exists   app/models/
exists   test/unit/
exists   test/fixtures/
create   app/models/australiancity.rb
create   test/unit/australiancity_test.rb
create   test/fixtures/australiancities.yml
create   db/migrate
create   db/migrate/001_create_australiancities.rb
```

Edit db/migrate/001_create_australiancities.rb. **The australiancities table requires an** id **and a** city **field. We use the** create **method to insert cities into the database:**

```
class CreateAustraliancities < ActiveRecord::Migration
    def self.up
        create_table :australiancities do |t|
            t.column :city, :string
        end
        Australiancity.create :city => "Brisbane"
        Australiancity.create :city => "Sydney"
        Australiancity.create :city => "Cairns"
        Australiancity.create :city => "Perth"
        Australiancity.create :city => "Gold Coast"
    end
    def self.down
        drop_table :australiancities
    end
end
```

Run the migration:

```
$ rake db:migrate
```

The australiancities table will be created:

```
(in C:/rails/ajax)
== CreateAustraliancities: migrating ========================================
-- create_table(:australiancities)
   -> 0.1090s
== CreateAustraliancities: migrated (0.1090s) ===============================
```

Generate a controller called `australiancity`:

```
$ ruby script/generate model australiancity
```

Edit the generated `australiancity_controller.rb` file. Add an index method to the controller. We need to include a call to `auto_complete_for`, which takes two parameters. The first parameter contains the model we are matching the input field from our view with. The second parameter specifies the name of the field we are matching to within the database table.

```
class AustraliancityController < ApplicationController
    auto_complete_for :australiancity, :city
    def index
    end
end
```

We now put the `text_field_with_auto_complete` helper to good use in our `index.rhtml` view.

```
<html>
<head>
<title>AutoCompletion: Australian Cities</title>
<%= javascript_include_tag :defaults %>
</head>
<body>
<h1>Select a City</h1>
<%= start_form_tag %>
<%= text_field_with_auto_complete :australiancity, :city %>
<%= submit_tag 'Add' %>
<%= end_form_tag %>
</body>
</html>
```

THE SORTABLE_ELEMENTS HELPER

Earlier in this chapter we learned to use Scriptaculous to create drag-and-drop sortable lists. We are now going to use this technique to reorder a list of items stored in a database. As usual there is an appropriate Rails helper available: the `sortable_elements` helper. Figure 8.11 shows a task list being reordered.

We start with a simple database table called tasks. The tasks table has an ID field, a `name` field, and a `position` field. Multiple tasks belong to a project. The second table we need to create is called projects. The projects table has an ID field and a `name` field.

Figure 8.11
A drag-and-drop sortable list.

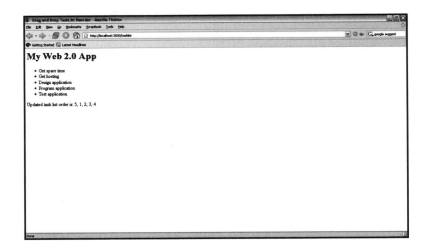

Generate a model called project:

```
$ ruby script/generate model project
```

The following will be output to the console:

```
exists   app/models/
exists   test/unit/
exists   test/fixtures/
create   app/models/project.rb
create   test/unit/project_test.rb
create   test/fixtures/projects.yml
exists   db/migrate
create   db/migrate/003_create_projects.rb
```

Edit the db/migrate/002_create_projects.rb **migration. The projects table needs a** name **field. We will create the first project as well:**

```
class CreateProjects < ActiveRecord::Migration
    def self.up
        create_table :projects do |t|
            t.column :name, :string
        end
        Project.create :name => "My Web 2.0 App"
    end
    def self.down
```

```
        drop_table :projects
    end
end
```

Generate a model called `task`:

```
$ ruby script/generate model task
```

The following will be output to the console:

```
exists   app/models/
exists   test/unit/
exists   test/fixtures/
create   app/models/task.rb
create   test/unit/task_test.rb
create   test/fixtures/tasks.yml
exists   db/migrate
create   db/migrate/002_create_tasks.rb
```

Edit the `db/migrate/002_create_tasks.rb` **migration. The tasks table needs** `name` **and** `position` **fields. We'll create some tasks at the same time:**

```
class CreateTasks < ActiveRecord::Migration
    def self.up
        create_table :tasks do |t|
            t.column :name, :string
            t.column :project_id, :integer
            t.column :position, :integer
        end
        Task.create :name => "Get hosting", :project_id => 1,
                    :position => 1
        Task.create :name => "Design application", :project_id => 1,
                    :position => 2
        Task.create :name => "Program application", :project_id => 1,
                    :position => 3
        Task.create :name => "Test application", :project_id => 1,
                    :position => 4
        Task.create :name => "Get spare time", :project_id => 1,
                    :position => 5
    end
```

```
      def self.down
          drop_table :tasks
      end
end
```

Run the rake task to create the database tables:

```
$ rake db:migrate
```

Enter `belongs_to :project` **in the** `model/task.rb` **file:**

```
class Task < ActiveRecord::Base
      belongs_to :project
end
```

A project has multiple tasks, so we add a `has_many` **relationship. We also specify the field used to order the tasks.**

```
class Project < ActiveRecord::Base
      has_many :tasks, :order => "position"
end
```

Generate a controller called `task`:

```
$ ruby script/generate controller tasklist
```

Edit the `controller/tasklist_controller.rb` **file. We need an index method that assigns the first project from the projects table to an instance variable available to the** `index.rhtml` **view. We also need an order method. The order method will be called each time a task is repositioned. The reordered sequence is sent back via the** `list` **parameter. We can use an** `each_with_index` **iterator to loop though the list and update the position field for each task.**

```
class TaskController < ApplicationController
      def index
          @project = Project.find(:first)
      end
      def order
          order = params[:list]
          order.each_with_index do |id, position|
                Task.find(id).update_attribute(:position, position + 1)
          end
          render :text => "Updated task list order is: #{order.join(', ')}"
```

```
        end
end
```

Finally, we use the `sortable_element` helper in our view. After the update, the order `div` will contain the reordered list. We also use a visual effect for the first time. When the database and the `div` tag have been updated, we use the `highlight` visual effect to give the user a visual indication that an update has occurred.

```
<html>
<head>
<title>Drag and Drop TaskList Reorder</title>
<%= javascript_include_tag :defaults %>
</head>
<body>
<h1><%= @project.name %></h1>
<ul id="list">
<% for task in @project.tasks -%>
<li id="task_<%= task.id %>" style="cursor:move;"><%= task.name %></li>
<% end %>
</ul>
<div id="order"></div>
<%= sortable_element 'list',
:update => 'order',
:complete => visual_effect(:highlight, 'list'),
:url => { :action => "order" } %>

</body>
</html>
```

THE `periodically_call_remote` HELPER

We don't need to rely on user interaction to make AJAX requests. We can also periodically poll a method within a controller. This technique is useful to update information on a page periodically such as stock quotes or messages in a multi-user chat room. The `periodically_call_remote` helper takes the following parameters:

❄ `update`, which specifies the `div` tag that must be updated

❄ `url`, which assigns a controller action to respond to the request

❄ `frequency`, which sets the interval between calls in seconds

Here is an example:

```
<%= periodically_call_remote(
:update => 'process-list',
:url => { :action => :ps },
:frequency => 2 )
%>
```

 Warning

Continuously polling a server can cause load and performance issues. Use the `periodically_call_remote` helper with great care.

Updating Multiple Page Elements with RJS

The AJAX helpers are great, but they are only able to call or update a single page element. This is where Rails JavaScript (RJS) templates come to the rescue. An RJS template maps to a controller's action. If no `.rhtml` template is available that matches the name of the action, Rails looks for a view with the `.rjs` extension. Within an RJS template, we are able to use Ruby to control page elements—no JavaScript is required. The Ruby code is converted to JavaScript automatically when it is sent to the browser. We will now look at some simple RJS commands.

Hide an element on a page:

```
page.hide 'header'
```

Show an element on a page:

```
page.show 'header'
```

Redirect to another controller and action:

```
page.redirect_to :controller => 'faq', :action => 'show'
```

Redirect to an external site:

```
page.redirect_to 'http://www.google.com'
```

Reset a form:

```
page.form.reset 'sample form'
```

Display a visual effect:

```
page.visual_effect :highlight, 'text_entry'
```

Inject HTML or text into a `div` from a partial template:

```
page.insert_html :bottom, 'text_entry', :partial => 'text_entry'
```

We are going to create a simple example to illustrate the power of Rails Javascript templates. The example is called IdeaPad. IdeaPad displays a log of all your great ideas. IdeaPad also provides a text input box for you to enter new ideas (see Figure 8.12).

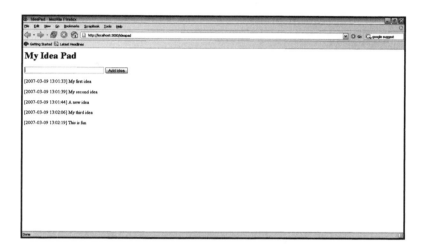

Figure 8.12
The IdeaPad in action.

Generate a controller called `ideapad`:

```
$ ruby script/generate controller ideapad
```

The controller (`ideapad_controller.rb`) has an index action, which will display the `index.rhtml`. The `add_idea` action maps to the `add_idea.rjs` template. The `@idea` instance variable contains the posted back `idea` field:

```
class IdeapadController < ApplicationController
    def index
    end
    def add_idea
        @idea = params[:idea]
    end
end
```

The `index.rhtml` template displays the form for you to enter your idea, which will be appended to the log contained in the `"ideas"` div. The `form_remote_tag` helper is used to post the idea to the `add_idea` action:

```
<html>
<head>
<title>IdeaPad</title>
<%= javascript_include_tag :defaults %>
</head>
<body>
<h1>My Idea Pad</h1>
<%= form_remote_tag :url => { :action => 'add_idea' }, :html => { :id => 'idea-
form' } %>
<%= text_field_tag 'idea', nil, :size => 40 %>
<%= submit_tag 'Add Idea' %>
<%= end_form_tag %>
<div id="ideas"></div>
</body>
</html>
```

The `add_idea.rjs` **injects the HTML generated by the idea partial (`_idea.rhtml`), highlights the** `"ideas"` **div, and resets the form:**

```
page.insert_html :bottom, 'ideas', :partial => 'idea'
page.visual_effect :highlight, 'ideas'
page.form.reset 'idea-form'
```

The `_idea.rhtml` **partial simply timestamps the** `@idea` **instance variable (i.e., the idea posted with the form):**

```
<p>
[<%= Time.now.to_s(:db) %>] <%=h idea %>
</p>
```

> ❄ **Tip**
>
> We can use RJS to make a printer friendly version of a page by hiding appropriate page elements, such as a header and footer, and then print the page by calling `window.print()`:
>
> ```
> page.hide 'header'
> page.hide 'footer'
> page.<<'javascript:window.print()'
> ```

> ❋ **Tip**
>
> We can use the `render` method to render an RJS template directly:
>
> ```
> def task
>     # skip task.rhtml or task.rxml
>     render :action => "product.rjs"
> end
> ```

Conclusion

Ruby on Rails incorporates impressive AJAX functionality. Everything from auto-completing text input boxes to drag-and-drop sortable lists is available as a Rails helper method. This chapter aims to give you a good understanding of the `XMLHttpRequest` object, but as you might have realized, you really don't need to write any JavaScript to create AJAX-enabled Web 2.0 applications. Rails JavaScript (RJS) templates add yet another dimension to the mix. RJS allows us to use Ruby to generate JavaScript. We are able to update multiple page elements using RJS. In the next chapter, "Flex on Rails," we will explore an alternate Flash-based user interface technology.

9 Flex on Rails

The Adobe Flex 2 Software Development Kit (SDK) is designed to help programmers build Rich Internet Applications in Flash. In Flex, MXML markup is used to declaratively author an interface that can then be compiled into Flash. Flex includes numerous useful components and makes it much easier to build Flash interfaces than using the Flash IDE, which was primarily designed as an animator's tool. Ruby on Rails is an ideal choice as a backend for Flex interfaces. In Rails it is easy to build database enabled applications. We will use this functionality to integrate a Flex interface with a Rails exposed database backend.

In this chapter you'll learn to:

* ❀ Download and install the Flex 2 SDK
* ❀ Write Flex MXML markup and compile to Flash
* ❀ Design Flex user interfaces
* ❀ Write basic ActionsScript
* ❀ Expose an ActiveRecord model as XML
* ❀ Build Flex interfaces for Ruby on Rails

Download and Install the Flex 2 SDK

We start our journey by downloading the Flex 2 SDK from the Adobe web site (http://www.adobe.com/products/flex/). The Flex SDK is free and allows you to compile MXML markup into a Flash file. Figure 9.1 shows the directory structure of the Flex 2 SDK after it has been unzipped. The samples folder contains example Flex applications including a Flex Store and PhotoViewer. These examples will give you a good idea of what is possible with Flex. Before you can explore these applications, you will need to compile the MXML markup into Flash (`.swf`) files by executing the `build-samples.bat` file. The `build-samples.bat` file takes a few minutes to run because it compiles all the Flex examples included in the SDK.

Figure 9.1
The Flex 2 SDK.

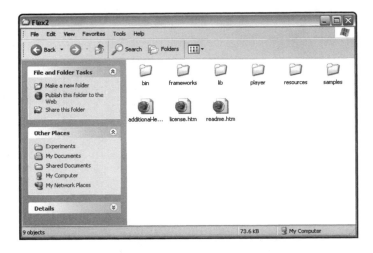

Note

The Flash files that Flex 2 generates require Flash Player 9. If your web browser does not have Flash Player 9, Flash files generated by Flex will not render or function properly. You can upgrade to Flash Player 9 by visiting the Adobe web site. The Flex 2 SDK includes a version of Flash Player with debugging support in the `player/debug` folder.

Once the sample applications are compiled, they can be viewed within a web browser. The Flex Store application is shown in Figure 9.2.

Figure 9.2
The Flex 2 Store in action.

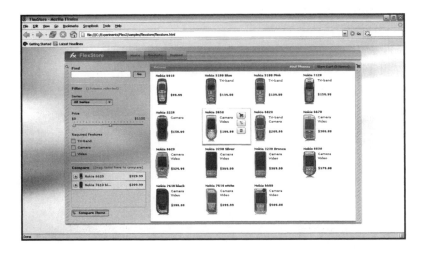

Flex Explorer, found in the `samples/explorer` folder, allows you to experiment with all of the available interface components as well as view the MXML markup used to build the examples. In Figure 9.3 the DataGrid component is displayed.

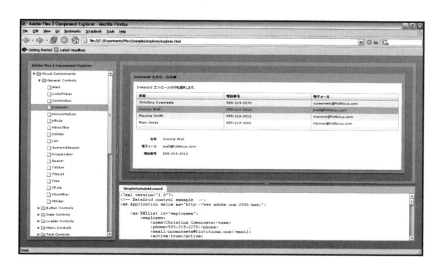

Figure 9.3
The DataGrid component viewed in Flex Explorer.

A Simple Flex Interface with MXML

We are going to use MXML to build a simple interface in Flex. The interface will use the `Panel`, `TextInput`, `Label`, and `Button` controls. Create a new folder called `FlexExample` in the `samples` folder of your Flex 2 SDK installation. Create a file called `FlexExample.mxml`. Copy the markup that follows into this file:

```
<?xml version="1.0"?>
<!-- Simple Flex Example. -->
<mx:Application xmlns:mx="http://www.adobe.com/2006/mxml">
    <mx:Panel title="Flex Example" height="75%" width="75%" paddingTop="10"
            paddingLeft="10">
        <mx:TextInput id="src" text="Hello World!"/>
        <mx:Button label="Copy Input" click="lbldest.text = src.text"/>
        <mx:Label id="lbldest" text=""/>
    </mx:Panel>
</mx:Application>
```

MXML is a proprietary XML format used by Flex. With MXML, you can declaratively author an interface. The `<mx:Application>` opening and closing tags must be present in an MXML file. All controls used in your interface must be placed in the opening and closing

`<mx:Application>` tags. A tag is used to represent each control. The example contains the `<mx:TextInput>`, `<mx:Button>`, `<mx:Label>`, and `<mx:Panel>` tags because our interface requires the `TextInput`, `Button`, `Label`, and `Panel` controls. The tags used to represent the controls also have attributes. It is important to include an `id` attribute for each control.

> **Note**
>
> The `<!--` and `-->` delimiters are used to include code comments in an MXML file.

The example we are creating allows the user to enter text into a `TextInput` control (`id="src"`) and when the Copy Input button is clicked, the `Label` control (`id="lbldest"`) will display the text. The `Button` control has a click attribute. We can use some simple ActionScript code to retrieve the text property of the `TextInput` box and assign this value to the text property of the `Label` control. ActionScript is an object-oriented scripting language that runs in the Flash Player.

We are now ready to compile our simple example into a Flash file (`.swf`). The `mxmlc.exe` file in the `bin` folder of the Flex SDK is the compiler. We will make a simple `bat` file to execute the compiler. The `bat` file must be placed in the same folder as your MXML files. The contents of the `build.bat` file:

```
@echo off
SET OPTS=-use-network=false
for /R . %%f in (*.mxml) do  ..\..\bin\mxmlc.exe %OPTS% "%%f"
```

We now need to create a web page to view our `swf` file (see Figure 9.4). The page uses the `<object>` tag to display Flash in Internet Explorer and the `<embed>` tag for Firefox. The `FlexExample.html` file is displayed below:

```
<html>
<head>
<title>Example Flex Interface</title>
</head>
<body>
<table width='100%' height='100%' cellspacing='0' cellpadding='0'><tr>
<td valign='top'>
     <object classid="clsid:D27CDB6E-AE6D-11cf-96B8-444553540000"
id="FlexExample" width="100%" height="100%"
codebase="http://download.macromedia.com/pub/shockwave/cabs/flash/swflash.cab">
               <param name="movie" value="FlexExample.swf" />
```

```
                <param name="quality" value="high" />
                <param name="bgcolor" value="#5c5f45" />
                <param name="allowScriptAccess" value="sameDomain" />
                    <embed src="FlexExample.swf " quality="high"
bgcolor="#5c5f45"
                            width="100%" height="100%" name="FlexExample"
align="middle"
                        play="true"
                        loop="false"
                        quality="high"
                        allowScriptAccess="sameDomain"
                        type="application/x-shockwave-flash"
pluginspage="http://www.macromedia.com/go/getflashplayer">
                    </embed>
        </object>
</td></tr></table>
</body>
</html>
```

Figure 9.4
Viewing the generated
Flash file in a web browser.

We are now going to make the click handler of the Button control call a method and place the code that copies the text entered into the `TextInput` to the Label control within this method. The method will be called `CopyText()`. ActionScript code is placed within the `<mx:script>` tags. The method must be place within a `<![CDATA[...]]>` element.

```xml
<?xml version="1.0"?>
<!-- Simple Flex Example. -->
<mx:Application xmlns:mx="http://www.adobe.com/2006/mxml">


    <mx:Script>
    <![CDATA[
        private function copytext():void {
            lbldest.text = src.text;
        }
    ]]>
    </mx:Script>
    <mx:Panel title="Flex Example" height="75%" width="75%" paddingTop="10"
paddingLeft="10">
        <mx:TextInput id="src" text="Hello World!"/>
        <mx:Button label="Copy Input" click="lbldest.text = src.text"/>
        <mx:Label id="lbldest" text=""/>
    </mx:Panel>
</mx:Application>
```

Interface Design with Flex

Flex provides a wide variety of components that can be assembled using the MXML declarative syntax. With MXML, creative, intuitive, and user friendly interfaces can be created. It is impossible to cover every Flex component in a single chapter. I could actually dedicate an entire book to Flex. This section will, however, detail a variety of examples, each using a different set of controls and showcasing the unique possibilities of Flex. The following types of controls are available for inclusion in your own applications:

* **Data entry controls.** These include TextInput boxes, TextAreas, Labels, Color selectors, Calendar entry controls, and even sliders.

* **Buttons.** Flex includes Buttons, Toggle Buttons, Checkboxes, and Radio boxes.

* **Validators.** These work with TextInput boxes and display in-place messages to inform the user that a field is required or check if the data entered matches the format of an email address or regular expression.

* **Loader controls.** These controls are able to load images, Flash files (in `.swf` format), and Flash Video.

- ❊ **Containers.** Controls can be placed inside containers. Panels, DividedBoxes, Accordions, and Tab bars are example container controls.
- ❊ **Effects and transitions.** Flex provides numerous effects such as fade or blur for use in your applications.

Using a Slider Control to Resize an Image

In this example, we will be using a slider control to dynamically resize an image (see Figure 9.5). We will be using the `<mx:Slider>` and `<mx:Image>` tags. Some basic ActionScipt is all that's required to set the width and height of the image to the value that matches the position of the slider.

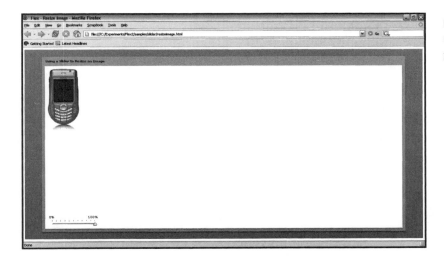

Figure 9.5
Using a slider to resize an image.

The Panel control is used as the container in this example. The slider and image will be placed in the panel. We give the `title` attribute to give the example a meaningful heading.

```
<mx:Panel id="panel" title="Using a Slider to Resize an Image"
height="100%" width="95%" paddingTop="10" paddingBottom="10"
paddingLeft="10" paddingRight="10">
```

Images can either be embedded in the generated `swf` file or dynamically loaded. We use the `embed` syntax to specify the image and embed it in the generated `swf` file. The `creationComplete` event is fired when the image is first displayed, and we calculate the width and height of the image and set these attributes.

```
<mx:Image id="img" source="@Embed('assets/Nokia_6630.png')"
creationComplete="imgWidth=img.width; imgHeight=img.height;" />
```

We will use an HSlider control. This is a horizontal slider. We could also use a VSlider, which displays a vertical slider. We need to set the minimum and maximum attributes, and we need to set liveDragging to true to allow the slider to be dragged. When a slider change event is triggered, the ResizeImage() method is called.

```
<mx:HSlider id="Slider" minimum="0" maximum="100" value="100"
            dataTipPlacement="top"
            tickColor="red"
            snapInterval="1" tickInterval="10"
            labels="['0%','100%']"
            allowTrackClick="true"
            liveDragging="true"
            change="ResizeImg();"
/>
```

The ResizeImage() method sets the width and height of the image to the slider's percentage value. We need to use uint to convert the value returned to a whole number.

```
        private function ResizeImg():void
        {
                img.width=uint(imgWidth*Slider.value/100);
                img.height=uint(imgHeight*Slider.value/100);
        }
```

Here is the full source listing:

```
<?xml version="1.0"?>
<mx:Application xmlns:mx="http://www.adobe.com/2006/mxml">
    <mx:Script>
    <![CDATA[
        private var imgWidth:Number=0;
        private var imgHeight:Number=0;

        private function ResizeImage():void
        {
                img.width=uint(imgWidth*Slider.value/100);
                img.height=uint(imgHeight*Slider.value/100);
        }
    ]]>
    </mx:Script>
```

```
     <mx:Panel id="panel" title="Using a Slider to Resize an Image"
height="100%" width="95%" paddingTop="10" paddingBottom="10" paddingLeft="10"
paddingRight="10">
          <mx:HBox height="100%" width="100%">
               <mx:Image id="img" source="@Embed('assets/Nokia_6630.png')"
creationComplete="imgWidth=img.width; imgHeight=img.height;" />
          </mx:HBox>
          <mx:HSlider id="Slider" minimum="0" maximum="100" value="100"
               dataTipPlacement="top"
               tickColor="red"
               snapInterval="1" tickInterval="10"
               labels="['0%','100%']"
               allowTrackClick="true"
               liveDragging="true"
               change="ResizeImg();"/>
     </mx:Panel>
</mx:Application>
```

Displaying a Series of Images

The TileList control displays elements in a series of rows and columns. We will use TileList to display images in a scrollable grid (see Figure 9.6). We will be using `<mx:Panel>`, `<mx:TileList>`, `<mx:DataProvider>`, and `<mx:Array>`.

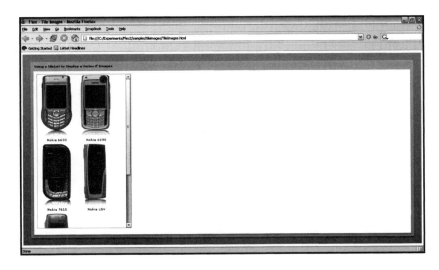

Figure 9.6
Using the TileList control.

First we set up the images that will be displayed. We will again be embedding them within the generated `swf`. This time we will use annotation in ActionScript. The `[Bindable]` annotation means the image can be assigned or bound to an image control. The `[Embed]` annotation sets the location of the image. We repeat the following code for each image we include.

```
[Bindable][Embed(source="assets/Nokia_6630.png")]
public var phone1:Class;
<mx:TileList id="TileImages" height="500" width="300"
maxColumns="2" rowHeight="225" columnWidth="125">
```

The `<mx:TileList>` is placed within a Panel control. We want to display images in two columns, so we set the `maxColumns` attribute to 2.

```
<mx:TileList id="TileImages" height="500" width="300"
             maxColumns="2" rowHeight="225" columnWidth="125">
```

We use the `<mx:DataProvider>` and the `<mx:Array>` to bind a list of images to the TileList control. The `<mx:Object>` tag is used to set a label and the image. The `icon` attribute of the first `<mx:Object>` tag is set to `{phone1}`. The `{` and `}` characters indicate that the attribute must be bound to `phone1`, which was set via annotations to an embedded image. This data binding is repeated for all the `<mx:Object>` tags until all images are included.

```
<mx:dataProvider>
<mx:Array>
<mx:Object label="Nokia 6630" icon="{phone1}"/>
<mx:Object label="Nokia 6680" icon="{phone2}"/>
<mx:Object label="Nokia 7610" icon="{phone3}"/>
<mx:Object label="Nokia LGV" icon="{phone4}"/>
<mx:Object label="Nokia LMV" icon="{phone5}"/>
</mx:Array>
</mx:dataProvider>
The MXML source for the TileList example:
<?xml version="1.0"?>
<mx:Application xmlns:mx="http://www.adobe.com/2006/mxml">
    <mx:Script>
    <![CDATA[
        [Bindable]
        [Embed(source="assets/Nokia_6630.png")]
        public var phone1:Class;
        [Bindable]
```

```
            [Embed(source="assets/Nokia_6680.png")]
            public var phone2:Class;
            [Bindable]
            [Embed(source="assets/Nokia_7610.png")]
            public var phone3:Class;
            [Bindable]
            [Embed(source="assets/Nokia_lg_v_keypad.png")]
            public var phone4:Class;
            [Bindable]
            [Embed(source="assets/Nokia_sm_v_keypad.png")]
            public var phone5:Class;
        ]]>
    </mx:Script>
    <mx:Panel title="Using a TileList to Display a Series if Images"
height="100%" width="100%"
        paddingTop="10" paddingBottom="10" paddingLeft="10" paddingRight="10">
        <mx:TileList id="TileImages" height="500" width="300"
            maxColumns="2" rowHeight="225" columnWidth="125">
            <mx:dataProvider>
                <mx:Array>
                    <mx:Object label="Nokia 6630" icon="{phone1}"/>
                    <mx:Object label="Nokia 6680" icon="{phone2}"/>
                    <mx:Object label="Nokia 7610" icon="{phone3}"/>
                    <mx:Object label="Nokia LGV" icon="{phone4}"/>
                    <mx:Object label="Nokia LMV" icon="{phone5}"/>
                </mx:Array>
            </mx:dataProvider>
        </mx:TileList>
    </mx:Panel>
</mx:Application>
```

Creating a Drag-and-Drop Image Classifier

We now focus our attention on some of the drag-and-drop functionality built into Flex. It is amazingly simple to enable drag-and-drop functionality in a Flex application. The Drag and Drop Image Classifier displays a set of images that need to be classified or dragged into an appropriate TileList control (see Figure 9.7). To make this example more challenging, the list of images will be loaded from an XML file and we will create a Flex component.

Figure 9.7
The Drag and Drop Image Classifier.

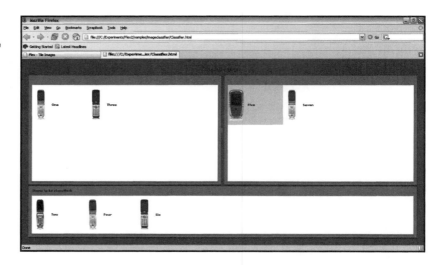

First we create an XML file that contains a list of all images and their respective locations:

```
<?xml version="1.0" encoding="utf-8"?>
<activity title="Classification" type="Classification">
        <items>
                <item title="One" imageurl="assets/products/DoCoMo_901_ic.png" />
                <item title="Two" imageurl="assets/products/DoCoMo_F900_i.png" />
                <item title="Three" imageurl="assets/products/Casio_W21CA.png" />
                <item title="Four" imageurl="assets/products/DoCoMo_901_ic.png" />
                <item title="Five" imageurl="assets/products/Siemens_SX1.png" />
                <item title="Six" imageurl="assets/products/Casio_W21CA.png" />
                <item title="Seven" imageurl="assets/products/DoCoMo_901_ic.png" />
        </items>
</activity>
```

The `Item.mxml` **file will be our first Flex component. Flex components can be re-used a number of times in Flex applications. Components also help to reduce the size and complexity of the main MXML file in applications. In the** `Item.mxml` **component we place an image in an HBox control. We databind the source of the image to** `{data.imageurl}`**. We also include a label that is set to** `{data.title}`**. The component displays only a single image and receives the** `{data.imageurl}` **and** `{data.title}` **fields, which it will bind. The** `title` **and** `imageurl` **fields are from the XML file.**

```
<mx:HBox xmlns:mx="http://www.adobe.com/2006/mxml"  backgroundAlpha="0"
    borderStyle="none" width="165" height="120" verticalAlign="middle"
```

```
verticalGap="0" verticalScrollPolicy="off">
    <mx:Image id="img" height="100" width="50" source="{data.imageurl}"/>
    <mx:VBox width="100%" paddingTop="0" horizontalGap="4">
        <mx:Label text="{data.title}" fontWeight="bold"/>
    </mx:VBox>
</mx:HBox>
```

We are now ready to code our main MXML file. The `<mx:HTTPService>` tag is extremely powerful, and we will use it extensively in the remainder of this chapter. In this instance, we use HTTPService to load the XML file. HTTPService is triggered when the `creationComplete` event is fired in the applications. The `<mx:Model>` tag provides an intuitive way to reference the data in the XML file, e.g. `activityModel.title` and `activityModel.items.item`, the latter of which will be databound to our component.

Images can be dragged onto a TileList by setting the `dragEnabled`, `dropEnabled`, and `dragMoveEnabled` attributes to true. Our application has two TileLists, both placed in Panel controls, which are in an `HDividedBox` control. The `HDividedBox` makes each panel resizable.

A HorizontalList control displays the images that need to be classified (i.e., dragged to an appropriate TileList control). The `dataProvider` attribute is set, `{activityModel.items.item}`, to bind it to the data from the XML file. The `itemRenderer` attribute is set to the name of the component we have designed to display a labeled image. We called our component `Item.mxml`, so this is set to `Item`. Finally, the `dragEnabled`, `dropEnabled`, and `dragMoveEnabled` attributes are set to true.

The source code listing for the Drag and Drop Classifier:

```
<?xml version="1.0" encoding="utf-8"?>
<mx:Application xmlns:mx="http://www.adobe.com/2006/mxml"  backgroundAlpha="0"
    creationComplete="srv.send();">
<mx:HTTPService id="srv" url="Classifier.xml" useProxy="false" />
<mx:Model id="activityModel">{srv.lastResult.activity}</mx:Model>
<mx:Label id="Title" text="{activityModel.title}" fontSize="16" />
    <mx:VBox width="100%" height="100%">
        <mx:HDividedBox width="100%" height="75%">
            <mx:Panel id="cat1" width="100%" height="100%" >
                <mx:TileList
                    height="100%"
                    width="100%"
                    id="tl_Category1"
                    itemRenderer="Item"
```

```
                                rowHeight="130"
                                columnWidth="175"
                                allowMultipleSelection="false"
                                dragEnabled="true"
                                dropEnabled="true"
                                dragMoveEnabled="true" />
                </mx:Panel>
                <mx:Panel id="cat2" width="100%" height="100%" >
                    <mx:TileList
                            height="100%"
                            width="100%"
                            id="tl_Category2"
                            itemRenderer="Item"
                            rowHeight="130"
                            columnWidth="175"
                            allowMultipleSelection="false"
                            dragEnabled="true"
                            dropEnabled="true"
                            dragMoveEnabled="true"/>
                </mx:Panel>
        </mx:HDividedBox>
        <mx:Panel title="Items to be classified:"
                width="100%" height="25%" >
            <mx:HorizontalList
                id="ItemsDsp"
                width="100%"
                dataProvider="{activityModel.items.item}"
                itemRenderer="Item"
                allowMultipleSelection="true"
                dragEnabled="true"
                dropEnabled="true"
                dragMoveEnabled="true" />
        </mx:Panel>
    </mx:VBox>
</mx:Application>
```

Using the DataGrid Control to Display XML

In this example, we will be using the DataGrid control (see Figure 9.8). The DataGrid is a table-like control with columns and rows. Rows of data retrieved from a database can be displayed, edited, and removed from a DataGrid. We will bind XML to a DataGrid. The XML, however, will not be loaded from an external file; rather, we will use the <mx:XMLList> control to embed the XML in the application. This is a very valuable feature if dynamic data is not required.

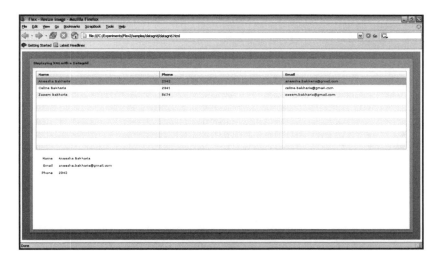

Figure 9.8
Displaying XML in a DataGrid.

An excerpt from the XMLList control is shown below. We can simply place this tag within our MXML file. The employees' XMLList has name, phone, and email fields for each employee. These fields will need to be databound to the DataGrid control.

```
<mx:XMLList id="employees">
        <employee>
              <name>Aneesha Bakharia</name>
              <phone>2342</phone>
              <email>aneesha.bakharia@gmail.com</email>
        </employee>
...
</mx:XMLList>
```

The DataGrid control is placed in a panel. The dataProvider attribute is set to the id of the XMLList control—this binds the XML to the DataGrid. Within the <Mx:columns> tag, we can define the columns in the DataGrid and also set the fields to which they are bound. We need three <mx:DataGridColumn> tags to display the name, phone, and email fields.

```
<mx:DataGrid id="dg" width="100%" height="100%" rowCount="5"
dataProvider="{employees}">
     <mx:columns>
                <mx:DataGridColumn dataField="name" headerText="Name"/>
                <mx:DataGridColumn dataField="phone"
                        headerText="Phone"/>
                <mx:DataGridColumn dataField="email"
                        headerText="Email"/>
     </mx:columns>
</mx:DataGrid>
```

The source code for displaying XML in a DataGrid control:

```
<?xml version="1.0"?>
<mx:Application xmlns:mx="http://www.adobe.com/2006/mxml">
     <mx:XMLList id="employees">
          <employee>
               <name>Aneesha Bakharia</name>
               <phone>2342</phone>
               <email>aneesha.bakharia@gmail.com</email>
          </employee>
          <employee>
               <name>Celine Bakharia</name>
               <phone>2341</phone>
               <email>celine.bakharia@gmail.com</email>
          </employee>
          <employee>
               <name>Zaeem Bakharia</name>
               <phone>5674</phone>
               <email>zaeem.bakharia@gmail.com</email>
          </employee>
     </mx:XMLList>
     <mx:Panel title="Displaying XML with a Datagrid"
          height="100%" width="100%"
          paddingTop="10"
          paddingLeft="10"
          paddingRight="10">
          <mx:DataGrid id="dg" width="100%" height="100%"
```

```
        rowCount="5" dataProvider="{employees}">
        <mx:columns>
            <mx:DataGridColumn dataField="name" headerText="Name"/>
            <mx:DataGridColumn dataField="phone"
                headerText="Phone"/>
            <mx:DataGridColumn dataField="email"
                headerText="Email"/>
        </mx:columns>
    </mx:DataGrid>
    <mx:Form width="100%" height="100%">
        <mx:FormItem label="Name:">
            <mx:Label text="{dg.selectedItem.name}"/>
        </mx:FormItem>
        <mx:FormItem label="Email">
            <mx:Label text="{dg.selectedItem.email}"/>
        </mx:FormItem>
        <mx:FormItem label="Phone">
            <mx:Label text="{dg.selectedItem.phone}"/>
        </mx:FormItem>
    </mx:Form>
    </mx:Panel>
</mx:Application>
```

Building a Flex Interface for a Ruby on Rails Project

We are going to build a Flex interface to display, update, and delete employee details as well as add the contact details of new employees. The Flex interface will interact with Rails, which will perform the database tasks. I guarantee that we will accomplish this ambitious project in record time and only 19 lines of Ruby code. The Staff Directory project takes advantage of the REST features built into Rails and the <mx:HTTPService> tag in Flex, which allows us to get and post data to a web service.

Exposing an Active Record Model as XML

Our first task involves publishing a list of employees to XML from Rails. Once this feed is created, we can use an HTTPService in Flex to retrieve the XML and bind it to a DataGrid control. We start by creating a new rails application called staffdirectory:

```
$ rails staffdirectory
```

Move into the `staffdirectory` **folder and then create a model:**

```
$ ruby script/generate model employee
```

The following is output to the console:

```
exists   app/models/
exists   test/unit/
exists   test/fixtures/
create   app/models/employee.rb
create   test/unit/employee_test.rb
create   test/fixtures/employees.yml
create   db/migrate
create   db/migrate/001_create_employees.rb
```

Edit the `db/migrate/001_create_employees.rb` **migration. We need** `name`, `email`, **phone, and** `department` **fields in the employees table. The migration is also used to insert two records into the database:**

```
class CreateEmployees < ActiveRecord::Migration
    def self.up
        create_table :employees do |t|
            t.column :name, :string
        t.column :email, :string
            t.column :phone, :string
            t.column :department, :string
        end
    Employee.create :name => "Aneesha Bakharia",
                        :email => 'aneesha.bakharia@gmail.com',
                        :phone => "1234",
                        :department => "IT"
    Employee.create :name => "Celine Bakharia",
                        :email => 'c.b@randomsyntax.com',
                        :phone => "1244",
                        :department => "Design"
    end
    def self.down
        drop_table :employees
    end
end
```

Run the migration:

```
$ rake db:migrate
```

The following is output to the console:

```
(in C:/rails/staffdirectory)
== CreateEmployees: migrating ============================================
-- create_table(:employees)
   -> 0.1560s
== CreateEmployees: migrated (0.1560s) ===================================
```

Create the `employees` **controller:**

```
$ ruby script/generate controller employees
```

The following is output to the console:

```
      exists  app/controllers/
      exists  app/helpers/
      create  app/views/employees
      exists  test/functional/
      create  app/controllers/employees_controller.rb
      create  test/functional/employees_controller_test.rb
      create  app/helpers/employees_helper.rb
```

Open the `app/controllers/employees_controller.rb` **file and add a** `list` **action. This action retrieves all the employees from the employees table and then renders this list to XML. The** `to_xml` **method is used to convert the** `employees` **data to the XML format:**

```
class EmployeesController < ApplicationController
    def list
      @employees = Employee.find :all
      render :xml => @employees.to_xml
    end
end
```

We start the Webrick web server on port 80 and point our browser to http://localhost/ employees/list to view the Employee XML feed (see Figure 9.9):

```
$ ruby script/server -p 80
```

Figure 9.9
Converting a model to XML.

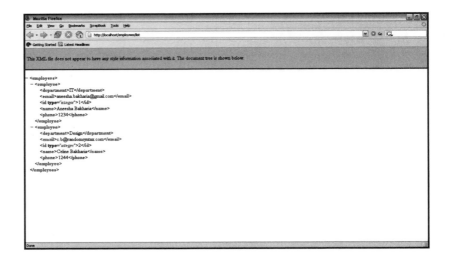

We can now use the `<mx:HTTPService>` tag to retrieve the dynamic XML feed and bind the data to a DataGrid (see Figure 9.10). The Flash file and the web page need to be placed within the `public` folder of your Rails application.

```
<?xml version="1.0"?>
<mx:Application xmlns:mx="http://www.adobe.com/2006/mxml"
                xmlns="*" layout="absolute"
                creationComplete="employeeRequest.send()">
    <mx:HTTPService
        id="employeeRequest"
        url="http://localhost/employees/list" useProxy="false"/>
    <mx:Panel title="Displaying XML with a Datagrid"
              height="100%"
              width="100%"
              paddingTop="10"
              paddingLeft="10"
              paddingRight="10">
        <mx:DataGrid id="dg"
            width="100%"
            height="100%"
            rowCount="5"
            dataProvider="{employeeRequest.lastResult.employees.employee}">
            <mx:columns>
```

```
        <mx:DataGridColumn dataField="name" headerText="Name"/>
        <mx:DataGridColumn dataField="phone" headerText="Phone"/>
        <mx:DataGridColumn dataField="email" headerText="Email"/>
    <mx:DataGridColumn
            dataField="department"
            headerText="Department"/>
        </mx:columns>
      </mx:DataGrid>
    </mx:Panel>
</mx:Application>
```

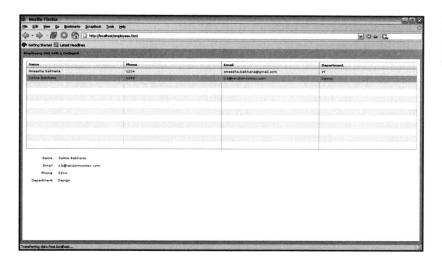

Figure 9.10
Retrieving and displaying
an XML feed in a DataGrid.

Adding an Employee

We will display a form when the Add an Employee button is clicked and use the `states` feature of Flex to do so. The form contains fields where a user can enter the name, email, phone, and department of an employee. The Add button will trigger the state change. This form will be sent to Rails via an HTTPService, which has the method attribute set to `post`. We are, in fact, sending the data back to Rails in an XML format:

```
<mx:HTTPService contentType="application/xml"
                id="employeeCreateRequest"
                result="employeeRequest.send();"
                url="http://localhost/employees/create"
                useProxy="false" method="POST">
```

```
    <mx:request xmlns="">
        <employee>
            <name>{fName.text}</name>
            <email>{fEmail.text}</email>
            <phone>{fPhone.text}</phone>
            <department>{fDepartment.text}</department>
        </employee>
    </mx:request>
</mx:HTTPService>
```

The `Employees` **controller needs to respond to the** `create` **request. We need to publish the XML feed after we save the data so that the new data is returned to the HTTPService and the DataGrid control is in turn updated. Here is the code to do so:**

```
def create
    @employee = Employee.new(params[:employee])
    @employee.save
    render :xml => @employee.to_xml
end
```

Figure 9.11 shows the Flex interface being used to add new employees. Here is the source code:

```
<?xml version="1.0" encoding="utf-8"?>
<mx:Panel title="Staff Directory"
        xmlns:mx="http://www.adobe.com/2006/mxml"
        xmlns="*"
        creationComplete="employeeRequest.send()">
    <mx:HTTPService id="employeeRequest"
                url="http://localhost/employees/list"
                useProxy="false"/>
    <mx:HTTPService contentType="application/xml"
                id="employeeCreateRequest"
                result="employeeRequest.send();"
                url="http://localhost/employees/create"
                useProxy="false"
                method="POST">
        <mx:request xmlns="">
            <employee>
                <name>{fName.text}</name>
```

```
                <email>{fEmail.text}</email>
                <phone>{fPhone.text}</phone>
                <department>{fDepartment.text}</department>
            </employee>
        </mx:request>
    </mx:HTTPService>
<mx:DataGrid id="dg"
            width="800"
            dataProvider="{employeeRequest.lastResult.employees.employee}"
            editable="false" >
            <mx:columns>
                <mx:DataGridColumn headerText="Name"
                                   dataField="name"
                                   width="480"/>
                <mx:DataGridColumn headerText="Email"
                                   dataField="email"
                                   width="240"/>
                <mx:DataGridColumn headerText="Phone"
                                   dataField="phone"
                                   width="80"/>
                <mx:DataGridColumn headerText="Department"
                                   dataField="department"
                                   width="80"/>
            </mx:columns>
</mx:DataGrid>
<mx:ControlBar id="EmployeeControlBar">
    <mx:Button label="Add Employee" id="btnAdd" click="currentState='Add'" />
</mx:ControlBar>
<mx:states>
        <mx:State name="Add">
            <mx:AddChild position="lastChild">
            <mx:Form width="800" id="frmCreate">
            <mx:FormHeading label="Add a new Employee"/>
            <mx:FormItem label="Name" required="true">
                <mx:TextInput width="260" id="fName"/>
            </mx:FormItem>
           <mx:FormItem label="Email" required="true">
```

```
            <mx:TextInput width="260" id="fEmail"/>
        </mx:FormItem>
        <mx:FormItem label="Phone" required="true">
            <mx:TextInput width="260" id="fPhone"/>
        </mx:FormItem>
      <mx:FormItem label="Department" required="true">
            <mx:TextInput width="260" id="fDepartment"/>
        </mx:FormItem>
        <mx:FormItem direction="horizontal">
            <mx:Button label="Submit"
                click="employeeCreateRequest.send();currentState=''"/>
            <mx:Button label="Cancel" click="currentState=''"/>
        </mx:FormItem>
        </mx:Form>
        </mx:AddChild>
      </mx:State>
    </mx:states>
</mx:Panel>
```

Figure 9.11
Adding an Employee.

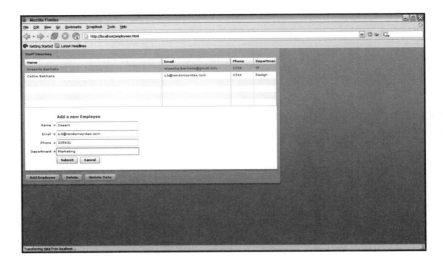

Deleting an Employee

Deleting an employee requires an additional HTTPService that can pass the `id` of the employee to the `delete` method:

```
<mx:HTTPService id="employeeDeleteRequest"
                result="employeeRequest.send();"
                url="http://localhost/employees/delete"
                useProxy="false"/>
```

The `delete` method needs to be added to the `Employees` controller:

```
def delete
    @employee = Employee.find(params[:id])
    @employee.destroy
    render :xml => @employee.to_xml
end
```

A delete button is added to the ControlBar control. When the button is clicked, the `deletehandler()` method must be executed.

```
<mx:Button label="Delete" click="deleteHandler(event);"/>
```

The `deleteHandler()` method displays an Alert box to confirm that the selected resource must be deleted (see Figure 9.12). If the user clicks on OK, the `id` is passed to the `send` method of the `employeeDeleteRequest` HTTPService. The full source code is included:

```
<?xml version="1.0" encoding="utf-8"?>
<mx:Panel title="Staff Directory"
        xmlns:mx="http://www.adobe.com/2006/mxml"
        xmlns="*"
        creationComplete="employeeRequest.send()">
 <mx:Script>
        <![CDATA[
            import mx.controls.Alert;
            import mx.events.CloseEvent;
            private function deleteHandler(event:Event) : void
            {
            Alert.show("Are you sure you want to delete this item?",
                    "Delete Item", 3, this,
             function(event:CloseEvent):void
            {
            if (event.detail==Alert.YES)
              employeeDeleteRequest.send({id: dg.selectedItem.id});
            });
```

```
            }
        ]]>
    </mx:Script>
  <mx:HTTPService id="employeeRequest"
                  url="http://localhost/employees/list"
                  useProxy="false"/>


  <mx:HTTPService contentType="application/xml"
                  id="employeeCreateRequest"
                  result="employeeRequest.send();"
                  url="http://localhost/employees/create"
                  useProxy="false"
                  method="POST">
    <mx:request xmlns="">
        <employee>
            <name>{fName.text}</name>
            <email>{fEmail.text}</email>
            <phone>{fPhone.text}</phone>
            <department>{fDepartment.text}</department>
        </employee>
    </mx:request>
  </mx:HTTPService>
<mx:HTTPService id="employeeDeleteRequest"
                  result="employeeRequest.send();"
                  url="http://localhost/employees/delete"
                  useProxy="false"/>
            <mx:DataGrid id="dg"
                width="800"
                dataProvider="{employeeRequest.lastResult.employees.employee}"
                editable="false" >
                <mx:columns>
                    <mx:DataGridColumn headerText="Name"
                                       dataField="name" width="480"/>
                    <mx:DataGridColumn headerText="Email"
                                       dataField="email" width="240"/>
                    <mx:DataGridColumn headerText="Phone"
                                       dataField="phone" width="80"/>
```

```
                    <mx:DataGridColumn headerText="Department"
                                    dataField="department" width="80"/>
                </mx:columns>
            </mx:DataGrid>
            <mx:ControlBar id="EmployeeControlBar">
                <mx:Button label="Add Employee"
                            id="btnAdd"
                            click="currentState='Add'" />
                <mx:Button label="Delete" click="deleteHandler(event);"/>
             </mx:ControlBar>
<mx:states>
        <mx:State name="Add">
            <mx:AddChild position="lastChild">
            <mx:Form width="800" id="frmCreate">
            <mx:FormHeading label="Add a new Employee"/>
             <mx:FormItem label="Name" required="true">
                <mx:TextInput width="260" id="fName"/>
            </mx:FormItem>
           <mx:FormItem label="Email" required="true">
                <mx:TextInput width="260" id="fEmail"/>
            </mx:FormItem>
            <mx:FormItem label="Phone" required="true">
                <mx:TextInput width="260" id="fPhone"/>
            </mx:FormItem>
           <mx:FormItem label="Department" required="true">
                <mx:TextInput width="260" id="fDepartment"/>
            </mx:FormItem>
            <mx:FormItem direction="horizontal">
                <mx:Button label="Submit"
click="employeeCreateRequest.send();currentState=''"/>
                <mx:Button label="Cancel" click="currentState=''"/>
            </mx:FormItem>
            </mx:Form>
            </mx:AddChild>
        </mx:State>
    </mx:states>
</mx:Panel>
```

Figure 9.12
Deleting an employee.

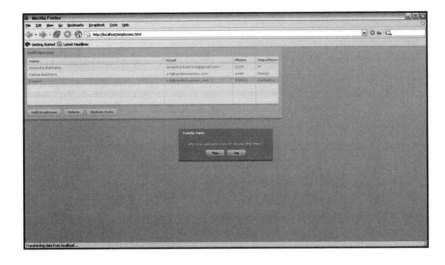

Updating an Employee

DataGrids in Flex are editable—TextInput box is placed within a cell when it is clicked (see Figure 9.13), and the data can be edited and sent back to be stored via an HTTPService post. We will add an Update button, which, when clicked, will make the DataGrid control editable.

Figure 9.13
Updating an employee.

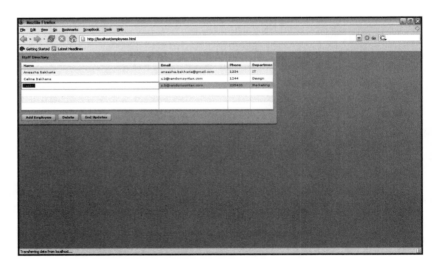

First we need to add an `update` method to our controller. This brings the total lines of Ruby code to only 19. Rails, Active Record, and the `to_xml` methods are tremendously powerful.

```
def update
     @employee = Employee.find(params[:id])
     @remployee.update_attributes(params[:employee])
     render :xml => @employee.to_xml
end
```

We create an `employeeUpdateRequest` **HTTPService. We don't need to send back XML as we did for the** `employeeCreateRequest`. **We will use ActionScript to send back each field in a row as it is edited.**

```
<mx:HTTPService id="employeeUpdateRequest"
                result="employeeRequest.send();"
                url="http://localhost/reviews/update"
                useProxy="false"
                method="POST"/>
```

An Update Employee Button is added to the ControlBar control. This button calls the `updateHandler()` **method when clicked:**

```
<mx:Button label="Update Data"
          click="updateHandler(event)"
          id="btnUpdateData"/>
public function checkUpdate(event:DataGridEvent) : void
{
    if (event != null)
    {
        var params:Object = new Object();
        params['id'] = event.currentTarget.editedItemRenderer.data['id']
        params['employee[' + event.dataField +']'] =
TextInput(event.currentTarget.itemEditorInstance).text
        employeeUpdateRequest.send(params);
    }
}
```

The editable attribute is set to false for the DataGrid control. The `itemEndEdit` **event calls the** `checkUpdate` **method. The** `checkUpdate` **method will send the updated data back to the** `Update` **controller in our Rails application.**

```
<mx:DataGrid id="dg"
            width="800"
            dataProvider="{employeeRequest.lastResult.employees.employee}"
```

```
        editable="false"
        itemEditEnd="checkUpdate(event);">
```

The updateHandler() method makes the DataGrid editable. It also changes the label of the Update Button and the click handler. The code for the updateHandler() method:

```
import mx.events.DataGridEvent
private function updateHandler(event:Event) : void
{
      dg.editable=true
      btnUpdateData.label = "End Updates"
      btnUpdateData.removeEventListener('click', updateHandler)
      btnUpdateData.addEventListener('click', endUpdateHandler)
}
```

The full source code listing:

```
<?xml version="1.0" encoding="utf-8"?>
<mx:Panel title="Staff Directory"
        xmlns:mx="http://www.adobe.com/2006/mxml"
        xmlns="*"
        creationComplete="employeeRequest.send()">
  <mx:Script>
      <![CDATA[
          import mx.controls.Alert;
          import mx.events.CloseEvent;
          private function deleteHandler(event:Event) : void
          {
          Alert.show("Are you sure you want to delete this item?",
                    "Delete Item", 3, this,
           function(event:CloseEvent):void
           {
           if (event.detail==Alert.YES)
             employeeDeleteRequest.send({id: dg.selectedItem.id});
           });
          }
          import mx.events.DataGridEvent
          private function updateHandler(event:Event) : void
          {
```

```
            dg.editable=true
            btnUpdateData.label = "End Updates"
            btnUpdateData.removeEventListener('click', updateHandler)
            btnUpdateData.addEventListener('click', endUpdateHandler)
            }
public function checkUpdate(event:DataGridEvent) : void
{
    if (event != null)
    {
        var params:Object = new Object();
        params['id'] = event.currentTarget.editedItemRenderer.data['id']
        params['employee[' + event.dataField +']'] =
        TextInput(event.currentTarget.itemEditorInstance).text
        employeeUpdateRequest.send(params);
    }
}

        ]]>
    </mx:Script>
  <mx:HTTPService id="employeeRequest"
                url="http://localhost/employees/list"
                useProxy="false"/>
  <mx:HTTPService id="employeeUpdateRequest"
                result="employeeRequest.send();"
                url="http://localhost/reviews/update"
                useProxy="false"
                method="POST"/>


  <mx:HTTPService contentType="application/xml"
                id="employeeCreateRequest"
                result="employeeRequest.send();"
                url="http://localhost/employees/create"
                useProxy="false"
                method="POST">
    <mx:request xmlns="">
        <employee>
            <name>{fName.text}</name>
            <email>{fEmail.text}</email>
```

```
            <phone>{fPhone.text}</phone>
            <department>{fDepartment.text}</department>
        </employee>
    </mx:request>
  </mx:HTTPService>
<mx:HTTPService id="employeeDeleteRequest"
              result="employeeRequest.send();"
              url="http://localhost/employees/delete"
              useProxy="false"/>
        <mx:DataGrid id="dg"
            width="800"
            dataProvider="{employeeRequest.lastResult.employees.employee}"
            editable="false"
            itemEditEnd="checkUpdate(event);">
            <mx:columns>
                <mx:DataGridColumn headerText="Name"
                                   dataField="name"
                                   width="480"/>
                <mx:DataGridColumn headerText="Email"
                                   dataField="email"
                                   width="240"/>
                <mx:DataGridColumn headerText="Phone"
                                   dataField="phone"
                                   width="80"/>
                <mx:DataGridColumn headerText="Department"
                                   dataField="department"
                                   width="80"/>
            </mx:columns>
        </mx:DataGrid>
        <mx:ControlBar id="EmployeeControlBar">
            <mx:Button label="Add Employee"
                       id="btnAdd"
                       click="currentState='Add'" />
            <mx:Button label="Delete" click="deleteHandler(event);"/>
            <mx:Button label="Delete" click="deleteHandler(event);"/>
            <mx:Button label="Update Data"
                       click="updateHandler(event)"
```

```
                        id="btnUpdateData"/>
            </mx:ControlBar>
<mx:states>
        <mx:State name="Add">
            <mx:AddChild position="lastChild">
            <mx:Form width="800" id="frmCreate">
            <mx:FormHeading label="Add a new Employee"/>
             <mx:FormItem label="Name" required="true">
                <mx:TextInput width="260" id="fName"/>
             </mx:FormItem>
            <mx:FormItem label="Email" required="true">
                <mx:TextInput width="260" id="fEmail"/>
             </mx:FormItem>
             <mx:FormItem label="Phone" required="true">
                <mx:TextInput width="260" id="fPhone"/>
             </mx:FormItem>
            <mx:FormItem label="Department" required="true">
                <mx:TextInput width="260" id="fDepartment"/>
             </mx:FormItem>
            <mx:FormItem direction="horizontal">
                <mx:Button label="Submit"
click="employeeCreateRequest.send();currentState=''"/>
                <mx:Button label="Cancel" click="currentState=''"/>
             </mx:FormItem>
            </mx:Form>
            </mx:AddChild>
        </mx:State>
    </mx:states>
</mx:Panel>
```

Conclusion

Flex provides a viable alternative to AJAX-powered interfaces. Flex has a wide variety of interface controls, it supports data binding from either XML or a web service, and it is very easy to integrate with an existing Rails application. Flex interfaces are authored in a declarative tag-like syntax known as MXML. This chapter highlights the superior capabilities of Rails that enable an Active Record model to be published to XML, as well as allow records to be updated and new records to be added via a web service.

10 } E-Mail, Image Processing, and Graphing

We will be using existing Ruby libraries to extend and enhance the capabilities of Rails applications. Ruby extensions such as TMail, Gruff, and RMagick add a professional touch to service-oriented web applications. The ability to send e-mail, convert and reduce images to an appropriate format, and generate meaningful graphs in a Web application is extremely important.

In this chapter you'll learn to:

- ※ Send and receive e-mails with Action Mailer and TMail
- ※ Use RMagick to create and process images
- ※ Generate line, bar, and pie charts with Gruff

Sending and Receiving E-Mail

The ability to send automated e-mail messages is extremely important and has many functional applications. Web-enabled applications send out e-mails to confirm registration, acknowledge product orders, advertise or inform consumers of new products, inform users of recent site activity, and so on. As a developer, you could even have bug or error reports e-mailed directly to you. E-mail is certainly an invaluable communication medium. It is hard to imagine a person not having an e-mail address.

Ruby on Rails includes the Action Mailer component, which facilitates the processing of e-mail messages. Action Mailer is built upon the TMail library to model and process e-mail messages. TMail is written by Minero Aoki.

Action Mailer Configuration

You will need to change the Action Mailer configuration settings to enable successful e-mail processing because the default Action Mailer settings may only work on certain hosts. If you are using the same configuration settings for your development, testing, and production setups, you can add the Action Mailer settings to the `/config/environment.rb` file. If your environments require different settings, then add the details to the appropriate `/config/environments` folder.

The `ActionMailer::Base.delivery_method` supports three e-mail delivery methods: `smtp`, `sendmail`, and `test`. Use the `test` method in your development environment, especially when you are running unit or functional tests. The `test` method does not send real e-mails; instead, the e-mails are placed in an array and are available via `ActionMailer::Base.deliveries`. The `sendmail` method uses the Sendmail program found in the `/usr/bin` folder. Unfortunately you can't always assume that the Sendmail program is installed and placed in the `/usr/bin` folder. The third option, `smtp`, uses a real SMTP server, is the default, and is the most reliable option. The SMTP server could reside on either the same server that houses your web application or another server. Table 10.1 contains required SMTP settings, along with a description.

Example Action Mailer syntax:

```
ActionMailer::Base.server_settings =
{
      :address => "smtp.hostname.com",
      :port => 25,
      :domain => "your.domain.com",
      :authentication => :login,
      :user_name => "aneesha",
      :password => "guess_my_password"
}
```

Table 10.1   SMTP Configuration Settings

`:address`	The address of the SMTP server. If the SMTP server is running on the same server as your web application, the default will be localhost.
`:port`	The port of the SMTP server. The default port is 25.
`:domain`	The domain name of your web server (the server sending the e-mail message).
`:authentication`	The following is supported: `:plain`, `:login`, or `:cram_md5`. Consult with your system administrator to determine which is appropriate.
`:user_name`	The username if authentication is required.
`:password`	The password if authentication is required.

Another way of turning e-mail delivery off for testing purposes is to set the `ActionMailer::Base.perform_deliveries` **method to** `false`:

```
ActionMailer::Base.perform_deliveries = false
```

The default character set for encoding e-mail messages is set with the `default_charset` property.

```
ActionMailer::Base.default_charset = "utf-8"
```

The default content type is text/plain. This setting is suitable only for plain text e-mail messages. Use the `text/html` setting if you are sending HTML formatted e-mail messages.

```
ActionMailer::Base.default_content_type = "text/html"
```

Sending E-Mail

A generator script (`script/generate mailer`) is used to create `Mailer` classes within the `app/models` folder. It might seem odd at first to have the `Mailer` classes placed in the `models` folder, but as this section unfolds it will all begin to make sense. Each method within the `Mailer` class has a corresponding `.rhtml` template file stored in the `app/views` folder. This is akin to having a view for each action within a controller class. The views provided for the methods within a `Mailer` class allow you to use ERb syntax to embed Ruby within an e-mail template.

We must pass the name of the `Mailer` class to the `script/generate mailer` generator followed by the e-mail action method names. If multiple e-mail action method names are specified, multiple methods within the class will be generated.

Generate the `NewsletterMailer` class and `confirm_subscription` e-mail action method:

```
$ ruby script/generate mailer NewsletterMailer confirm_subscription
```

The following files are created:

* ❊ `app/models/newsletter_mailer.rb`
* ❊ `app/views/newsletter_mailer/confirm_subscription.rhtml`

The `app/models/newsletter_mailer.rb` file contains the `NewsletterMailer` class, which inherits from `ActionMailer::Base`. The `confirm_subscription()` method sets up instance variables for the e-mail message. The e-mail instance variables (see Table 10.2) define the subject, body and e-mail recipients:

```
class NewsletterMailer < ActionMailer::Base
    def confirm_subscription(sent_at = Time.now)
        @subject    = 'NewsletterMailer#confirm_subscription'
        @body       = {}
        @recipients = ''
        @from       = ''
        @sent_on    = sent_at
```

```
        @headers      = {}
    end
end
```

Table 10.2   E-Mail Message Instance Variables

Variable	Data Type	Description
@recipients	Array or String	One or more e-mail addresses for recipients, such as aneesha.bakharia@gmail.com or @recipients = ["aneesha.bakharia@gmail.com","Celine <aneesha.bakharia@gmail.com>"].
@cc	Array or String	Recipients that receive a carbon copy of the e-mail.
@bcc	Array or String	Recipients that receive a blind copy of the e-mail.
@from	Array or String	The e-mail address of the sender that a recipient can reply to.
@subject	String	A brief description of the e-mail message.
@body	Hash	A hash containing values that must be passed to the e-mail template file within the `views` folder.
@charset	String	The character set of the e-mail. Defaults to the `default_charset = "utf-8"` setting variable.
@sent_on	Time	The time the e-mail was sent is included within the e-mail's header.

An example e-mail template (`.rhtml` view file) that has been passed the first name of a user who has just subscribed to a newsletter follows:

```
Dear <%= @first_name %>
Thank you for subscribing to Rails News.
A monthly newsletter will be e-mailed to you.
Sincere thanks
The Rails News Team
```

 Note

Partials can be called from within an e-mail template file, but you will need to pass the explicit path to the template. You need to do this because the partial is not being invoked from a controller action. Here is an example:

```
<%= render(:partial => "./item", :collection => @order.items) %>
```

Now that we have modeled the e-mail message and its associated template file, we need a controller to send the e-mail. We can accomplish this in two ways using class methods: Create an e-mail object and then call the deliver method or send the e-mail to the defined recipients. The class methods are called `create_xxx` and `deliver_xxx`, where `xxx` is the name of the action method, such as `create_ confirm_subscription` and `deliver_ confirm_subscription` for the `NewletterMailer` class.

The `create_ confirm_subscription()` call invokes `confirm_subscription()` within our `NewletterMailer` class, and an e-mail template will be rendered. The `encoded()` method returns the generated template as text. Let's create an e-mail message and preview it in a web browser (see Figure 10.1) before we send it off:

```
class EmailController < ApplicationController
    def sent_confirmation_email
        name = "Aneesha"
        email = NewletterMailer.create_confirm_subscription(name)
        render(:text => "<pre>" + email.encoded + "</pre>")
    end
end
```

Figure 10.1
Previewing an e-mail message.

We are now ready to send the e-mail message by calling

```
NewletterMailer.deliver_confirm_subscription(name)
```

HTML Formatted E-Mails

Since we are already using `.rhtml` template files to create the body of the e-mail, we can easily generate HTML formatted messages. We just need to insert the appropriate HTML tags within our view and set the content type to `text/html`:

```
email.set_content_type("text/html")
```

 Tip

Always either prefix or suffix a mailer class with the word `mailer` so as not to confuse your e-mail models with regular Active Record models.

In the following example, multiple values are passed to the e-mail template via the `@body` instance variable, which takes a hash data structure.

```
class NewletterMailer < ActionMailer::Base
    def welcome_message(first_name, email_address)
        @subject = "Rails News"
        @body = {:name => first_name, :email => email_address}
        @recipients = email_address
        @from = "clientsupport@yourdomain.com"
        @sent_on = Time.now
    end
end
```

Attaching Files to E-Mail Messages

Files are attached to an e-mail message with the `part()` method. The `part()` method takes a hash structure containing the MIME type of the file, its file name, and transfer encoding method (such as base64). We can include numerous calls to the `part()` method, thereby attaching multiple files. In this example, a JPEG image is attached to an e-mail message:

```
class NewletterMailer < ActionMailer::Base
    def welcome_message(first_name, email_address)
        @subject = "Rails News"
        @body = {:name => first_name, :email => email_address}
        @recipients = email_address
        @from = "clientsupport@yourdomain.com"
        @sent_on = Time.now
part(:content_type => "image/jpeg",
    :disposition => "attachment; filename=rails_news_newletter.jpg",
```

```
          :transfer_encoding => "base64") do |attachment.body =
File.read("header.jpg")

          end
end
```

 Note
The attached file will have the name assigned within the disposition key.

Receiving E-Mail

Action Mailer also makes it possible to process incoming e-mail. This might be handy if you want to log bug report e-mails to an issue tracking database and send out a confirmation e-mail that contains the support ticket number. Once you are able to capture the e-mail with Rails, it is very easy to process the TMail::Mail object that corresponds to the incoming message. Intercepting the message from a mail server, however, can be quite difficult, and varies depending upon the setup and software used as an e-mail server.

Let's deal with the easy bit first. Action Mailer is able to process a TMail::Mail object. Your Action Mailer class requires a receive() method, which must be passed a TMail::Mail object. You then can retrieve the e-mail's subject line, body, file attachments, and recipient list. Here is an example:

```
class NewletterMailer < ActionMailer::Base
      def receive(email)
            bugreport = Bugreport.new
            bugreport.from   = email.from[0]
            bugreport.desciption = email.body
            if email.has_attachments?
                  email.attachments.each do |attachment|
                        filecollection = FileCollection.new(
                        :name => attachment.original_filename,
                        :body => attachment.read)
                        bugreport.FileCollection << filecollection
                  end
            end
            bugreport.save
      end
end
```

Now we can move on to the not so easy task of intercepting the e-mail before it is delivered by the mail server. Essentially we need a script to grab the e-mail message (as raw text) and pass it to the `receive()` method located within the Action Mailer class. If Sendmail was being used, the script would need to be executed when an e-mail was placed in a mailbox (associated with an e-mail address). There are, however, many different e-mail servers. The Ruby on Rails Wiki provides possible solutions for mailman, QMail, POP3, and imap (see http://wiki.rubyonrails.com/rails/show/HowToReceiveEmailsWithActionMailer).

Image Processing with RMagick

Free, open source, and commercial image editors are available in abundance, so why is there a need for image processing within a web application? The answer is simple—not all users are familiar with image editing and conversion concepts or software. You can't rely on all users to upload an image optimized for display within a web page or a thumbnail image to the exact dimensions. Failing to post process an image after it has been uploaded is a recipe for disaster because you could be storing large files and eating up valuable bandwidth each time the image is viewed. There also are more creative applications such as a dynamic postcard (e-card) builder, photo sharing service, and easy- to-use online image editing wizards.

RMagick is a robust and feature-rich image conversion, manipulation, and effects toolkit for Ruby. The image manipulation that you are able to achieve programmatically with RMagick is simply breathtaking. RMagick provides an interface to the ImageMagick (http://www.imagemagick.org) and GraphicsMagick (http://www.graphicsmagick.org) image processing libraries. More than 90 popular image formats such as PNG, GIF, and JPEG are supported.

An RMagick gem is available but not downloadable from the gem server at RubyForge. You will need to download and install the gem manually:

* Download RMagick from http://rubyforge.org/projects/rmagick/.
* Unzip to a folder.
* Navigate to the folder that contains all the unzipped files.
* **Run** `Run ImageMagick-6.2.9-3-Q8-windows-dll.exe` and follow the onscreen instructions.
* Type the following at the command prompt:

```
$ C:\yourinstallfolder\RMagick-1.9.1-IM-6.2.3-win32>gem install rmagick-1.13.0-win32.gem
>> Successfully installed rmagick, version 1.13.0
```

We are now ready to try our first RMagick example in Ruby. We will simply create an `Image` object with a red background and set both its width and height to 100 pixels. The `write()` method is used to save the image to the format specified in the file extension. The generated image will be saved to the same folder where the script is located. The resulting red square is shown in Figure 10.2.

```
require 'rubygems'
require 'RMagick'
include Magick
test_image = Image.new(100,100) { self.background_color = "red" }
test_image.write("testimage.jpg")
exit
```

Figure 10.2
Using RMagick to create a red square.

Converting an Image to Another Format

RMagick supports 90 image formats and allows for one format to be converted to another. This comes in handy when you need to convert an image to a web-friendly format such as to convert a bitmap (`.bmp`) to either the GIF, JPEG, or PNG format. All we need to do is pass the filename of the image to the `Image.read()` method and then use the `Image.write()` method to save the file to an alternate format. The file extension passed to the `Image.write()` method determines the saved format.

In the following example, a PNG file is converted to both the GIF and JPEG formats:

```
require 'rubygems'
require 'RMagick'
img = Magick::Image.read('sample.png').first        #Return the first image
img.write('sample.jpg')
img.write('sample.gif')
```

 Note
The `Image.read()` method returns an array of images because some image formats contain a sequence of multiple images, such as an animated GIF. To access the first image or only image stored in a file, call the `first` property.

We can also explicitly set or retrieve the image format:

```
img.format = "GIF"
```

Creating an Animated GIF

Animated GIFs were much more popular in the mid 1990s. Animated GIFs were to 90s web site design what reflected logos are to Web 2.0. Animated GIFs would not be covered if RMagick did not make them so easy to create:

```
img_list = ImageList.new("image1.gif", "image2.gif", "image3.gif")
img_list.write("animatedgif.gif")
```

As you can see, we need only to pass the `ImageList.new()` method a comma-delimited list of the images that need to be included in the animation and then use the `write()` method to save to the GIF format.

Adding Text to an Image

The `annotate()` method of the `Draw` object is able to overlay formatted text on an image. You could use this functionality to insert a copyright symbol, watermark, or textual description on an image. Choose the color of text added to an image carefully so as to avoid antialiasing and color conflicts that influence the readability of text.

In this example, "Rmagick" is drawn on top of a 200 × 100 pixels wide blue background (see Figure 10.3). The text is white, 20 points in size, and bold.

```
require 'rubygems'
require 'RMagick'
include Magick
test_image = Image.new(200,100) { self.background_color = "blue" }
text = Magick::Draw.new
text.pointsize = 20
text.fill = 'white'
text.font_weight = Magick::BoldWeight
text.annotate(test_image,20,20,50,50, "RMagick")
test_image.write("Text.jpg")
exit
```

Figure 10.3
Using RMagick to insert text into an image.

In the next example, we insert a copyright symbol in the lower-right side of an image. The `Magick::SouthEastGravity` property is used to help position the text at the desired position. Table 10.3 lists gravity settings, which are useful to help position an image or text in relation to another.

```
require 'rubygems'
require 'RMagick'
img = Magick::Image.read("sunset.png").first
copyright_text = '\251 Your Inc'
copyright_symbol = Magick::Draw.new
copyright_symbol.pointsize = 14
copyright_symbol.font_weight = Magick::BoldWeight
copyright_symbol.fill = 'white'
copyright_symbolgravity = Magick::SouthEastGravity
copyright_symbol.annotate(img, 0, 0, 3, 18, copyright_text)
img.write('sunsetwithcopyright.png')
```

Table 10.3 Gravity Settings

Gravity Type	Description
ForgetGravity	Gravity not required
NorthWestGravity	Top left position
NorthGravity	Top center position
NorthEastGravity	Top right position
WestGravity	Left center position
CenterGravity	Center position
EastGravity	Right center position
SouthWestGravity	Left bottom position
SouthGravity	Bottom center position
SouthEastGravity	Bottom right position

Image Manipulation

RMagick provides access to a variety of filters and effects. Filters such as `reduce_noise`, `enhance`, and `despeckle` help to refine defects (such as noise) in an image. Effects such as `sepiatone`, `vignette`, `solarize`, and `sketch` might not be all that useful, but they are fun to play with and require only a single method.

`despeckle` preserves edges within an image while reducing noise:

```
require 'rubygems'
require 'RMagick'
img = Magick::Image.read('sunset.jpg').first
img = img.despeckle
img.write('despeckledimage.jpg')
```

enhance **uses a digital filter to improve the overall image appearance:**

```
require 'rubygems'
require 'RMagick'
img = Magick::Image.read('sunset.jpg').first
img = img.enhance
img.write('enhancedimage.jpg')
```

The reduce_noise() **method softens an image without affecting edges or boundaries within the image. The method takes a single parameter (the radius), but if you pass a value of 0, the method is smart enough to calculate a value for you.**

```
require 'rubygems'
require 'RMagick'
img = Magick::Image.read('sunset.jpg').first
img = img.reduce_noise(0)
img.write('reducednoiseimage.jpg')
```

vignette **masks an image with a circle and then fades the edges to match a background color (see Figure 10.4).**

```
require 'rubygems'
require 'RMagick'
img = Magick::Image.read('sample.jpg').first
img = img.vignette
img.write('vignetteimage.jpg')
```

solarize **produces an interesting effect by overexposing an image.**

```
require 'rubygems'
require 'RMagick'
img = Magick::Image.read('sample.jpg').first
img = img.solarize(127.5)
img.write('solarizedimage.jpg')
```

Figure 10.4
The vignette effect
applied to an image.

The `sepiatone` effect is able to make your photographs look like they are from an older era (see Figure 10.5).

Figure 10.5
The sepiatone effect
applied to an image.

```
require 'rubygems'
require 'RMagick'
img = Magick::Image.read('sample.jpg').first
img = img.sepiatone(255) #MaxRGB
img.write('sepiatoneimage.jpg')
```

We can even make an image almost look like it was painted with water colors (see Figure 10.6).

```
require 'rubygems'
require 'RMagick'
img = Magick::Image.read('sample.jpg').first
img = img.oil_paint(2)
img.write('oilpaintedimage.jpg')
```

Figure 10.6
RMagick does oil painting.

Creating Thumbnails

In this section we discuss different techniques to change the size of an image. A thumbnail is a reduced (both dimensions and file size) version of an image. RMagick provides the Resize(), Scale(), Sample(), and Thumbnail() methods, all of which are capable of reducing the dimensions of an image. All of these methods take two parameters: the required width and height.

The `thumbnail()` method is optimized to produce images that are roughly 10% of their original size:

```
require 'rubygems'
require 'RMagick'
img = Magick::Image.read('sunset.jpg').first
width = 100
height = 100
thumb = img.thumbnail(width, height)
thumb.write('thumbnail.jpg')
```

The `thumbnail()` method does not preserve the original aspect ratio. An image that is rectangular in shape will be square when reduced in size. We will explore a few techniques to preserve aspect ratio. A scale factor could be applied to the image's width and height. We use the `Magick::Image#columns` and `Magick::Image#rows` properties of an `Image` object to retrieve an image's width and height:

```
require 'rubygems'
require 'RMagick'
img = Magick::Image.read('sunset.jpg').first
thumb = img.thumbnail(img.columns*0.1, img.rows*0.1)
thumb.write('thumbnail.jpg')
```

We could also scale an image to 10% of its original size. The scale factor is passed to the `scale()` method as a single parameter. The desired width and height can also be passed to the `scale()` method.

```
require 'rubygems'
require 'RMagick'
img = Magick::Image.read('sunset.jpg').first
thumb = img.scale(0.10)
thumb.write('thumbnail.jpg')
```

The `resize_to_fit()` method takes the width and height as parameters. The `resize_to_fit()` method resizes an image to be within the bounds of the specified dimensions while maintaining the original aspect ratio.

```
require 'rubygems'
require 'RMagick'
img = Magick::Image.read('sunset.jpg').first
thumb = img.resize_to_fit(100,100)
thumb.write('thumbnail.jpg')
```

Rather than shrinking an image, extracting a portion of the image might be a viable alternative that allows more detail to be preserved. The `crop()` method is used to cut out a square or rectangular segment of an image.

The following code extracts a 200 × 300 pixel rectangle taken from the center of the image:

```
cropped_img = img.crop(Magick::CenterGravity, 200, 300)
```

Generating Thumbnails from a Rails Application

We have thus far explored the graphics manipulation functionality included in RMagick from within a standalone Ruby file. In this section we will focus on using RMagick from a Rails application and build a web-based thumbnailing tool.

The thumbnailing tool will allow users to upload an image. The uploaded image will be reduced in size, converted to an appropriate format (either GIF or JPEG), and saved to a database. In previous chapters we have explored saving an uploaded file to the file system. It makes sense to cover the storage and retrieval of binary image files within a database in this section.

First we'll need to create a database with `Items` and `Pics` folders. The Items table must have `id` and name fields. The pics table will store and relate an image to an item. The pics table requires `id`, `item_id`, `name`, `content_type`, and `data` fields. The `data` field needs to store binary data and must be of type `blob`. The uploaded image, after it has been processed and reduced in size, will be stored in the `data` field.

Create a new Rails application called `thumbnailer`:

```
$ rails thumbnailer
```

Generate a model for the items table:

```
$ ruby script/generate model item
```

The following will be output to the console:

```
exists   app/models/
exists   test/unit/
exists   test/fixtures/
create   app/models/item.rb
create   test/unit/item_test.rb
create   test/fixtures/items.yml
create   db/migrate
create   db/migrate/001_create_items.rb
```

Edit the `db/migrate/001_create_items.rb` migration. The items table must have a `name` field:

```
class CreateItems < ActiveRecord::Migration
    def self.up
        create_table :items do |t|
            t.column :name, :string
        end
    end
    def self.down
        drop_table :items
    end
end
```

Generate a model for the pics table:

```
$ ruby script/generate model pic
```

The following will be output to the console:

```
exists   app/models/
exists   test/unit/
exists   test/fixtures/
create   app/models/pic.rb
create   test/unit/pic_test.rb
create   test/fixtures/pics.yml
exists   db/migrate
create   db/migrate/002_create_pics.rb
```

Edit the db/migrate/002_create_pics.rb **migration. The pics table requires** name, content_type, data, **and** item_id **fields:**

```
class CreatePics < ActiveRecord::Migration
    def self.up
        create_table :pics do |t|
            t.column :name, :string
            t.column :content_type, :string
            t.column :data, :binary
            t.column :item_id, :integer
        end
    end
    def self.down
        drop_table :pics
```

```
      end
end
```

Run the migrations to create the database tables:

```
$ rake db:migrate
```

The following is output to the console:

```
(in C:/rails/thumbnailer)
== CreateItems: migrating =====================================================
-- create_table(:items)
   -> 0.0930s
== CreateItems: migrated (0.0930s) ============================================

== CreatePics: migrating ======================================================
-- create_table(:pics)
   -> 0.1250s
== CreatePics: migrated (0.1250s) =============================================
```

Generate a controller called `imageprocessor`:

```
$ ruby script/generate controller imageprocessor
```

The following is output to the console:

```
      exists  app/controllers/
      exists  app/helpers/
      create  app/views/imageprocessor
      exists  test/functional/
      create  app/controllers/imageprocessor_controller.rb
      create  test/functional/imageprocessor_controller_test.rb
      create  app/helpers/imageprocessor_helper.rb
```

Edit the `apps/model/item.rb` **file. Establish a** `has_many` **relationship with the** `pic` **model:**

```
class Item < ActiveRecord::Base
      has_many :pics
end
```

Edit the `apps/model/pic.rb` **file. The RMagick library must be referenced. We need to add functionality to the** `Pic` **class or model so that it is able to reduce the size of an image and save the resulting image as a** `blob` **in the data field. Also, we need to establish a** `belongs_to` **relationship with the item model.**

```
require 'RMagick' # if used in multiple locations add to environment.rb
include Magick
class Pic < ActiveRecord::Base
    belongs_to :item
    def pic=(image_field)
        self.name =
File.basename(image_field.original_filename).gsub(/[^\w._-]/, '')
        self.content_type = image_field.content_type.chomp
        img =
Magick::Image::read_inline(Base64.b64encode(image_field.read)).first
        self.data = img.resize_to_fit(100, 100).to_blob
    end
end
```

The `pic` method retrieves the filename, content type, and image in binary format. The image data is base64 encoded, resized, and then converted to a `blob`. The `to_blob()` method converts the uploaded image to a `blob` data type so that it can be inserted into the database. Internet Explorer returns the full path to the file as stored on a user's local drive, so we need to strip out the path details before we save the filename.

Create the following actions within the `imageprocessor_controller.rb` file:

* index

This action will render the `index.rhtml` file, which displays an image upload form.

* show

The `show` action links to the `show.rhtml` file. The `show.rhtml` file will display a thumbnail within a web page. An `<img>` tag is used to display the thumbnail. The `src` attribute of the `<img>` tag calls the `render_pic` controller.

* render_pic

The `render_pic` action retrieved a data field from the Pics table and uses the send method to push the image, its associated filename, and its content type to a web browser.

* create

The `create` action saves an `item` object and checks that the uploaded image is of the correct MIME type. The `pic` model has been enhanced to process the image, so all we need to do from within the `controller` action is call the `save()` method.

The full source code listing of `imageprocessor_controller.rb` is as follows:

```ruby
class ImageprocessorController < ApplicationController
    def index
    end
    def show
    end
    def render_pic
        @pic = Pic.find(params[:id])
        send_data(@pic.data,
                :filename => @pic.name,
                :type => @pic.content_type,
                :disposition => "inline")
    end
    def create
        @item = Item.new(params[:item])
        @item.save
        unless params[:pic]['pic'].content_type =~ /^image/
            flash[:error] = 'Please select an image file to upload.'
            render :action => 'index'
            return
        end
        @pic = Pic.new(params[:pic])
        @pic.item_id = @item.id
        if @pic.save
            flash[:notice] = 'Item was successfully created.'
            redirect_to :action => 'show'
        else
            flash[:error] = There was a problem saving the image.'
            render :action => 'index'
        end
    end
end
```

The `index.rhtml` **template uses the** `file_field` **helper to insert a file upload input box in the form (see Figure 10.7):**

```html
<html>
<head>
<title>Image Thumbnailer</title>
</head>
<body>
```

```
<h1>Image Thumbnailer</h1>
<%= form_tag( {:action=>'create'}, :multipart=>true ) %>
<% if @flash[:error] %>
<div class="error"><%= @flash[:error] %></div>
<% end %>
<p>Name: <%= text_field 'item', 'name' %></p>
<p>Description: <br/> <%= text_area 'item', 'description', :rows => 5 %></p>
<p>Image:<%= file_field("pic", "pic", :class => 'textinput') %>
<br/>
<%= submit_tag "Create Thumbnail" %>
<%= end_form_tag %>
</body>
</html>
```

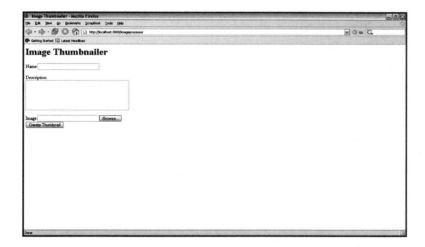

Figure 10.7
Creating a thumbnail from within a Rails application.

In the `show.rhtml` **template we can just use a** `<img>` **tag to display the thumbnail :**

```
<html>
<head>
<title>Show Image Thumbnail</title>
</head>
<body>
<h1>Show Image Thumbnail</h1>
<img src="<%= url_for(:controller => "imageprocessor",
:action => "render_pic",
```

```
:id => 3) %>" />
</body>
</html>
```

Graphs

Reviewing rows and rows of data is a tedious task. Graphs provide us with an intuitive visual representation that is helpful when searching for trends and relationships. This section discusses the graphing capabilities of the Gruff library. Gruff (http://rubyforge.org/projects/gruff/) is written by Geoffrey Grosenbach (of Ruby on Rails podcast fame) and is powered by RMagick. Gruff is able to draw bar (Gruff::Bar), line (Gruff::Line), and pie (Gruff::Pie) charts. Gruff also supports themes and customized colors.

A Gruff gem is available from RubyForge, so it can easily be installed:

```
$ gem install gruff
```

A pie graph object (see Figure 10.8) is created with the Gruff::Pie.new method. We can then set the title, theme, and datasets. The write() method saves the graph to the specified path, file, and image format:

```
require 'rubygems'
require 'Gruff'
include Gruff
p = Gruff::Pie.new
p.theme_37signals
p.title = "Product Line Sales"
p.data('Laptops', [25])
p.data('Desktops', [20])
p.data('Mobile Devices', [65])
p.write('c:/rmagick/graphs/pie_graph.png')
```

The following creates a line graph (see Figure 10.9):

```
require 'rubygems'
require 'Gruff'
include Gruff
g = Gruff::Line.new
g.title = "A Line Graph"
g.data("DataSet 1", [1, 6, 8, 4, 7, 9])
g.data("DataSet 2", [6, 7, 7, 2, 6, 8])
g.data("DataSet 3", [3, 1, 1, 3, 2, 10])
```

```
g.labels = {0 => '2001', 1 => '2002', 2 => '2003', 3 => '2004', 4 => '2005', 5
=> '2006'}
g.write('c:/rmagick/graphs/line_graph.jpg')
```

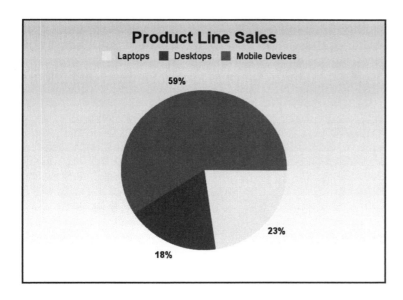

Figure 10.8
A pie chart.

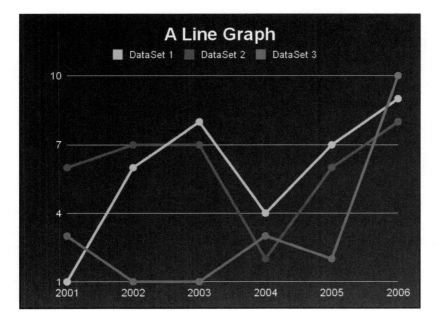

Figure 10.9
A line graph.

A bar graph is created by the following (see Figure 10.10):

```
require 'rubygems'
require 'Gruff'
include Gruff
g = Gruff::Bar.new
g.title = "A Bar Graph"
g.data("DataSet 1", [1, 6, 8, 4, 7, 9])
g.data("DataSet 2", [6, 7, 7, 2, 6, 8])
g.data("DataSet 3", [3, 1, 1, 3, 2, 10])
g.labels = {0 => '2001',
            1 => '2002',
            2 => '2003',
            3 => '2004',
            4 => '2005',
            5 => '2006'}
g.write('c:/rmagick/graphs/bar_graph.jpg')
```

Figure 10.10
A bar graph.

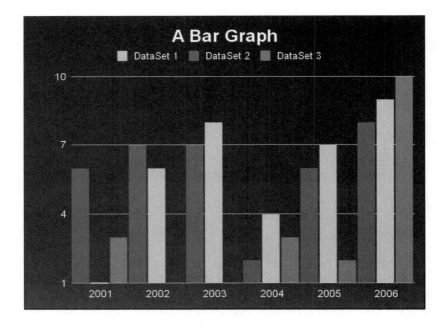

Note

Gruff::Pie.new, Gruff::Bar.new, and Gruff::Line.new also accept a single parameter, which specifies the width of the generated graph.

Generating Graphs in Rails

Gruff can easily be integrated with Rails to produce powerful web-based reports. We can either include the Gruff library with the require directive wherever it is required or place the reference in the config/environment.rb file. In the render_graph action within the GraphController code that follows, the pie chart object is converted to a blob (with the to_blob() method) and passed to a web browser via the send_data method:

```
class GraphController < ApplicationController
    def render_graph
        p = Gruff::Pie.new
        p.theme_37signals
        p.title = "Product Line Sales"
        p.data('Laptops', [25])
        p.data('Desktops', [20])
        p.data('Mobile Devices', [65])
        send_data(p.to_blob,
                :disposition => 'inline',
                :type => 'image/png',
                :filename => "graph.png")
    end
end
```

An <img> tag can then display the rendered graph (see Figure 10.11):

```
<img src="<%= url_for
(:controller => " GraphController",
 :action => " render_graph "
) %>" />
```

Figure 10.11
Using Gruff to display
graphs.

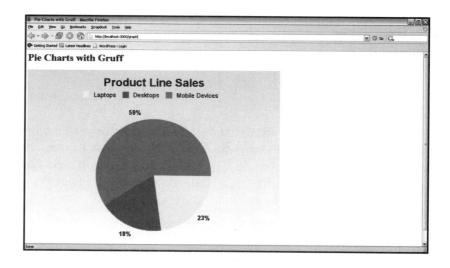

Conclusion

Action Mailer is a Rails component equipped with a script generator to help model e-mail messages that can be rendered with dynamic `.rhtml` templates (views). RMagick has some impressive image manipulation functionality. We are able to create thumbnail versions of an uploaded image file. In this chapter, Gruff was used with a Ruby on Rails application to produce line, bar and pie charts.

Although only three Ruby libraries were covered in this chapter, the concepts covered lend themselves to incorporating other libraries as well. The capabilities available at your fingertips are endless. Have fun!

11 } Rails Plug-Ins

Rails is completely extensible. This is illustrated by the huge number of available plug-ins. This chapter concentrates on plug-ins that extend Active Record and simplify the integration of comments, tags, versions, and full-text search into an application. We will also look at an extension to Action View that allows Rails to render a PDF document as a view. Plug-ins are particularly useful for prototyping applications. In this chapter we will build a bookmark manager with tagging support, an article manager with support for comments and full-text search, and a note manager that versions all notes as they are edited.

In this chapter you'll learn to:

* ❋ Install plug-ins
* ❋ Version content with `acts_as_versioned`
* ❋ Add tagging with `acts_as_taggable`
* ❋ Add comments with `acts_as_commentable`
* ❋ Add full text search with `acts_as_ferret`
* ❋ Generate PDF documents

Plug-In Installation

Plug-ins are listed on the Rails wiki at http://wiki.rubyonrails.org/rails/pages/Plugins. Rails uses this page to get a list of valid plug-in subversion repositories by looking for URLs with `/plugins` in the path. We can get Rails to parse the Wiki page for new plug-ins by typing:

```
$ ruby script/plugin discover
```

We can then display a list of plug-in repositories:

```
$ ruby script/plugin list --remote
```

We can view a list of currently installed plug-ins:

```
$ ruby script/plugin list --local
```

We can add a plug-in manually:

```
$ ruby script/plugin source
```

And we can delete a plug-in:

```
$ ruby script/plugin delete
```

Plug-ins are placed within the `vendor/plugins` directory after installation. Once a plug-in is installed, you will need to restart the Webrick web server, if it is already running. Each plug-in has an `init.rb` file that is executed when the application is started. Plug-in initialization code is placed within the `init.rb` file.

> ※ **Tip**
>
> You can use the `script/generate plugin` command to create a skeleton structure for a plug-in:
>
> ```
> $ ruby script/generate plugin acts_as_madonna
> ```

Versioning with acts_as_versioned

`acts_as_versioned` is an Active Record extension that stores a new version of a record each time the content is updated. `acts_as_versioned` maintains a history of edits, and with some code we will be able to allow users to view and swap between versions.

The following code will install `acts_as_versioned`:

```
$ ruby script/plugin install acts_as_versioned
```

The following files will be installed:

```
+ ./acts_as_versioned/CHANGELOG
+ ./acts_as_versioned/MIT-LICENSE
+ ./acts_as_versioned/README
+ ./acts_as_versioned/RUNNING_UNIT_TESTS
+ ./acts_as_versioned/Rakefile
+ ./acts_as_versioned/init.rb
+ ./acts_as_versioned/lib/acts_as_versioned.rb
+ ./acts_as_versioned/test/abstract_unit.rb
+ ./acts_as_versioned/test/database.yml
```

```
+ ./acts_as_versioned/test/fixtures/authors.yml
+ ./acts_as_versioned/test/fixtures/locked_pages.yml
+ ./acts_as_versioned/test/fixtures/locked_pages_revisions.yml
+ ./acts_as_versioned/test/fixtures/migrations/1_add_versioned_tables.rb
+ ./acts_as_versioned/test/fixtures/page.rb
+ ./acts_as_versioned/test/fixtures/page_versions.yml
+ ./acts_as_versioned/test/fixtures/pages.yml
+ ./acts_as_versioned/test/fixtures/widget.rb
+ ./acts_as_versioned/test/migration_test.rb
+ ./acts_as_versioned/test/schema.rb
+ ./acts_as_versioned/test/versioned_test.rb
```

We will build an application to arbitrary notes—when notes are edited a new version will be stored. `acts_as_versioned` **has certain conventions that must be followed. The table that stores the item being versioned must contain a version field.**

The following will create a Notes table with a version field:

```
class CreateNotes < ActiveRecord::Migration
    def self.up
        create_table 'notes' do |t|
        t.column 'title', :string
        t.column 'body', :text
        t.column 'version', :int
    end
    end
    def self.down
        drop_table 'notes'
    end
end
```

Next we need to create a second table called `note_versions`, **the singular form of the table name suffixed with** _versions. **This table will store older versions:**

```
class AddVersions < ActiveRecord::Migration
    def self.up
        create_table 'note_versions' do |t|
        t.column 'note_id', :int
        t.column 'title', :string
        t.column 'body', :text
```

```
      t.column 'version', :int
   end
   def self.down
      drop_table 'note_versions'
   end
end
```

Within the app/models/note.rb **file we just need to call** acts_as_versioned:

```
class Statement < ActiveRecord::Base
      acts_as_versioned
end
```

On the edit form we can add some code to allow a user to revert to a previous version. The code will call the 'revert_version' **action:**

```
<h1>Editing note</h1>
<%= start_form_tag :action => 'update', :id => @note %>
  <%= render :partial => 'form' %>
<p><label for="note_version">Version</label>:
<% if @note.version > 0 %>
<% (1..@note.versions.length).each do |v| %>
<% if @note.version == v %>
<%= v %>
<% else %>
<%= link_to v, :action => 'revert_version', :id => @note, :version => v %>
<% end %>
<% end %>
<% end %>
</p>
  <%= submit_tag 'Edit' %>
<%= end_form_tag %>
<%= link_to 'Show', :action => 'show', :id => @statement %> |
<%= link_to 'Back', :action => 'list' %>
```

An excerpt from the Note **controller with only the** revert_version **action listed follows. The** revert_to! **method is called:**

```
class NoteController < ApplicationController
    def revert_version
        @note = Note.find(params[:id])
        @note.revert_to!(params[:version])
        redirect_to :action => 'edit', :id => @note
    end
end
```

Folksonomy with acts_as_taggable

Tags are keywords that are associated with a content item. Tags are entered by users and are known as a folksonomy because the keywords used are not predefined. Tags can be thought of as a type of category and are usually displayed as a list or a tag cloud. The acts_as_taggable plug-in is an Active Record plug-in. We are now able to add tags to any Active Record model:

Installing acts_as_taggable:

```
$ ruby script/plugin install http://dev.rubyonrails.com/svn/rails
```

The following files are installed:

```
/plugins/acts_as_taggable/
+ ./acts_as_taggable/init.rb
+ ./acts_as_taggable/lib/README
+ ./acts_as_taggable/lib/acts_as_taggable.rb
+ ./acts_as_taggable/lib/tag.rb
+ ./acts_as_taggable/lib/tagging.rb
+ ./acts_as_taggable/test/acts_as_taggable_test.rb
```

The use of acts_as_taggable **will be illustrated by a simple bookmark (or link storing) application. A bookmark consists of a title, body, and URL. The** tag_with **method is part of** acts_as_taggable **and takes a comma-delimited list of tags to associate with a bookmark. The** tags **method returns a list of tags associated with an Active Record object. The** find_tagged_with **method will return all bookmarks with a specified tag. The** bookmark.rb **model file only needs to call** acts_as_taggable **for us to take advantage of the plug-in:**

```
class Bookmark < ActiveRecord::Base
    acts_as_taggable
end
```

We can use the Rails console to get some experience with the `acts_as_taggable` plug-in. We are able to create a bookmark object and add tags to the object as well as list all the tags associated with an object:

```
>> c= Bookmark.create(:title => "Link", :body => "a link", :url =>
"http://www.google.com")
=> #<Bookmark:0x3982904 @attributes={"body"=>"a link", "title"=>"Link",
"url"=>"
http://www.google.com", "id"=>1}, @new_record=false,
@errors=#<ActiveRecord::Errors:0x3924818 @base=#<Bookmark:0x3982904 ...>,
@errors={}>, @new_record_before_save=true>
>> c.tag_with("search, rank, hello")
=> ["search", "rank", "hello"]
>> c.tags
=> [#<Tag:0x38e4600 @attributes={"name"=>"search", "id"=>"1"}>,
#<Tag:0x38e45c4@attributes={"name"=>"rank", "id"=>"2"}>,
#<Tag:0x38e4588 @attributes={"name"=>"hello", "id"=>"3"}>]
>> c2 = Bookmark.create(:title => "Link 2", :body => "link 2",
:url => "http://www.madonna.com")
=> #<Bookmark:0x38cec60 @attributes={"body"=>"link 2",
"title"=>"Link 2", "url"=>"http://www.madonna.com",
"id"=>2}, @new_record=false, @errors=#<ActiveRecord::
Errors:0x38ca638 @base=#<Bookmark:0x38cec60 ...>,
@errors={}>, @new_record_before_save=true>
>> c2.tag_with("search, madonna")
=> ["search", "madonna"]
>> c2.tags
=> [#<Tag:0x3895c1c @attributes={"name"=>"search", "id"=>"1"}>,
 #<Tag:0x3895a00
@attributes={"name"=>"madonna", "id"=>"4"}>]
>> exit
```

The `bookmark_controller.rb` file can now be enhanced to include support for tagging. The `list` action assigns a list of all tags to the `@tags` instance variable:

```
    def list
        @bookmarks =  Bookmark.find(:all)
        @tags = Tag.tags(:limit => 100, :order => "name desc")
    end
```

The `create` **action saves the bookmark and uses the** `tag_with` **method to assign the tags to the bookmark:**

```ruby
def create
    @bookmark = Bookmark.new(params[:bookmark])
    if @bookmark.save
        @bookmark.tag_with(params[:tags])
        flash[:notice] = 'Bookmark was successfully created.'
        redirect_to :action => 'list'
    else
        render :action => 'new'
    end
end
```

We even provide a `tag_search` **action that facilitates searching for all bookmarks with a particular tag:**

```ruby
def tag_search
    @bookmarks = Bookmark.find_tagged_with(params[:id])
end
```

The full source code listing for `bookmark_controller.rb`:

```ruby
class BookmarkController < ApplicationController
    def index
        list
        render :action => 'list'
    end
    # GETs should be safe
    #(see http://www.w3.org/2001/tag/doc/whenToUseGet.html)
    verify :method => :post, :only => [ :destroy, :create, :update ],
            :redirect_to => { :action => :list }

    def list
        @bookmarks =  Bookmark.find(:all)
        @tags = Tag.tags(:limit => 100, :order => "name desc")
    end


    def tag_search
```

```ruby
    @bookmarks = Bookmark.find_tagged_with(params[:id])
end

def show
    @bookmark = Bookmark.find(params[:id])
end

def new
    @bookmark = Bookmark.new
    @tags = ""
end

def create
    @bookmark = Bookmark.new(params[:bookmark])
    if @bookmark.save
        @bookmark.tag_with(params[:tags])
        flash[:notice] = 'Bookmark was successfully created.'
        redirect_to :action => 'list'
    else
        render :action => 'new'
    end
end

def edit
    @bookmark = Bookmark.find(params[:id])
end

def update
    @bookmark = Bookmark.find(params[:id])
    if @bookmark.update_attributes(params[:bookmark])
        flash[:notice] = 'Bookmark was successfully updated.'
        redirect_to :action => 'show', :id => @bookmark
    else
        render :action => 'edit'
    end
end
```

```
    def destroy
        Bookmark.find(params[:id]).destroy
        redirect_to :action => 'list'
    end
end
```

Following is the `_form.rb` partial with support for the entry of tags. The partial is used by the create and update forms. The tags associated with a bookmark are displayed as a comma-separated list by the `text_field_tag` helper:

```
<%= error_messages_for 'bookmark' %>
<!--[form:bookmark]-->
<p><label for="bookmark_title">Title</label><br/>
<%= text_field 'bookmark', 'title'  %></p>
<p><label for="bookmark_body">Body</label><br/>
<%= text_area 'bookmark', 'body'  %></p>
<p><label for="bookmark_url">Url</label><br/>
<%= text_field 'bookmark', 'url'  %></p>
<p><label for="tags">Tag</label><br/>
<%= text_field_tag 'tags', @bookmark.tags.collect{|t| t.name}.join(", ") %></p>
<!--[eoform:bookmark]-->
```

A comma-delimited list of tags associated with a bookmark is displayed by calling `bookmark.tags.collect{|tag| tag.name}.join(", ")`. This code can be added to edit and update forms as well as the tag search results view:

```
<li> <a href="<%=bookmark.url%>"><%=bookmark.title%></a>
    (<%= link_to 'Edit', :action => 'edit', :id => bookmark %> |
    <%= link_to 'Destroy', { :action => 'destroy',
                             :id => bookmark },
                           :confirm => 'Are you sure?',
                           :post => true %>)
    <br>
    <%=bookmark.body%> <br>
    Tags:
<%=
if bookmark.tags.blank?
" "
```

```
else
 bookmark.tags.collect{|tag| tag.name}.join(", ")
end
%>
```

Commenting with acts_as_commentable

In Chapter 3, "Prototyping Database-Driven Applications with Rails," we built a simple weblog with support for comments within each post. We will now explore the acts_as_commentable plug-in, which extends any model to support commenting. We have a Rails application that allows articles to be stored. We will allow site visitors to add comments to the articles.

Installing acts_as_commentable:

```
$ ruby script/plugin install http://juixe.com/svn/acts_as_commentable
+ ./acts_as_commentable/MIT-LICENSE
+ ./acts_as_commentable/README
+ ./acts_as_commentable/init.rb
+ ./acts_as_commentable/install.rb
+ ./acts_as_commentable/lib/acts_as_commentable.rb
+ ./acts_as_commentable/lib/comment.rb
+ ./acts_as_commentable/tasks/acts_as_commentable_tasks.rake
+ ./acts_as_commentable/test/acts_as_commentable_test.rb
```

acts_as_commentable **requires a table called comments with specific fields as outlined in the migration below:**

```
def self.up
  create_table :comments, :force => true do |t|
    t.column :title, :string, :limit => 50, :default => ""
    t.column :comment, :string, :default => ""
    t.column :created_at, :datetime, :null => false
    t.column :commentable_id, :integer, :default => 0, => false
    t.column :commentable_type, :string, :limit => 15,
      :default => "", :null => false
    t.column :user_id, :integer, :default => 0, :null => false
  end
  add_index :comments, ["user_id"], :name => "fk_comments_user"
end
```

```
def self.down
  drop_table :comments
end
```

We have generated a scaffold for the `articles` **model. To enable commenting, we need to add** `acts_as_commentable` **to our model:**

```
class Article < ActiveRecord::Base
    acts_as_commentable
end
```

Within the `article_controller.rb` **file, we need to add a** `comment` **action that creates a new** `comment` **object and associates the object with an article:**

```
class ArticleController < ApplicationController
    def comment
        comment = Comment.new(params[:comment])
        Article.find(params[:id]).add_comment(comment)
        flash[:notice] = "Your comment has been added!"
        redirect_to :action => "show", :id => params[:id]
    end
end
```

The `show.rhtml` **view template is called to display an article and list all associated comments. We also include a form to add a comment by posting to the** `comment` **action.**

```
<%= render :partial => "article", :object => @article  %>
<h2>Comments</h2>
<% for comment in @article.comments %>
<strong><%= comment.title %> </strong> <br />
<%= comment.comment %>
<hr />
<% end %>
<%= form_tag :action => "comment", :id => @article %>
<p><label for="comment_title">Title</label><br/>
<%= text_field 'comment', 'title'  %></p>
<%= text_area "comment", "comment" %> <br />
<%= submit_tag "Comment!" %>
</form>
```

Searching with acts_as_ferret

Lucene provides an API for integrating full-text search into a Java application. Ferret is a port of Lucene to the Ruby language. Lucene is both extremely customizable and powerful. A full-text search engine breaks a document down into words and creates an index. The index is organized in such a manner that no matter what search terms you use, the time it takes to return matching documents will always be the same. Lucene allows you to determine the fields that are stored in the index, making it easy to add full-text search to a web application.

We use gem to install Ferret:

```
$ gem install ferret
```

Some simple Ruby code is needed to store the index on the file system, tokenize two documents, and insert the tokens within the file-based index. The documents are actually hashes; this allows us to separate the documents into fields. In this example, the documents have a title field and a body field. This could easily be expanded to include a unique ID and other fields retrieved from a database.

The create_index.rb file:

```
require 'ferret'
include Ferret
index = Index::Index.new(:path => '/index')
index << {:title => "Power Ruby", :body => "The Ruby port of Lucene is
awesome."}
index << {:title => "This is great", :body => "full text search at my finger
tips."}
```

In true Ruby style, we can use a code block to search the index:

```
require 'ferret'
include Ferret
index = Index::Index.new(:path => '/index')
index.search_each('body:"Lucene"') do |id, score|
     puts "Document #{index[id][:title]} found with a score of #{score}"
end
```

The previous two code snippets are very impressive in terms of functionality, but full-text searching gets even better because the acts_as_ferret plug-in integrates Ferret with any Active Record model.

acts_as_ferret can be installed with the script/plugin install command:

```
$ ruby script/plugin install
svn://projects.jkraemer.net/acts_as_ferret/tags/stable/acts_as_ferret
```

We just need to make a call to `acts_as_ferret` from within our model and tell it which fields from our model must be indexed:

```
class Article < ActiveRecord::Base
    acts_as_ferret :fields => ['title', 'body' ]
end
```

Within our `Article` controller, the `find_by_contents` method will return search results from the `Ferret` index:

```
class ArticleController < ApplicationController
    def search
        @results = Article.find_by_contents("Lucene")
    end
end
```

The `@results` variable is passed to the `search.rhtml` view template, which lists all search results:

```
<h1>Article Search</h1>
<% if @results %>
<p>Your search for returned <%= @results.size %> Results:</p>
<ul>
<% @results.each { |result| %>
<li><%= link_to result.title, :action => 'show', :id => result %></li>
<% } %>
</ul>
<% end %>
<br />
```

Generating PDF Documents

PDF is a universally supported format that preserves formatting when viewed and printed. The PDF Writer library brings PDF reports to Ruby. The PDF Writer library can be used within a Rails application to generate PDF reports. `Railspdf` is a plug-in that allows a view template to render and send a PDF file to a web browser.

We use `gem` to install PDF Writer:

```
$ gem install pdf-writer
```

Enter y for required dependencies:

```
Bulk updating Gem source index for: http://gems.rubyforge.org
Install required dependency color-tools? [Yn]  y
Install required dependency transaction-simple? [Yn]  y
Need to update 1 gems from http://gems.rubyforge.org
Successfully installed pdf-writer-1.1.3
Successfully installed color-tools-1.3.0
Successfully installed transaction-simple-1.3.0
Installing ri documentation for pdf-writer-1.1.3...
Installing ri documentation for color-tools-1.3.0...
Installing ri documentation for transaction-simple-1.3.0...
Installing RDoc documentation for pdf-writer-1.1.3...
Installing RDoc documentation for color-tools-1.3.0...
Installing RDoc documentation for transaction-simple-1.3.0...
```

Note

Documentation for PDF Writer is also installed with the PDF Writer library. Information on PDF Writer can be found at http://www.artima.com/rubycs/articles/pdf_writer2.html.

PDF Writer can be used directly within a controller. We need to include a reference to require `"pdf/writer"` in the controller. A `PDF::Writer` object is created by calling the `new` method. Properties such as `font`, `text`, and `justification` can be set. The `render` method generates the PDF file that is passed to the `send_data` method. The `send_data` method sends the PDF document to a web browser. When the `report` action in the `HelloController` controller is called, a PDF document will be generated and sent to a web browser for download. The `send_data` method also requires a filename and MIME type. In this case the MIME type is set to `"application/pdf"`.

```
require "pdf/writer"
class HelloController < ApplicationController
    def report
        pdf_report = PDF::Writer.new
        pdf_report.select_font "Times-Roman"
        pdf_report.text "Hello, Ruby.", :font_size => 72,
            :justification => :center
        send_data pdf_report.render, :filename => "hello.pdf",
```

```
                :type => "application/pdf"
        end
end
```

This all works, but we are doing document generation in the controller. It makes sense to take HTML and XML out to the view. The same benefits apply to generating the PDF document in the view. An action can be routed to a `.rhtml` or `.rxml` template to generate HTML and XML, respectively. `railspdf` is a plug-in that allows actions to map to `.rpdf` template files. Let's install the `railspdf` plug-in:

```
ruby script/plugin install svn://rubyforge.org//var/svn/railspdfplugin/railspdf
```

We can now pass data from an action to a `.rpdf` view. No `send_data` method call is required:

```
class HelloController < ApplicationController
      def report
            @name = "Ruby"
      end
end
```

The code for the `pdf.rpdf` template is reduced to just two lines. There is no need to initialize `PDF::Writer` because this is already done:

```
pdf.select_font "Times-Roman"
pdf.text "Hello, #{@name}.", :font_size => 72, :justification => :center
```

Conclusion

Many more useful plug-ins are available. This chapter has served as an introduction to popular and useful plug-ins (`acts_as_versioned`, `acts_as_commentable`, `acts_as_taggable`, and `acts_as_ferret`) that will be of great assistance for prototyping applications. The concepts taught, however, apply to other plug-ins, so you should have no trouble installing a plug-in and using it within either a model, a view, or a controller in your Rails application.

12 } Filters, Caching, and Active Support

This chapter pulls together key Rails features that will not only make Ruby programming more enjoyable but also help you to centralize code and improve performance. Filters are supported by Action Controller and allow code to be run before and after actions in a controller are executed. Practical examples of filter usage will be covered including basic authentication. Instead of dynamically rendering content for each page request, we will use the caching mechanisms provided by Rails to improve performance for content that is rarely updated. Active Support is yet another Rails component, albeit a special component that Active Record, Action Controller, and Action View all themselves utilize. Active Support extends base Ruby classes and has impressive functionality that you can use directly in your own applications' models and controllers.

In this chapter you'll learn to:

❋ Use filters to authenticate users and to track and time actions being accessed

❋ Use page and action caching to help improve your application's performance

❋ Use the array, string, date, and pluralization extensions provided by Active Support

Filters
A *filter* is a method in a controller that can be executed before, after, or before and after all actions within the controller are executed. Filters can even be placed within a class of their own and shared across many controllers in your application. Filters are specified in a controller by the `before_filter`, `after_filter`, and `around_filter` directives. The filter directive is passed the name of the method that must be executed as the first parameter. The `:except` parameter is optional and allows us to specify actions that must be excluded from the filter. In the sections that follow, example filter usage will be illustrated.

A `before_filter` **directive added to a controller:**

```
class AdminController < ApplicationController
      before_filter :sample_method
end
```

An `after_filter` **directive added to a controller:**

```
class AdminController < ApplicationController
      after_filter :sample_method
end
```

An `around_filter` **directive added to a controller:**

```
class AdminController < ApplicationController
      around_filter :sample_method
end
```

A before filter that executes the `authentication_check` method for all action requests in a controller except the login action:

```
before_filter :authentication_check, :except => [:login]
```

Authentication with Filters

The most important use of filters is for authentication. With a `before_filter`, you will be able to enforce authentication against all actions that require restricted access. In this example, we will set up a database to store user credentials and enforce authentication on an admin controller.

We start by generating a model called `user`:

```
$ ruby script/generate model user
```

The following files and folders will be created:

```
      exists   app/models/
      exists   test/unit/
      exists   test/fixtures/
      create   app/models/user.rb
      create   test/unit/user_test.rb
      create   test/fixtures/users.yml
      create   db/migrate
      create   db/migrate/001_create_users.rb
```

You will notice that when we create a model called `user`, a migration called `001_create_users.rb` is generated for us as well. Because I knew this would be done for us, I did not generate a migration first. We can now edit the `001_create_users.rb` file and add the fields required by the users table. We only need a `user_name` and `hashed_password` field:

```
class CreateUsers < ActiveRecord::Migration
    def self.up
        create_table :users do |t|
            t.column :username, :string
            t.column :hashed_password, :string
        end
    end

    def self.down
        drop_table :users
    end
end
```

We now run our migration and create the users table:

```
$ rake db:migrate
(in C:/rails/authentication)
== CreateUsers: migrating ======================================================
-- create_table(:users)
   -> 0.1250s
== CreateUsers: migrated (0.1250s) =============================================
```

We edit the `user.rb` file. The username must be unique, so we set the `validates_uniqueness_of` directive. We will use the `digest/sha2` library to create the password hash. We include a method to set the password that will be inserted in the database:

```
require 'digest/sha2'
class User < ActiveRecord::Base
    validates_uniqueness_of :username
    def password=(pass)
        self.hashed_password = Digest::SHA256.hexdigest(pass)
    end
end
```

Ideally, we would create an interface to add a user or a self registration form. Because this is an example to illustrate filters, we will just create a new user with the Rails console:

```
$ ruby script/console
Loading development environment.
>> aneesha = User.create(:username => "aneesha")
=> #<User:0x39bdf04 @attributes={"hashed_password"=>nil, "username"=>"aneesha",
"id"=>1}, @new_record=false, @errors=#<ActiveRecord::Errors:0x396a19c @base=#<Us
er:0x39bdf04 ...>, @errors={}>>
>> aneesha.password ="donttellme"
=> "donttellme"
>> aneesha.hashed_password
=> "47c105d8c2634273e04dcd76aa5fdeff732586bb8814277a7a3a47a5c9a1338f"
>> aneesha.save
=> true
>> exit
```

We can now generate a controller called admin:

```
$ ruby script/generate controller admin
```

The admin **controller needs to display a login form. The first action we add to the controller is**
called login, which renders the login.rhtml **template if called by a** get **request. If login is**
called by a post **request, it is assumed that the login form has been posted and we check to see**
if the username and password combination are stored in the users table. If the password or
username is not found, we store the error message in flash[:info] **and redirect back to the**
login page. If the username and password are valid, we set session[:username] **and**
return to the action and controller that was originally requested. The
session[:intended_controller] **and** session[:intended_action] **need to be set by**
the authentication filter so that all actions are caught.

```
def login
      if request.post?
    user = User.find(:first,
                :conditions => ['username = ?', params[:username]])
    if user.blank? || Digest::SHA256.hexdigest(params[:password])
                          != user.hashed_password
       flash[:info] = "Invalid Username or Password!"
       redirect_to :action => "login"
       return
    end
```

```
            session[:username] = user.username
            redirect_to :action => session[:intended_action],
                    :controller => session[:intended_controller]
        end
    end
```

The `login.rhtml` template displays the login form, which has a username and password field. The form posts to the `login` action. If `flash[:info]` is set, this means that the invalid username or password error message must be displayed.

```
<html>
<head>
<title>Admin: Login Form</title>
</head>
<body>
<h2>Admin: Login Form</h2>
<% if @flash[:info] %>
    <p><div id="info">
        <%= @flash[:info] %>
    </div></p>
<% end %>
<%= start_form_tag :action => "login" %>
<label for="username">Username:</label>
<%= text_field_tag "username" %><br />
<label for="password">Password:</label>
<%= password_field_tag "password" %><br />
<%= submit_tag "Login" %>
<%= end_form_tag %>
</body>
</html>
```

Next we add the `logout` and `show_admin` actions to the controller. The `show_admin` action just needs to display the `show_admin` template. The `logout` action resets `session[:username]` to log the user out:

```
    def logout
        session[:username] = nil
    end
```

```
def show_admin
end
```

The `show_admin.rhtml` **template informs users that they have access to the admin area. It also includes a Logout link:**

```
<html>
<head>
<title>Admin</title>
</head>
<body>
You have access to the Admin area.
<p>
<%= link_to 'Logout', :action => 'logout' %>
</p>
</body>
</html>
```

The `logout.rhtml` **template includes a link that will force users to login before they can access the admin area again:**

```
<html>
<head>
<title>Admin: Logout</title>
</head>
<body>
You have logged out.
<p>
<%= link_to 'Try to access the Admin area.', :action => 'show_admin' %>
</p>
</body>
</html>
```

We are now ready to implement a filter to enforce authentication. The method will be called `authentication_check`. **If** `session[:username]` **is not set, the method sets** `session[:intended_action]` **and** `session[:intended_controller]` **and then redirects the user to the login form.**

```
def authentication_check
    unless session[:username]
        session[:intended_action] = action_name
```

```
                     session[:intended_controller] = controller_name
                     redirect_to :action => "login"
               end
         end
```

The authentication filter needs to be run before the user is allowed to access all actions, especially show_admin, but not the login action. We use the `before_filter` directive and its optional except parameter to achieve the required functionality. The final source code listing for the admin controller (`admin_controller.rb`) follows:

```ruby
require 'digest/sha2'
class AdminController < ApplicationController
    before_filter :authentication_check, :except => [:login]
    def authentication_check
        unless session[:username]
                session[:intended_action] = action_name
                session[:intended_controller] = controller_name
                redirect_to :action => "login"
        end
    end


    def login
        if request.post?
    user = User.find(:first,
                :conditions => ['username = ?', params[:username]])
    if user.blank? || Digest::SHA256.hexdigest(params[:password])
                        != user.hashed_password
        flash[:info] = "Invalid Username or Password!"
        redirect_to :action => "login"
        return
    end
        session[:username] = user.username
        redirect_to :action => session[:intended_action],
                    :controller => session[:intended_controller]
        end
    end

    def logout
```

```
        session[:username] = nil
    end


    def show_admin
    end
end
```

Using a before_filter to Log Actions

The before_filter can also be used to track all actions that have been accessed. The controller in the example below implements a filter called ActionLoggerFilter. ActionLoggerFilter is actually a class. Placing the code for a filter in a class allows us to implement the filter across all controllers in the application. The showform and show_formdata actions can be tracked by ActionLoggerFilter.

```
class MyappactionsController < ApplicationController
    before_filter ActionLoggerFilter
    def showform
    end
    def show_formdata
        @name = params[:name]
        @prog_languages = params[:prog_languages] || []
        @operating_systems = params[:operating_systems] || []
    end
end
```

The action_logger_filter.rb contains the ActionLoggerFilter class. The action_logger_filter.rb file is placed in the app/controllers folder. We create a new Logger object and then use log.info to add to our log file. We even store posted form data (from the params hash) in the actions.log file:

```
require 'logger'
class ActionLoggerFilter
    def self.filter(controller)
        log = Logger.new('C:/rails/authentication/log/actions.log')
        log.info("Action: " + controller.action_name +
                " Params: "+controller.params.to_json)
    end
end
```

After requesting the actions in our controller we can view the actions.log file:

```
# Logfile created on Mon Jan 01 14:03:02 E. Australia Standard Time 2007 by
logger.rb/1.5.2.7
Action: showform Params: {"action": "showform", "controller": "myappactions"}
Action: show_formdata Params: {"name": "Aneesha", "commit": "Submit Form",
"prog_languages": ["Ruby", "Java", "C#"], "action": "show_formdata",
"controller": "myappactions", "operating_systems": ["Windows", "Linux", "Mac"]}
```

Using an around_filter to Time Actions

The around_filter runs code before and after an action is executed. We will use an around filter to calculate and log the time each action takes to execute. This is useful to determine slow-running actions that may need performance enhancements.

Use the around_filter directive to create a new instance of the DurationLogger:

```
class MyappactionsController < ApplicationController
    around_filter DurationLogger.new
    def showform
    end
    def show_formdata
        @name = params[:name]
        @prog_languages = params[:prog_languages] || []
        @operating_systems = params[:operating_systems] || []
    end
end
```

Within the DurationLogger class we need before and after methods. In the before method we set @start, which stores the time prior to the execution of an action. The after method determines the amount of time it took the action to run using @start and then writes the details to duration.log.

```
require 'logger'
class DurationLogger
  def before(controller)
    @start = Time.now
  end

  def after(controller)
    log = Logger.new('C:/rails/authentication/log/duration.log')
    duration = Time.now.to_f - @start.to_f
```

```
      log.info(controller.action_name + ", Duration: %.2f" % duration)
    end
end
```

The `duration.log` file after a few actions have been requested:

```
# Logfile created on Mon Jan 01 14:07:57 E. Australia Standard Time 2007
by logger.rb/1.5.2.7
showform, Duration: 0.00
show_formdata, Duration: 0.00
show_formdata, Duration: 0.02
```

Caching

Most applications you build will be viewed by many but updated by a select few who have the appropriate rights. The owner of a blog, for example, would add new entries and possibly update an entry, but all visitors would only view entries. It probably takes a few queries to view the blog entries within a themed interface. These queries will be run for each visitor and unless blog entries have been added, updated, or deleted, each visitor will see the same content. This is not really a problem until the blog becomes popular and receives heavy traffic—then it becomes a performance issue. The solution is to cache the content and only update the cache when a change (edit, update, delete, or new entry) occurs.

Caching is only turned on in production mode. We will need to enable caching to test within a development environment. We need to set `config.action_controller.perform_caching` to true in `development.rb`:

```
config.action_controller.perform_caching = true
```

We are going to create a News application using the `scaffold` command to generate the controller code and interface. The News application is an ideal candidate for caching because once an item is added, it is rarely changed, and most site traffic will be requests to view the news items. We start by generating a migration to create the newsitem table:

```
$ ruby script/generate migration add_newsitem_table
      create  db/migrate
      create  db/migrate/001_add_newsitem_table.rb
```

The newsitems table only requires `title` and `type` fields to be used in our caching example. If this was a real application, more fields such as a `body` would be required. The migration to create the newsitems table:

```
class AddNewsitemTable < ActiveRecord::Migration
    def self.up
        create_table :newsitems do |t|
            t.column "title", :string
            t.column "type", :string
        end
    end

    def self.down
        drop_table :newsitems
    end
end
```

Run the `rake` **command to create the table:**

```
$ rake db:migrate
(in C:/rails/caching)
== AddNewsitemTable: migrating ================================================
-- create_table(:newsitems)
   -> 0.0940s
== AddNewsitemTable: migrated (0.0940s) =======================================
```

Next we use a `scaffold` **to generate the** `newsitem` **model and controller:**

```
$ ruby script/generate scaffold newsitem newsitem
```

The first type of caching that we will use is called page caching. With page caching the entire page or request, as defined by a unique URL, is cached. The `caches_page` **directive must be added to a controller to enable page caching. The name of the action to be cached must be passed to the** `caches_page` **directive. The list action in the** `newsitem` **controller displays all news items. The following directive will cache the list action:**

```
caches_page :list
```

The first time http://localhost:3000/newsitem/list is requested, a static version will be stored as `public\newsitem\list.html`**. A folder in the public directory has been created corresponding to the name of the cached controller. The action name has** `.html` **appended and is the filename of the cached content.**

All seems to work fine and a speed improvement is noted immediately. However, when we add a new item, delete an item, or update an item, the list action always displays the out of date version that was cached. We need to determine all the actions involved in changing news items

and then add code in these actions to delete the cached version of the content rendered by the list action. The `expire_page` directive is used to achieve this:

```
expire_page :action => "list"
```

The `newsitem` controller with the `expire_page` directive added to all actions that alter content is as follows:

```
class NewsitemController < ApplicationController
    caches_page :list
  def index
    list
    render :action => 'list'
  end

  # GETs should be safe (see http://www.w3.org/2001/tag/doc/whenToUseGet.html)
  verify :method => :post, :only => [ :destroy, :create, :update ],
         :redirect_to => { :action => :list }

  def list
    @newsitem_pages, @newsitems = paginate :newsitems, :per_page => 10
  end

  def show
    @newsitem = Newsitem.find(params[:id])
  end

  def new
    @newsitem = Newsitem.new
    expire_page :action => "list"
  end

  def create
    @newsitem = Newsitem.new(params[:newsitem])
    if @newsitem.save
      expire_page :action => "list"
      flash[:notice] = 'Newsitem was successfully created.'
      redirect_to :action => 'list'
    else
```

```
    render :action => 'new'
    end
  end

  def edit
    @newsitem = Newsitem.find(params[:id])
    expire_page :action => "list"
  end

  def update
    @newsitem = Newsitem.find(params[:id])
    if @newsitem.update_attributes(params[:newsitem])
      expire_page :action => "list"
      flash[:notice] = 'Newsitem was successfully updated.'
      redirect_to :action => 'show', :id => @newsitem
    else
      render :action => 'edit'
    end
  end

  def destroy
    Newsitem.find(params[:id]).destroy
    expire_page :action => "list"
    redirect_to :action => 'list'
  end
end
```

> ❋ **Tip**
>
> It makes no sense to cache content that is rapidly updated such as stock quotes. If the display of this data is causing a performance problem, cache the data but don't delete the cache when the data is updated. Instead, run a batch process that periodically deletes the cached content—you can do this by deleting the folder that contains the cached version.

We can also cache actions by using the `caches_action` directive. Caching an action is beneficial if we want to run some code before or after an action is run (i.e., execute a filter).

If we wanted to ensure that a user was authenticated before the cached version was retrieved, the `caches_action` should be used instead of the `caches_page` directive:

```
caches_action :list
```

Note

The `around_filter` runs code before and after an action in a controller. The `action` cache is an example of an `around` filter.

Active Support

Active Support is a library of extremely useful extensions to the Ruby language. Active Support is used by other Rails components such as Active Record, Action Controller, and Action View. You can take advantage of Active Support's functionality and syntactic magic in your Rails application.

Active Support encompasses a diverse range of extensions—everything from pluralization to enumeration. Each extension will be illustrated with a simple example in the sub-sections that follow. The Rails console will be used in all examples. The Rails console is like the Interactive Ruby Shell (irb), first introduced in Chapter 1 and used in Chapter 2 to help you to learn the essential ingredients of the Ruby language.

Starting the Rails console:

```
$ ruby script/console
```

The `>>` prompt will be displayed. This indicates that you are ready to start trying Active Support:

```
Loading development environment.
>> _
```

Useful String Extensions

In Ruby, `string[4]` returns an integer value when we really want the character at position 4 returned. Active Resource extends the string class with an `at()` method, which does return the character at a given position:

```
>> a_string = "Rails is fun"
=> "Rails is fun"
>> a_string.at(4)
=> "s"
```

We can get the characters of a string up to a specified position with the `to` method:

```
>> a_string.to(7)
=> "Rails is"
```

The `from` method gets all characters from a specified position:

```
>> a_string.from(9)
=> "fun"
```

We can also get the first and last characters of a string:

```
>> a_string.first()
=> "R"
>> a_string.first(4)
=> "Rail"
>> a_string.last(3)
=> "fun"
>> a_string.last
=> "n"
```

Date and Time Calculations

The `to_s` method helps format both `Date` and `Time` objects. The `to_s` method takes `:short` and `:long` as formatting options. The `to_s` method applied to a `Date` object looks like this:

```
>> the_date = Date.today
=> #<Date: 4908201/2,0,2299161>
>> the_date.to_date
=> #<Date: 4908201/2,0,2299161>
>> the_date.to_s
=> "2006-12-31"
>> the_date.to_s(:short)
=> "31 Dec"
>> the_date.to_s(:long)
=> "December 31, 2006"
>> the_date.to_s(:db)
=> "2006-12-31"
```

The `to_s` method applied to a `Time` object:

```
>> the_time = Time.now
=> Sun Dec 31 17:28:55 E. Australia Standard Time 2006
>> the_time.to_s
```

```
=> "Sun Dec 31 17:28:55 E. Australia Standard Time 2006"
>> the_time.to_s(:short)
=> "31 Dec 17:28"
>> the_time.to_s(:long)
=> "December 31, 2006 17:28"
>> the_time.to_s(:db)
=> "2006-12-31 17:28:55"
```

Date and time calculations can now be done in a breeze:

```
>> 30.minutes.ago
=> Sun Dec 31 17:01:08 E. Australia Standard Time 2006
>> 10.hours.ago
=> Sun Dec 31 07:31:22 E. Australia Standard Time 2006
>> 10.hours.from_now
=> Mon Jan 01 03:31:31 E. Australia Standard Time 2007
>> 1.day.from_now
=> Mon Jan 01 17:31:46 E. Australia Standard Time 2007
>> 3.months.ago
=> Mon Oct 02 17:31:57 E. Australia Standard Time 2006
>> Time.days_in_month(2)
=> 28
>> Time.days_in_month(2,2000)
=> 29
```

Convert an Object to JSON or YAML

JavaScript Object Notation (JSON) is a data-interchange format with a small footprint. Like YAML, JSON is easy to read and write. JSON and YAML are good replacements for XML. Active Support extends objects in Ruby with `to_json` and `to_yaml` methods. This is especially useful if we wish to pass objects to Javascript.

```
>> person = Struct.new(:name, :address, :zip)
=> #<Class:0x39c05d8>
>> me = person.new("Aneesha Bakharia","Somewhere, Australia",4122)
=> #<struct #<Class:0x39c05d8> name="Aneesha Bakharia", address="Somewhere, Aust
ralia", zip=4122>
>> me.to_json
=> "[\"Aneesha Bakharia\", \"Somewhere, Australia\", 4122]"
>> me.to_yaml
```

```
=> "--- !ruby/struct: \nname: Aneesha Bakharia\naddress: Somewhere, Australia\nz
ip: 4122\n"
```

Convert XML to a Hash

The `from_xml` method takes a string containing XML and stores each XML element as a key in a hash data structure. This is great because hashes are familiar and easy to work with in Ruby.

```
>> Hash.from_xml
'<blog><blogpost><id>2</id></blogpost><blogpost><id>5</id></blogpost></blog>'
=>{"blog"=>{"blogpost"=>[{"id"=>"2"}, {"id"=>"5"}]}}
```

Fun with Arrays

Active Support array extensions are pure magic. I keep using these in my Rails applications, and I am sure you will find them handy as well. Sometimes I am left wondering why these extensions are not part of the Ruby core.

Add all values in an array:

```
>> [5,10,15].sum
=> 30
```

We can make smart comma-delimited lists with `to_sentence`:

```
>> %w[Aneesha Celine Zaeem Tess].to_sentence
=> "Aneesha, Celine, Zaeem, and Tess"
```

That is great, but you may not want the last comma before the `'and'`. The `:skip_last_comma` option does what its name suggests:

```
>> %w[Aneesha Celine Zaeem Tess].to_sentence(:skip_last_comma => true)
=> "Aneesha, Celine, Zaeem and Tess"
```

The `:connector` option lets us replace the `'and'`:

```
>> %w[Aneesha Celine Zaeem Tess].to_sentence(:connector=> '&')
=> "Aneesha, Celine, Zaeem & Tess"
```

We can break up an array with `in_groups_of`. We pass the number of elements per group to the `in_groups_of` method. Let's split an array with eight elements into groups of two:

```
>> [1,2,3,4,5,6,7,8].in_groups_of(2) {|slice| puts slice.inspect}
=> [1, 2]
[3,4]
[5,6]
[7,6]
```

What if the number of elements isn't divisible by the number of groups we require:

```
>> [1,2,3,4,5,6,7,8].in_groups_of(3) {|slice| puts slice.inspect}
=> [1, 2, 3]
[4, 5, 6]
[7, 8, nil]
```

If 'nil' is not acceptable, we can pass another parameter to the in_group_of **method and provide a replacement:**

```
>> [1,2,3,4,5,6,7,8].in_groups_of(3, "-") {|slice| puts slice.inspect}
=> [1, 2, 3]
[4, 5, 6]
[7, 8, "-"]
```

Setting the second parameter to false **just removes blank elements from the resulting array:**

```
>> [1,2,3,4,5,6,7,8].in_groups_of(3, false) {|slice| puts slice.inspect}
=> [1, 2, 3]
[4, 5, 6]
[7, 8]
```

Numeric Enhancements

I used to write logic to handle the ordinance of a number but then I discovered the ordinalize method. Needless to say I have never looked back.

```
>> 1.ordinalize
=> "1st"
>> 2.ordinalize
=> "2nd"
>> 3.ordinalize
=> "3rd"
>> 4.ordinalize
=> "4th"
>> 5.ordinalize
=> "5th"
>> 21.ordinalize
=> "21st"
```

We can check whether a number is even or odd:

```
>> 8.even?
=> true
```

```
>> 8.odd?
=> false
>> 3.even?
=> false
>> 3.odd?
=> true
```

Using the `multiple_of` **method:**

```
>> 100.multiple_of? 5
=> true
>> 3.multiple_of? 2
=> false
```

Getting the size in `bytes`:

```
>> 20.bytes
=> 20
>> 30.bytes
=> 30
>> 30.kilobytes
=> 30720
>> 30.megabytes
=> 31457280
>> 30.gigabytes
=> 32212254720
>> 30.terabytes
=> 32985348833280
```

Pluralization

Pluralization in Rails is pretty smart—Rails has a good handle on the pluralization rules for the English language. Let's see just how smart it really is:

```
>> "dog".pluralize
=> "dogs"
>> "cake".pluralize
=> "cakes"
>> "chocolate".pluralize
=> "chocolates"
>> "box".pluralize
```

```
=> "boxes"
>> "horse".pluralize
=> "horses"
>> "mouse".pluralize
=> "mice"
>> "leaf".pluralize
=> "leafs"
```

Oops! The plural of leaf is not leafs. Let's try a few more:

```
>> "man".pluralize
=> "men"
>> "criterion".pluralize
=> "criterions"
```

The plural of criterion is criteria. Rails does a good job but is admittedly not perfect. Hopefully, thorough testing will reveal the words of incorrect pluralizations and we can add rules to the inflector module. We can define words that have irregular or no plurals as well as a new plural for a word with an incorrect plural. In the `confide` directory, you will find the `environment.rb` file. We will add a new inflector rule to deal with the incorrect `"leaf"` plural:

```
Inflector.inflections do |inflect|
      inflect.irregular "leaf", "leaves"
end
```

To get Rails to pick up the new rules, we need to exit and restart the Rails console:

```
$ ruby script/console
Loading development environment."
>> "leaf".pluralize
=> "leaves"
>> "leaves".singularize
=> "leaf"
```

Conclusion

Three diverse but nonetheless important Rails features were covered in this chapter: filters, caching, and Active Resource. This is the last chapter in which additional Rails functionality will be introduced. In the chapter that follows, we will change our focus to implementing real-world web applications. Enjoy the ride!

13 } Testing and Debugging

Rails is fully integrated with `Test::Unit`, Ruby's unit testing framework. Models, controllers, actions, and even complex user scenarios that span multiple controllers are able to be tested. The model and controller generators create stub test files to remove all barriers of entry. Testing is now fully part of the development process. Testing uncovers bugs, so a few techniques to help you debug your application are also included.

In this chapter you'll learn to:

* Use the Ruby unit testing framework (`Test::Unit`)
* Set up a database for testing
* Unit test models
* Functional test controllers
* Write integration tests across controllers and actions
* Determine the percentage of code covered during testing
* Display debug information
* Write debug statements to log files
* Check code for syntax errors

Using the Ruby Unit Testing Framework (Test::Unit)

`Test::Unit` is the unit testing framework that is included in the Ruby standard library. Rails uses `Test::Unit` behind the scenes for unit, functional, and integration testing, so it makes sense to first learn to use `Test::Unit` to unit test a simple class.

Our class is called `Employee` and is saved to a directory called `employee/app`. The employee directory can be thought of as the project directory. Application code within a project is saved to the `/app` directory. The `Employee` class has accessor methods for `firstname` and lastname. **It also has a method that concatenates the** firstname **and** lastname **and returns a** fullname.

```
class Employee
     attr_accessor :firstname, :lastname
     def initialize(firstname, lastname)
          @firstname, @lastname = firstname, lastname
     end
     def fullname
          firstname + ' ' + lastname
     end
end
```

The unit test for the Employee **class is placed in a directory called** test. **The unit test filename is the name of the class being unit tested with** _test **appended. The name of the class is just the class name appended with** Test. **The unit test class extends the** Test::Unit::TestCase **framework class. We require the** Employee **class and** test/unit. **Each method in the** EmployeeTest **class is a test and is able to make numerous assertions. The names of methods must be prefixed with** test_. **An assertion simply checks that a value returned by the class being tested matches what we determine to be the correct response.**

```
# test/employee_test.rb
require File.join(File.dirname(__FILE__), '..', 'app', 'employee')
require 'test/unit'
class EmployeeTest < Test::Unit::TestCase
     def test_firstname
          employee = Employee.new('Aneesha', 'Bakharia')
          assert_equal 'Aneesha', employee.firstname
     end
     def test_lastname
          employee = Employee.new('Celine', 'Bakharia')
          assert_equal 'Bakharia', employee.lastname
     end
     def test_fullname
          employee = Employee.new('Celine', 'Bakharia')
          assert_equal 'Celine Bakharia', employee.fullname
     end
end
```

The `test_firstname` test initializes an `Employee` object with a first and last name. It then retrieves the `firstname` attribute and checks if the returned value matches the value that was passed to the constructor. The `assert_equal` method is used to check that the values match. The `test_lastname` asserts that the `lastname` attribute is working. The `test_fullname` method checks that the `lastname` and `firstname` attributes are concatenated.

> **Tip**
>
> A *test suite* consists of a number of test cases.

We now are able to run the test. Because the test is just a Ruby file, we can just type:

```
$ ruby test/employee_test.rb
```

We receive feedback that three tests, three assertions, zero failures, and zero errors have occurred:

```
Loaded suite test/employee_test
Started
..
Finished in 0.0 seconds.

3 tests, 3 assertions, 0 failures, 0 errors
```

Let's alter the `Employee` class so that the test will fail. Suppose that another developer wants to use the `fullname` method but requires that a comma be placed between the first and last names. The other developer does not realize that the code might be used in multiple places. This is a fairly trivial example, but it often occurs in real life.

```
class Employee
     attr_accessor :firstname, :lastname
     def initialize(firstname, lastname)
          @firstname, @lastname = firstname, lastname
     end
     def fullname
          firstname + ', ' + lastname
     end
end
```

Before the code is deployed, the test case is run again—this time with a failed test:

```
$ ruby test/employee_test.rb
Loaded suite test/employee_test
Started
.F.
Finished in 0.125 seconds.
  1) Failure:
test_fullname(EmployeeTest) [test/employee_test.rb:16]:
<"Celine Bakharia"> expected but was <"Celine, Bakharia">.
3 tests, 3 assertions, 1 failures, 0 errors
```

> ❄ **Tip**
> A version control system such as Subversion or CSV will help you track down where a change has occurred and by whom when a test case does eventually fail.

The `assert_equal` is one example of an assertion method; there are many more at your disposal. Table 13.1 displays a list of assertion methods that `Test::Unit` supports. Some methods take a message as an optional argument. The message gets displayed if the assertion fails.

Table 13.1   Test::Unit Assertions

Assertion	Description
`assert(boolean, [message])`	Assertion is passed if the Boolean is true. The `message` parameter is optional.
`assert_equal(expected, actual, [message])`	Assertion is passed if `expected` is equal to `actual`.
`assert_not_equal(expected, actual, [message])`	Assertion is passed if `expected` is not equal to `actual`.
`assert_match(pattern, string, [message])`	Assertion is passed if `string` matches `pattern`.
`assert_no_match(pattern, string, [message])`	Assertion is passed if `string` does not match `pattern`.
`assert_nil(object, [message])`	Assertion is passed if `object` is nil.
`assert_not_nil(object, [message])`	Assertion is passed if `object` is not nil.

Assertion	Description
`assert_instance_of(class, object, [message])`	Assertion is passed if `object` is of type `class`.
`assert_raise(Exception1, Exception2, ... ) {block}`	Assertion is passed if one of the exceptions is raised by the block.
`assert_nothing_raised(Exception1, Exception2, ... ) {block}`	Assertion is passed if none of the exceptions are raised by the block.

> ❋ **Tip**
>
> Within a test case, we can include `setup` and `teardown` methods. Use the `setup` method to load data that will be used by the tests or establish database connections. The `teardown` method gets executed after all tests have been run. The `teardown` method is the ideal place to put clean-up code and close database connections.

Setting Up the Test Database

Testing in Rails requires its own database. Before a test begins, the data in the test database gets deleted and repopulated. It is wise to create a database that is named after your project and has _test appended when you create your development database. This will allow you to start writing tests from the very beginning and instill a practice of continual testing. The test database is specified in the `config/database.yml` file. In this example, the `testingrails_development` and `testingrails_test` database connections are specified:

```
development:
  adapter: mysql
  database: testingrails_development
  username: root
  password: secret
  host: localhost
# Warning: The database defined as 'test' will be erased and
# re-generated from your development database when you run 'rake'.
# Do not set this db to the same as development or production.
test:
  adapter: mysql
  database: testingrails_test
  username: root
```

```
   password: secret
   host: localhost
production:
   adapter: mysql
   database: testingrails_production
   username: root
   password: secret
   host: localhost
```

The test database is an empty database. We will use migrations to create tables and columns in the development database. When we are ready to test, we need to copy the schema to the test database. This is easily achieved by a `rake` command:

```
$ rake db:test:prepare
```

Testing in Rails

Rails has been encouraging us to write tests from the moment we created our very first application. All new Rails applications have a `tests` directory. Within the `tests` directory, the following subdirectories are found:

fixtures: The `fixtures` directory contains YAML files (`.yml`) that are used to populate a test database prior to running the actual tests.

unit: The `unit` directory contains unit tests. In Rails, unit tests are used to test models.

functional: Functional tests are placed in the `functional` directory. Functional tests are used to test controllers and actions in Rails.

integration: Integration tests simulate user activity on your site and test functionality across controllers and actions.

Create a Rails application called `testingrails`:

```
$ rails testingrails
```

The `test/unit` and `test/test_helper.rb` file is created:

```
   create  test/unit
   create  test/test_helper.rb
```

Each time you create a model or a controller, the generator script also creates a skeleton file for the unit and functional tests:

```
$ ruby script/generate model user
     exists   app/models/
     exists   test/unit/
     exists   test/fixtures/
     create   app/models/user.rb
     create   test/unit/user_test.rb
     create   test/fixtures/users.yml
     create   db/migrate
     create   db/migrate/001_create_users.rb
$ ruby script/generate controller users
     exists   app/controllers/
     exists   app/helpers/
     create   app/views/users
     exists   test/functional/
     create   app/controllers/users_controller.rb
     create   test/functional/users_controller_test.rb
     create   app/helpers/users_helper.rb
```

Unit Testing Models

In Rails, models are unit tested. Unit tests use `Test::Unit` and are placed in the `tests/unit` folder. A common test to perform on models is to check if the validation works as desired. We will create a table called `users` in our database with four columns: firstname, lastname, username, and email.

Generate a user model:

```
$ ruby script/generate model user
```

Now we can edit the migration (`001_create_users.rb`) and create the users table:

```
class CreateUsers < ActiveRecord::Migration
  def self.up
    create_table :users do |t|
      t.column :username, :string
      t.column :firstname, :string
      t.column :lasttname, :string
      t.column :email, :string
    end
  end
end
```

```
    def self.down
        drop_table :users
    end
end
```

We run the migration:

```
$ rake db:migrate
(in C:/rails/testingrails)
== CreateUsers: migrating ========================================================
-- create_table(:users)
    -> 0.0790s
== CreateUsers: migrated (0.0790s) ===============================================
```

We add validation helpers to the user model (app/models/user.rb):

```
class User < ActiveRecord::Base
      validates_presence_of :firstname, :lastname, :username
      validates_format_of :email,
                            :with => /^([^@\s]+)@((?:[-a-z0-9]+\.)+[a-z]{2,})$/i
end
```

We are just about to start writing tests, but because our test database is empty, we need to copy the schema from the development database:

```
$ rake db:test:prepare
```

The test/unit/user_test.rb **file was created by the model generator. The file is a skeleton for a unit test. The class inherits from** Test::Unit::TestCase **as expected. It also includes a dummy test that always passes. The reason for the inclusion of** test_truth **is to allow you to run tests even if a test was just added:**

```
require File.dirname(__FILE__) + '/../test_helper'
class UserTest < Test::Unit::TestCase
  fixtures :users
  # Replace this with your real tests.
  def test_truth
    assert true
  end
end
```

We edit the `test/unit/user_test.rb` file and add a `test_validation` method. We initialize a user and then assert that the object is not valid. It won't be valid because the mandatory fields (`firstname`, `lastname`, and `username`) have not been set. We also assert that the `errors` object contains error messages for the invalid fields:

```
require File.dirname(__FILE__) + '/../test_helper'
class UserTest < Test::Unit::TestCase
     fixtures :users
     def test_validation
          user = User.new
          assert !user.valid?
          assert user.errors.invalid?(:firstname)
          assert user.errors.invalid?(:lastname)
     end
end
```

We run the test:

```
$ ruby test/unit/user_test.rb
```

Our one test and one assertion have passed:

```
Loaded suite test/unit/user_test
Started
.
Finished in 0.219 seconds.

1 tests, 1 assertions, 0 failures, 0 errors
```

Let's add another test called `test_email_validation`. In this test we will use the `assert_equal` method to make sure that the appropriate message is returned if an invalid email address is assigned to the `email` attribute:

```
require File.dirname(__FILE__) + '/../test_helper'
class UserTest < Test::Unit::TestCase
     fixtures :users
     def test_validation
          user = User.new
          assert !user.valid?
          assert user.errors.invalid?(:firstname)
          assert user.errors.invalid?(:lastname)
```

```
        end
    def test_email_validation
            user = User.new(:email => "invalidemail.com")
            assert !user.valid?
            assert_equal "is invalid", user.errors.on(:email)
    end
end
```

Now we will have two successful tests and five successful assertions:

```
$ ruby test/unit/user_test.rb
Loaded suite test/unit/user_test
Started
..
Finished in 1.031 seconds.

2 tests, 5 assertions, 0 failures, 0 errors
```

> ❄ **Tip**
>
> You will no doubt have multiple unit tests (one for each model). All tests can be run by typing rake
> test:units at the command line.

Using Fixtures

We have thus far used Active Record objects to help simulate the addition and validation of data. What if we need to perform tests on data already in a database? Fixtures allow us to prepopulate a test database with data. Each time we run a test, the test database will be returned to the state specified by the fixture. Fixtures are placed in the tests/fixtures directory. A fixture for the user model is created by the model generator (users.yml):

```
# Read about fixtures at http://ar.rubyonrails.org/classes/Fixtures.html
first:
  id: 1
another:
  id: 2
```

A fixture could use the YAML or CSV format. The default file that has been generated uses YAML because this is the preferred format. The file is named after the database table and not the model—it is a plural word.

Each row of data that will be inserted into the table is labeled. This allows us to refer to it within the test case. The name/value pairs are not indented—spaces are used. Be very careful to preserve the spaces when you edit or insert more rows, because the YAML parser will throw errors if it can't parse the file.

To illustrate the usefulness of fixtures, we will use a fixture to help test that we can't add a duplicate username to the users table. The `validates_uniqueness_of` helper is used to enforce this validation:

```
class User < ActiveRecord::Base
     validates_uniqueness_of :username
     validates_presence_of :firstname, :lastname, :username
     validates_format_of :email,
                          :with => /^([^@\s]+)@((?:[-a-z0-9]+\.)+[a-z]{2,})$/i
end
```

We edit the `users.yml` fixture and create a record named `first_user`:

```
# Read about fixtures at http://ar.rubyonrails.org/classes/Fixtures.html
first_user:
  id: 1
  username: aneesha
  firstname: Aneesha
  lastname: Bakharia
  email: aneesha.bakharia@gmail.com
```

In the `test/unit/user_test.rb` file we add the fixture directive (`fixtures :users`) so that we can use the fixture in the test. The fixture directive will force all records in the users table to be deleted and populated with the data specified in the fixture before each test commences. We can use the labels in the `users.yml` file to return an Active Record object: Calling `users (:first_user)` returns a user model with the data defined for that row in the fixture. We now add a test to ensure no duplicate usernames can be stored:

```
require File.dirname(__FILE__) + '/../test_helper'
class UserTest < Test::Unit::TestCase
     fixtures :users
     def test_unique_username
          user = User.new(:username => users(:first_user).username)
          assert !user.save
          assert_equal "has already been taken", user.errors.on(:username)
```

```
      end
end
```

As a matter of interest this is what a CSV fixture looks like:

```
id, username, firstname, lastname, email
1, "aneesha", "Aneesha", "Bakharia", "aneesha.bakharia@gmail.com"
2, "celine", "Celine", "Bakharia", "cb@randomsyntax.com"
```

Functional Testing Controllers

In Rails, testing a controller and its actions is called a functional testing. Functional tests still use `Test::Unit` but are able to simulate HTTP requests to a controller's action (just like the ones made by a web browser) and inspect the response. When the controller generator is used, a skeleton functional test is created as well:

```
$ ruby script/generate controller users
      exists   app/controllers/
      exists   app/helpers/
      create   app/views/users
      exists   test/functional/
      create   app/controllers/users_controller.rb
      create   test/functional/users_controller_test.rb
      create   app/helpers/users_helper.rb
```

The generated functional test inherits from `Test::Unit::TestCase` and contains the `test_truth` method that always returns `true`. There is an extra method called `setup`. The `setup` method is run before the test methods. Within the `setup` method, a new instance of the controller is created. Request and response objects are also created and allow us to perform functional tests that would normally only be run from within a web browser.

```
require File.dirname(__FILE__) + '/../test_helper'
require 'users_controller'
# Re-raise errors caught by the controller.
class UsersController; def rescue_action(e) raise e end; end
class UsersControllerTest < Test::Unit::TestCase
  def setup
    @controller = UsersController.new
    @request    = ActionController::TestRequest.new
    @response   = ActionController::TestResponse.new
  end
```

```
    # Replace this with your real tests.
    def test_truth
      assert true
    end
end
```

Our sample controller called `UsersController` (`users_controller.rb`) is exceptionally simple but will illustrate key functional testing concepts. The controller has three actions. The `index` action displays the `index.rhtml` template. The `list` action just redirects to the `index` action. The `setflash` action stores a message in `flash[:notice]` and then redirects to the `index` action.

```
class UsersController < ApplicationController
    def index
    end
    def list
        redirect_to :action => 'index'
    end
    def setflash
        flash[:notice] = 'The item was successfully created.'
        redirect_to :action => 'index'
    end
end
```

In a test case we use the `get` method to call the `index` action and the `assert_response` method to ensure that the request was a success:

```
def test_index
  get :index
  assert_response :success
end
```

We could even use the `assert_template` method to check that the `index.rhtml` template was rendered:

```
def test_index_template
  get :index
  assert_response :success
  assert_template "index"
end
```

The `list` action redirects to the `index` action, so after using `get` to request the action, we use `assert_redirected_to` to make sure that we are redirected to the `index` action:

```
def test_list_redirection
  get :list
  assert_redirected_to :action => "index"
end
```

We can even check that the `flash` has the correct value with `assert_equal`:

```
def test_set_flash
  get :set_flash
  assert_redirected_to :action => "index"
  assert_equal "The item was successfully created.", flash[:notice]
end
```

Here is the full code listing for the `test/functional/users_controller_test.rb` file:

```
require File.dirname(__FILE__) + '/../test_helper'
require 'users_controller'
# Re-raise errors caught by the controller.
class UsersController; def rescue_action(e) raise e end; end
class UsersControllerTest < Test::Unit::TestCase
  def setup
    @controller = UsersController.new
    @request    = ActionController::TestRequest.new
    @response   = ActionController::TestResponse.new
  end
  def test_index
    get :index
    assert_response :success
  end
  def test_index_template
    get :index
    assert_response :success
    assert_template "index"
  end
  def test_list_redirection
    get :list
    assert_redirected_to :action => "index"
```

```
    end
  def test_list_redirection
    get :list
    assert_redirected_to :action => "index"
  end
  def test_set_flash
    get :set_flash
    assert_redirected_to :action => "index"
    assert_equal "The item was successfully created.", flash[:notice]
  end
end
```

The four tests and eight assertions all run successfully:

```
$ rake test:functionals
(in C:/rails/testingrails)
c:/ruby/bin/ruby-Ilib;test"c:/ruby/lib/ruby/gems/1.8/gems/rake-0.7.1/lib/rake/
rake_test_loader.rb" "test/functional/users_controller_test.rb"
Loadedsuitec:/ruby/lib/ruby/gems/1.8/gems/rake-0.7.1/lib/rake/rake_test_loader

Started
....
Finished in 0.875 seconds.

4 tests, 8 assertions, 0 failures, 0 errors
```

Rails adds several assertions to help with functional testing (see Table 13.2). In the previous example we used `assert_response`, `assert_redirected_to`, **and** `assert_template`.

Table 13.2 Rails-Specific Assertions

Assertion	Description
assert_dom_equal	Assertion returns true if two HTML strings are the same.
assert_dom_not_equal	Assertion returns true if two HTML strings are not the same.
assert_tag	Assertion returns true if the body of the response contains a tag/node/ element that matches the specified conditions.
assert_recognizes	Assertion returns true if the routing rules parse the specified URL path.
assert_redirected_to	Assertion returns true if a redirection occurs to the specified action.

Assertion	Description
assert_response	Assertion returns true if the specified HTTP response code is returned.
assert_template	Assertion returns true if the specified template file was used to generate the response.
assert_valid	Assertion returns true if the Active Record object is valid.

Posting Form Data

Within a functional test, we can simulate a form post and then check that the posted form data is displayed. In the previous section we used the get method to make a request; we will now use the post method in a functional test. The assert_tag will help us check whether the returned response contains the posted data.

We start by generating a controller:

```
$ ruby script/generate controller formprocessor
        exists   app/controllers/
        exists   app/helpers/
        create   app/views/formprocessor
        exists   test/functional/
        create   app/controllers/formprocessor_controller.rb
        create   test/functional/formprocessor_controller_test.rb
        create   app/helpers/formprocessor_helper.rb
```

The controller (formprocessor_controller.rb) has two actions. The showform action renders showform.rhtml, which displays a form with a single field called name. The show_formdata action receives the posted data, sets the @name variable, and then renders show_formdata.

```
class FormprocessorController < ApplicationController
    def showform
    end
    def show_formdata
        @name = params[:name]
    end
end
```

The show_formdata.rhtml template:

```
<h2>A Simple Form</h2>
<%= start_form_tag(:action => "show_formdata") %>
```

```
<p>Text Field:
<%= text_field_tag("name","Aneesha") %></p>
<%= submit_tag("Submit Form") %>
<%= end_form_tag %>
```

The `showform.rhtml` **template displays the** `@name` **variable within opening and closing** `<h2>` **tags:**

```
<h2>Name: <%= @name %></h2>
```

We now edit `formprocessor_controller_test.rb` **and add a** `test_show_formdata` **test. We use** `assert_tag` **to check that the text between the opening and closing** `<h2>` **tags matches the name posted to the form:**

```
require File.dirname(__FILE__) + '/../test_helper'
require 'formprocessor_controller'
# Re-raise errors caught by the controller.
class FormprocessorController; def rescue_action(e) raise e end; end
class FormprocessorControllerTest < Test::Unit::TestCase
  def setup
    @controller = FormprocessorController.new
    @request    = ActionController::TestRequest.new
    @response   = ActionController::TestResponse.new
  end
  def test_show_formdata
    post :show_formdata, :name => 'Aneesha'
    assert_response :success
    assert_template "show_formdata"
    assert_tag :tag => "h2", :content => "Name: Aneesha"
  end
end
```

We run the one test and three assertions:

```
$ ruby test/functional/formprocessor_controller_test.rb
Loaded suite test/functional/formprocessor_controller_test
Started
.
Finished in 0.141 seconds.

1 tests, 3 assertions, 0 failures, 0 errors
```

Scaffolding and Functional Testing

In Chapter 3, "Prototyping Database-Driven Applications with Rails," we created an FAQ Manager that primarily used the Rails scaffold generator. You'll be pleased to know that even the `scaffold` command generates a functional test, and it's not just a stub file. It actually has tests for each action, including `show`, `new`, `create`, and `destroy`. Please review the `faq_controller_test.rb` file; it is a useful learning tool for writing CRUD functional tests:

```ruby
require File.dirname(__FILE__) + '/../test_helper'
require 'faq_controller'
# Re-raise errors caught by the controller.
class FaqController; def rescue_action(e) raise e end; end
class FaqControllerTest < Test::Unit::TestCase
  fixtures :faqs
  def setup
    @controller = FaqController.new
    @request    = ActionController::TestRequest.new
    @response   = ActionController::TestResponse.new
  end
  def test_index
    get :index
    assert_response :success
    assert_template 'list'
  end
  def test_list
    get :list
    assert_response :success
    assert_template 'list'
    assert_not_nil assigns(:faqs)
  end
  def test_show
    get :show, :id => 1
    assert_response :success
    assert_template 'show'
    assert_not_nil assigns(:faq)
    assert assigns(:faq).valid?
  end
  def test_new
```

```ruby
    get :new
    assert_response :success
    assert_template 'new'
    assert_not_nil assigns(:faq)
  end
  def test_create
    num_faqs = Faq.count
    post :create, :faq => {}
    assert_response :redirect
    assert_redirected_to :action => 'list'
    assert_equal num_faqs + 1, Faq.count
  end
  def test_edit
    get :edit, :id => 1
    assert_response :success
    assert_template 'edit'
    assert_not_nil assigns(:faq)
    assert assigns(:faq).valid?
  end
  def test_update
    post :update, :id => 1
    assert_response :redirect
    assert_redirected_to :action => 'show', :id => 1
  end
  def test_destroy
    assert_not_nil Faq.find(1)
    post :destroy, :id => 1
    assert_response :redirect
    assert_redirected_to :action => 'list'
    assert_raise(ActiveRecord::RecordNotFound) {
      Faq.find(1)
    }
  end
end
end
```

Authentication

In Chapter 12, we used filters to force a user to log in before being allowed to see certain admin-only areas of a web site. We are now going to build a functional test to ensure that our authentication is working correctly.

Before we get started, let's take another look at the user model. Note that the password is encrypted and stored in the hash_password field:

```
require 'digest/sha2'
class User < ActiveRecord::Base
     validates_uniqueness_of :username

     def password=(pass)
          self.hashed_password = Digest::SHA256.hexdigest(pass)
     end
end
```

In the controller, the authentication_check method is applied as a filter for all actions except login. If the user has not logged in (session[:username] is not set) a login page is shown. The login page requires a username and password and posts back to the login action. If the username and password are in the database, the user is allowed access to the other actions. If they are invalid, a message is added to the flash and shown on the login form. Here is the source code for the Admin controller:

```
require 'digest/sha2'
class AdminController < ApplicationController
     before_filter :authentication_check, :except => [:login]
     def authentication_check
          unless session[:username]
               session[:intended_action] = action_name
               session[:intended_controller] = controller_name
               redirect_to :action => "login"
          end
      end
    def login
          if request.post?
       user = User.find(:first,
                         :conditions => ['username = ?',
                         params[:username]])
          if user.blank? || Digest::SHA256.hexdigest(params[:password]) !=
```

```
                              user.hashed_password
            flash[:info] = "Invalid Username or Password!"
            redirect_to :action => "login"
            return
        end
              session[:username] = user.username
              redirect_to :action => session[:intended_action], :controller =>
session[:intended_controller]
            end
      end
      def logout
          session[:username] = nil
      end
      def show_admin
      end
    end
end
```

With the fixture (`users.yml`) we add a username and password to validate against. The password is encrypted. This would present a problem except that fixtures are able to include Embedded Ruby. We can use the `<%=` and `%>` delimiters. This is very powerful, and we can encrypt the password using Ruby:

```
# Read about fixtures at http://ar.rubyonrails.org/classes/Fixtures.html
<% require 'digest/sha2' %>
aneesha:
  id: 1
  username: aneesha
  hashed_password: <%=Digest::SHA256.hexdigest('donttellme') %>
```

In the `test_login` method, we post the username and password to the `login` action and check that `session[:username]` has been set:

```
def test_login
  aneesha = users(:aneesha)
  post :login, :username => aneesha.username, :password => 'donttellme'
  assert_equal aneesha.username, session[:username]
end
```

The `test_invalid_password` method posts an incorrect password to the `login` action and checks that `flash[:info]` is set:

```
def test_invalid_password
  aneesha = users(:aneesha)
  post :login, :username => aneesha.username, :password => 'tellme'
  assert_redirected_to :action => "login"
  assert_equal "Invalid Username or Password!", flash[:info]
end
```

The full source code listing for the `admin_controller_test.rb`:

```
require File.dirname(__FILE__) + '/../test_helper'
require 'admin_controller'
# Re-raise errors caught by the controller.
class AdminController; def rescue_action(e) raise e end; end
class AdminControllerTest < Test::Unit::TestCase
  fixtures :users
  def setup
    @controller = AdminController.new
    @request    = ActionController::TestRequest.new
    @response   = ActionController::TestResponse.new
  end
  def test_login
    aneesha = users(:aneesha)
    post :login, :username => aneesha.username, :password => 'donttellme'
    assert_equal aneesha.username, session[:username]
  end
  def test_invalid_password
    aneesha = users(:aneesha)
    post :login, :username => aneesha.username, :password => 'tellme'
    assert_redirected_to :action => "login"
    assert_equal "Invalid Username or Password!", flash[:info]
  end
end
```

Integration Testing

Integration tests allow you to model tests based upon the activity performed by your users or web site visitors. Functional tests are able to test only a single controller. With integration tests, we can test across controllers and actions. Integration tests were first introduced in Rails 1.1.

Unlike unit and functional tests, integration tests are not created when a model or controller is generated. However, there is an integration test generator:

```
$ ruby script/generate integration_test user_scenario
```

Running the `intergration_test` **generator will create a test file:**

```
exists test/integration/
create test/integration/user_ scenario_test.rb
```

The stub file inherits from `IntegrationTest`. **You can include multiple fixtures:**

```
require "#{File.dirname(__FILE__)}/../test_helper"
class UserScenarioTest < ActionController::IntegrationTest
# fixtures :your, :models
# Replace this with your real tests.
  def test_truth
    assert true
  end
end
```

In the following example we test that a user can register and then log in:

```
require "#{File.dirname(__FILE__)}/../test_helper"
class UserScenarioTest < ActionController::IntegrationTest
    fixtures :user, :preferences
    def test_register_new_user
        get "/register"
        assert_response :success
        assert_template "register/regform"
        post "/register",
        :user_name => "aneesha",
        :password => "donttellme"
        assert_response :redirect
        follow_redirect!
        assert_response :success
    end
end
```

You can use `rake` **to run all tests found in the** `tests/integrations` **directory:**

```
rake test::integration
```

Tip

When a user reports a bug, write a test to reproduce the error. This will increase the number of integration tests and also give you ideas on the types of integration tests you should be building. When changes are made to your application, you can also ensure that the same bugs don't creep in again.

Tip

If you'd like to test AJAX within your application, try Selenium. Selenium runs inside a browser and has a recorder to help you design tests. More information on Selenium can be found at http://www.openqa.org/selenium/.

Code Coverage

It is good to get an indication of how much code you have written in relation to test code. Ideally you should aim to get close to a 1:1 ratio to make sure everything your code is doing gets tested. The `rake stats` command prints code and test statistics:

```
$ rake stats
(in C:/rails/authentication)
```

Name	Lines	LOC	Classes	Methods	M/C	LOC/M
Helpers	7	6	0	0	0	0
Controllers	74	58	5	9	1	4
Components	0	0	0	0	0	0
Functional tests	46	35	4	7	1	3
Models	9	7	1	1	1	5
Unit tests	10	7	1	1	1	5
Libraries	0	0	0	0	0	0
Integration tests	0	0	0	0	0	0
Total	146	113	11	18	1	4

```
  Code LOC: 71      Test LOC: 42      Code to Test Ratio: 1:0.6
```

The `rake stats` command traverses through all the folders in your application and prints the number of lines of code, number of classes, and number of methods in an ASCII table. The code to test ratio is also displayed.

How do we know that we have tested everything? Code is often made up of complex logic! How do we ensure that every scenario is tested? The `rake stats` command just gives us a ratio but can't tell us which segments of code have not been tested. A useful tool called `rcov` can run tests and then produce a report that will show the code segments that have not been tested.

A `gem` is used to install `rcov`:

```
$ gem install rcov
```

If your operating system is Windows, make sure you select the mswin32 version.

We now tell `rcov` to determine the code coverage of all the functional tests. We have removed a test to check if the `flash` was set before a redirection occurs. This means that not all code is tested. Let's see if `rcov` can pick this up:

```
$ rcov test/functional/*
Loaded suite c:/ruby/bin/rcov
Started
....
Finished in 0.141 seconds.

4 tests, 8 assertions, 0 failures, 0 errors
```

The output of `rcov` looks like that from a routine functional test, but behind the scenes `rcov` produces a coverage report and places it in the `/coverage/` directory. Open the `index.html` to view the report (see Figure 13.1). A list of files and their percentage of code coverage is shown. The `app/controllers/users_controller.rb` file has only 63% test

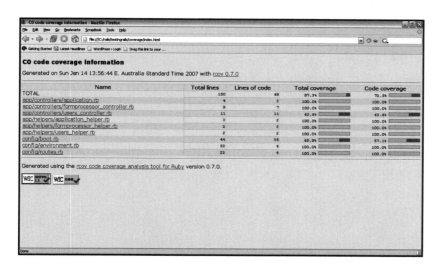

Figure 13.1
The rcov report.

coverage. We can click on the link to see the code segment that has not been tested (see Figure 13.2). In this case, the `setflash` action has not been tested.

Figure 13.2
Code not tested by a functional test.

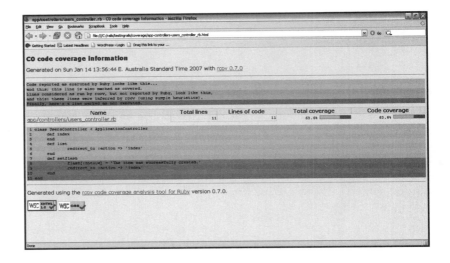

Debugging

This section includes some handy techniques to help you fix errors, whether they are detected while you are coding or after running a test suite.

Using the debug Helper

The `debug` helper can be used in a view (`.rthml`) template. The `debug` helper is able to output the contents of HTTP headers, the `params` hash, the `request` object, the `response` object, and all the data stored in a session.

An example template using all the `debug` variations:

```
<h2>Headers:</h2>
<%= debug(headers) %><br />
<h2>Environment Variables:</h2>
<%= debug(request.env) %><br />
<h2>Params hash:</h2>
<%= debug(params) %><br />
```

```
<h2>Request:</h2>
<%= debug(request) %><br />
<h2>Response:</h2>
<%= debug(response) %><br />
<h2>Session</h2>
<%= debug(session) %><br />
```

❋ **Tip**

The `raise` method can be used to convert any object into a string. This is a useful technique to print the attributes of an object. To make the result more readable we convert to YAML:

```
def index
    @user = User.find_by_firstname()
    raise @user.to_yaml
end
```

Using the Built-In Logger Class

Rails includes development and production log files. Log files are stored in the `#{RAILS_ROOT}/log` directory. The `Logger` class can be used to write custom entries into log files. The `Logger` class supports severity levels: debug, info, warn, error, and fatal.

Examples to add entries with varying severity:

```
logger.debug "A sample debug message"
logger.info "A sample info message"
logger.warn "A sample warn message"
logger.error "A sample error message"
logger.fatal "A sample fatal message"
```

The following will be inserted into the log:

```
DEBUG A sample debug message
INFO A sample info message
WARN A sample warn message
ERROR A sample error message
FATAL A sample fatal message
```

Within the `config/environment.rb` file, we can set the lowest severity level that we would like to output. All levels of greater severity will also be output:

```
Rails::Initializer.run do |config|
     config.log_level = :debug
end
```

There are also methods to test whether logger severity is supported in the current environment (development or production):

- ❋ `logger.debug?`
- ❋ `logger.info?`
- ❋ `logger.warn?`
- ❋ `logger.error?`
- ❋ `logger.fatal?`

We can therefore check if a severity level is supported before we try to write to the log:

```
if logger.debug? then
     logger.debug "A debug message"
end
```

> ❋ **Tip**
>
> Within the `config/environment.rb` file we can specify the format of a log entry. In this example we add a timestamp:
>
> ```
> class Logger
>     def format_message(severity, timestamp, progname, msg)
>         "[#{timestamp.strftime("%Y-%m-%d %H:%M:%S")}] #{severity} #{msg}\n
>     end
> end
> ```

Checking Code for Syntax Errors

In Chapter 2, "Ruby Essentials," we learned to use command switches for the Ruby interpreter. The -cw switch enables us to check the syntax of Ruby code and display warning messages. The -cw switch does not execute code. We can use the switch to check the code in models and controllers before we request an action in a browser:

```
$ ruby -cw app/models/user.rb
```

Conclusion

We have unit tests to test our models, functional tests to test actions in a controller, fixtures to help us load test data into the test database, and integration tests to simulate user activity that spans multiple controllers and actions. Testing in Rails is fully integrated! Generators even help you with skeleton files to help you get started. You don't have any excuse not to write test cases and improve the quality and reliability of your application as it is maintained and upgraded. This chapter also included some useful debugging techniques.

14 } Designing Rails Applications

In this chapter we apply all that we have learned throughout the book to design and build two Rails applications—a wiki and a forum. We start with a feature list for each application, install required plug-ins and libraries, use migrations to create the database, add validation rules to the model, program the logic for the controller, and design the view templates.

Designing a Wiki

A wiki allows web pages to be created, updated, and hyperlinked in a simple and intuitive manner. Wikipedia is the most well known wiki, but in recent years it is hard to find a web application, framework, or technology that does not use a wiki to allow for the collaborative creation and versioning of documentation. We are going to design and build a wiki with Rails.

Features

We are going to design a simple, yet functional wiki. The following key features are required:

* **Wiki markup.** We need to support textile formatting. Users have come to rely on and are familiar with wiki. We can easily implement this functionality by using the `textilize` helper. We need to install RedCloth before we are able to use the `textilize` helper.

* **The ability to create, edit, and version pages.** No problem with creating and updating pages in Rails. Versioning should not be too difficult but instead of making our own solution, we choose to use the `acts_as_versioned` plug-in that was introduced in Chapter 11.

* **Hyperlink CamelCased words.** CamelCased words are links to new or existing pages in a wiki. We will use a regular expression to hyperlink CamelCased words. If a page that is linked to is not found, a form allowing the user to create the page will be displayed.

* **List all wiki pages.** A list of all pages with links to edit and view each page.

❊ **Version history.** Display a list of versions and allow the user to revert to either a previous or more recent version of a page. The `acts_as_versioned` plug-in has a `revert_to` method, which we will use to implement this feature.

We would also like to use a differencing algorithm to compare two versions. We would like to see additions and deletions in a visual manner. A quick search on the Rails mailing list reveals a solution proposed by Beate Paland. The solution uses the `diff.rb` file from Instiki (a wiki built in to Ruby): http://dev.instiki.org/file/instiki/trunk/lib/diff.rb.

❊ **Intuitive navigation.** A navigation panel must be displayed on the right side of the page. The panel must be available on all pages and must provide links to show page history, edit the page, return to the home page, and display a list of all pages in the wiki.

Layout

We create a two-column layout in the style sheet. The wiki contents will be displayed in the left column while the navigation will be displayed on the right. Figure 14.1 shows the layout rendered in a web browser.

Figure 14.1
The wiki layout.

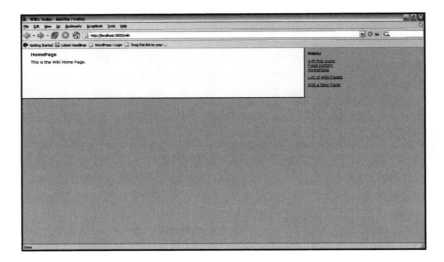

The `wiki.css` file:

```
body
{
        font:12px/1.2 Verdana, Arial, Helvetica, sans-serif;
        background:#CCCCCC;
        padding:0px;
```

```
        margin:0px;
}

#wikipagebody
{
        float:left;
        width:70%;
        background:#FFFFCC;
        border-right:2px solid #000;
        border-bottom:2px solid #000;
        margin-right:10px;
        padding-bottom:15px;
}

#menu
{

}

#rightcontent p
{
        font-size:10px;
        margin-left:0px;
}

div#flash
{
        border: thin groove #CC0000;
        margin:0px 30px 10px 30px;
        background-color: #CCCCCC;
        width: 80%;
}

p
{
        margin:0px 30px 10px 30px;
}
```

```
h1
{
        font-size:14px;
        padding-top:10px;
        margin:0px 30px 10px 30px;
}
```

>
> **Tip**
> We include the `div#flash` because we know that Flash messages will need to be displayed.

Setup

Key features of the wiki require the `acts_as_versioned` plug-in and RedCloth library. After we have created a Rails application called wiki, we will need to install the `acts_as_versioned` plug-in and RedCloth library.

Create a Rails application called `wiki`:

```
$ rails wiki
```

Change to the `wiki` **directory:**

```
$ cd wiki
```

Install the `acts_as_versioned` **plug-in:**

```
$ ruby script/plugin install acts_as_versioned
```

Install the RedCloth library:

```
$ gem install RedCloth
```

Create a database called `wiki_development` **and enter the database password in the** `database.yml` **file:**

```
development:
  adapter: mysql
  database: wiki_development
  username: root
  password: secret
  host: localhost
```

Creating the Model and Database

A wiki is made up of pages, so we create a table called pages. The pages table requires columns to store the `title`, `body`, `created_at`, and `edited_by` fields. Create the `page` model:

```
$ ruby script/generate model page
```

We can now edit the `001_create_pages.rb` migration and specify the column names required by the pages table:

```
class CreatePages < ActiveRecord::Migration
  def self.up
    create_table :pages do |t|
      t.column :title, :string, :limit => 100
      t.column :body, :text
      t.column :created_at, :datetime
      t.column :edited_by, :string
    end
  end
  def self.down
    drop_table :pages
  end
end
```

We add validation rules to the `page` model (`app/models/page.rb`). The `:title` must be unique and the `edited_by` field is mandatory. The `acts_as_versioned` declaration is also added:

```
class Page < ActiveRecord::Base
    validates_uniqueness_of :title
    validates_presence_of :title, :edited_by
    acts_as_versioned
end
```

We need to implement versioning with `acts_as_versioned`. The pages table requires a version column. We create a new migration called `002_add_version_column.rb`:

```
class AddVersionColumn < ActiveRecord::Migration
  def self.up
      add_column :pages, :version, :integer
  end
  def self.down
```

```
          remove_column :pages, :version
   end
end
```

The `acts_as_versioned` **plug-in requires a table called** `page_versions`. **The** `create_versioned_table` **method creates the required table** (`003_add_version_table.rb`):

```
class AddVersionTable < ActiveRecord::Migration
  def self.up
     Page.create_versioned_table
  end
  def self.down
     Page.drop_versioned_table
  end
end
```

We create a migration solely for the purpose of adding a `HomePage` **to the wiki** (`004_add_homepage.rb`):

```
class AddHomepage < ActiveRecord::Migration
  def self.up
     Page.create :title => "HomePage",
                     :body => 'This is the Wiki Home Page.',
                     :edited_by => "Aneesha"
  end
  def self.down
  end
end
```

Run the migrations:

```
$ rake db:migrate
```

Figure 14.2 shows the `page_versions` **table that the** `acts_as_versioned` **plug-in uses. A version for the** `HomePage` **has even been created.**

The Controller and View

The scaffold generator provides many of the features we require, so we use it and will customize its output to fit our needs:

```
$ ruby script/generate scaffold page wiki
```

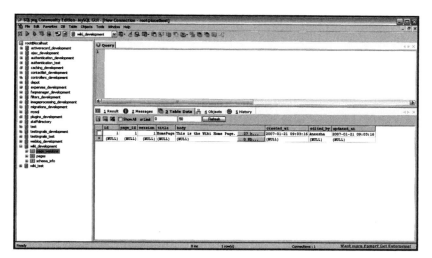

Figure 14.2
The page_versions
table will store versions of
pages in the wiki.

The wiki controller is the main controller of the application. We change the `config/routes.rb`
file so that http://localhost:3000 maps to the wiki controller:

```
ActionController::Routing::Routes.draw do |map|
    map.connect '', :controller => "wiki"
    map.connect ':controller/service.wsdl', :action => 'wsdl'
    map.connect ':controller/:action/:id'
end
```

We copy the `wiki.css` file we created earlier to the `public/stylesheets` folder. The
`apps/views/layouts/wiki.rhtml`, which will be applied to all the views rendered by the
wiki controller, needs to reference the `wiki.css` file—the `stylesheet_link_tag` helper is
used. The `wiki.rhtml` file will lay out the wiki page and the navigation panel. The navigation
panel includes links to actions within the wiki controller, namely `edit`, `history`, `list`,
and `new`:

```
<!DOCTYPE html PUBLIC "-//W3C//DTD XHTML 1.0 Transitional//EN"
"DTD/xhtml1-transitional.dtd">
<html>
<head>
  <title>Wiki: <%= controller.action_name %></title>
  <%= stylesheet_link_tag "wiki" %>
</head>
</head>
<body>
```

```
<div id="wikipagebody">
      <% if @flash[:notice] %>
              <div id="flash"><%= flash[:notice] %></div>
      <% end %>
      <%= yield %>
      <br/><br/><br/><br/><br/><br/>
</div>

<div id="menu">
    <h1>Menu</h1>
    <% if @page and @page.title %>
          <%= link_to "Edit this page", { :action => "edit",
                                          :id => @page.id } %>
<br/>
          <%= link_to "Page History", { :action => "history",
                                          :id => @page.id } %>
<br/>
        <% end %>
          <p><a href="/wiki">HomePage</a> </p>
      <p><%= link_to "List of Wiki Pages", :action => 'list' %></p>
      <p><%= link_to "Add a New Page", :action => 'new' %></p>
</div>
</body>
</html>
```

> ※ **Tip**
>
> We only display the `flash` `div` if a message has been set.

Displaying a Wiki Page

The index action is called when the wiki is accessed via http://localhost:3000 and http://localhost:3000/wiki. If the title is not included in the query string, `'HomePage'` is assumed. If the specified page does not exist, the user is redirected to the new action where she will be able to add a new page. When a page exists, a regular expression transforms all CamelCased words into hyperlinks and renders the show template. Figure 14.3 shows the `'HomePage'` of the wiki. The index action within the wiki controller is as follows:

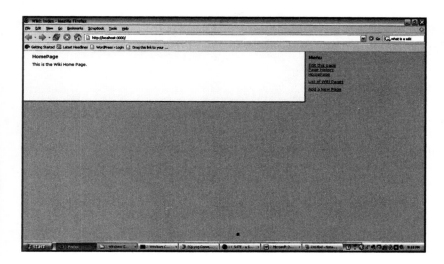

Figure 14.3
The wiki home page.

```ruby
def index
    @page = Page.find_by_title( params[:title] || 'HomePage' )
    if @page.nil?
        redirect_to :action => 'new', :title => params[:title]
    else
        @page.body.gsub!(
        Regexp.new( '\b((?:[A-Z]\w+){2,})' ),
'<a href="/wiki/index?title=\1">\1</a>' )
        render :action => 'show'
    end
end
```

The `show` action retrieves `@page` from the `id` and uses a regular expression to convert CamelCased words into hyperlinks:

```ruby
def show
    @page = Page.find(params[:id])
    @page.body.gsub!(
     Regexp.new( '\b((?:[A-Z]\w+){2,})' ),
'<a href="/wiki/index?title=\1">\1</a>' )
end
```

The show **template** (`views/wiki/show.rhtml`) **displays the title and the body of a page. The** `textilize` **helper is used to render wiki markup. Both the** `index` **and** `show` **actions call the** show **template:**

```
<h1><%= @page.title %></h1>
<div><%= textilize(@page.body) %></div>
```

Adding and Editing Wiki Pages

We believe in keeping things DRY and so we place all form elements in a partial (`_form.rhtml`) **that both the new and edit forms can utilize. The** `_form.rhtml` **partial includes the** `title`, `body`, `created_at`, **and** `edited_by` **fields:**

```
<%= error_messages_for 'page' %>
<!--[form:page]-->
<p><label for="page_title">Title</label><br/>
<%= text_field 'page', 'title'  %></p>
<p><label for="page_body">Body</label><br/>
<%= text_area 'page', 'body'  %></p>
<!--
<p><label for="page_created_at">Created at</label><br/>
<%= datetime_select 'page', 'created_at'  %></p>
-->
<p><label for="page_edited_by">Edited by</label><br/>
<%= text_field 'page', 'edited_by'  %></p>
<!--[eoform:page]-->
```

The `new` **action creates a new** `Page` **object. The** `title` **attribute of the new** `Page` **object is set to blank; if not,** `title` **key is in the** `params` **hash. We do this check because a hyperlinked CamelCased page link may be embedded within the body of another page. If this link is clicked, we want the title to match that of the CamelCased link:**

```
    def new
        @page = Page.new
        @page.title = params[:title] || ''
    end
```

The `new.rhtml` **template includes the form** `partial(_form.rhtml)` **(see Figure 14.4):**

```
<h1>New page</h1>
<%= start_form_tag :action => 'create' %>
  <%= render :partial => 'form' %>
```

```
<%= submit_tag "Create" %>
<%= end_form_tag %>
```

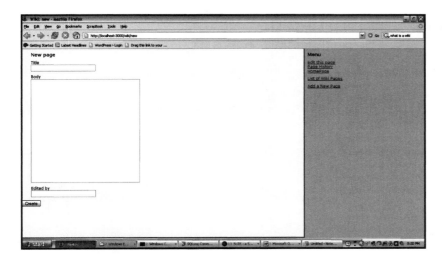

Figure 14.4
Add a new wiki page.

The new form is processed by the `create` action. The `@page` object is constructed from `params[:page]`. If `@page.save` is a success (i.e., no validation errors occur), `flash[:notice]` is set, and the page is displayed by redirecting to the `index` action and passing the title of the page as a parameter:

```
def create
      @page = Page.new(params[:page])
      if @page.save
            flash[:notice] = 'Page was successfully created.'
            redirect_to :action => 'index', :title => params[:title]
      else
            render :action => 'new'
      end
end
```

The `edit` action finds a page either by its `id` or `title`:

```
def edit
      @page = (Page.find(params[:id]) ||
Page.find_by_title(params[:title]))
end
```

The edit form (`edit.rhtml`) includes the `_form.rhtml` partial (see Figure 14.5):

```
<h1>Editing page</h1>
<%= start_form_tag :action => 'update', :id => @page %>
  <%= render :partial => 'form' %>
  <%= submit_tag 'Edit' %>
<%= end_form_tag %>
```

Figure 14.5
Editing a wiki page.

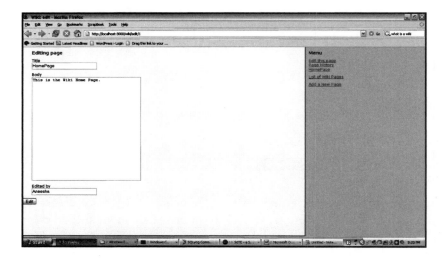

The edit form is processed by the `update` action. The `@page` object is found by its `id` and the `update_attributes` method is used to save the data back to the database. If successful, the user is redirected to the `show` action:

```
def update
    @page = Page.find(params[:id])
    if @page.update_attributes(params[:page])
        flash[:notice] = 'Page was successfully updated.'
        redirect_to :action => 'show', :id => @page
    else
        render :action => 'edit'
    end
end
```

Displaying a List of all Wiki Pages

The `list` action retrieves all pages in the wiki and displays them in sets of 10 (see Figure 14.6):

```
def list
    @page_pages, @pages = paginate :pages, :per_page => 10
end
```

The `list.rhtml` file displays links to view and edit each page:

```
<h1>Listing pages</h1>
<ul>
<% for page in @pages %>
  <li><%= link_to page.title, :action => 'show', :id => page %>
(<%= link_to 'Edit', :action => 'edit', :id => page %>)</li>
<% end %>
</ul>
<%= link_to 'Previous page',
{ :page => @page_pages.current.previous } if @page_pages.current.previous %>
<%= link_to 'Next page',
{ :page => @page_pages.current.next } if @page_pages.current.next %>
```

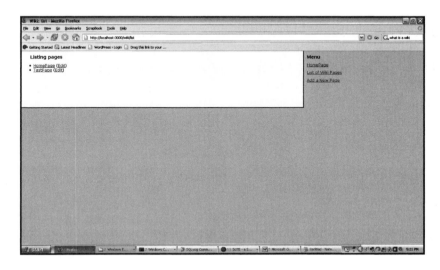

Figure 14.6
Displaying a list of all wiki pages.

Displaying Page History

The history action finds a Page object by its id and sets the @page instance object. We will be able to access the @page.version property to determine the current version of the page and the @page.versions.length attribute will return the number of versions being stored:

```
def history
     @page = Page.find(params[:id])
end
```

The history.rhtml template loops through the @page.versions.length collection and, if the version does not match that of the current object, prints a 'Revert' and 'Diff' link next to the name of the version (see Figure 14.7):

```
<h1>Version History:<%= @page.title %></h1>
<p>
<ul>
<% if @page.version > 0 %>
<% (1..@page.versions.length).each do |v| %>
<% if @page.version == v %>
<li><%= v %> [Current]
<% else %>
<li><%= v %> [<%= link_to 'Revert', :action => 'revert_version', :id => @page,
 :version => v %> | <%= link_to 'Diff', :action => 'diff_compare',
 :id => @page, :version => v %>]
<% end %>
<% end %>
<% end %>
</ul>
</p>
```

The revert_version action uses the revert_to method to go back to a previous version. The revert_to method is added to the page model when the acts_as_versioned declaration is added:

```
def revert_version
     @page = Page.find(params[:id])
     @page.revert_to!(params[:version])
     redirect_to :action => 'index', :title => @page.title
end
```

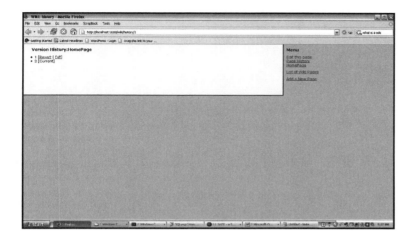

Figure 14.7
Displaying the history for
a page.

Comparing Versions

The History page displays a link next to each version that, when clicked, should compare the selected version to the current version. We will be using the `http://dev.instiki.org/file/instiki/trunk/lib/diff.rb` file. The downloaded `diff.rb` file must be placed in the `\lib` directory of the Rails application. We also need to include the diff library in the `config/environment.rb` file:

```
require 'diff'
include HTMLDiff
```

The current version of the page is retrieved by its `id`. The version we need to compare it to is retrieved using the `find_version` method. We pass the `@curr_page` and `@version_page` to the `HTMLDiff.diff` method.

```
def diff_compare
    @curr_page = Page.find(params[:id])
    @version_page = @curr_page.find_version(params[:version])
    @diff_results = HTMLDiff.diff(@curr_page.body,@version_page.body)
end
```

The `diff_compare.rhtml` template displays the insertions and deletions that have been made between versions (see Figure 14.8):

```
<h1>Version Diff: <%= @curr_page.title %> </h1>
<p>
<%= @diff_results %>
</p>
```

Figure 14.8
The output of comparing two versions of a wiki page.

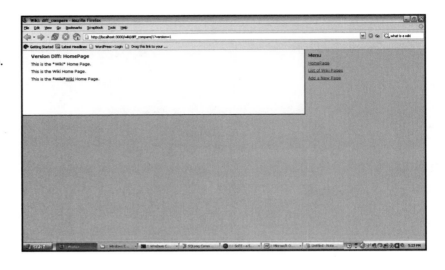

Source Code for the Wiki Controller
Here is the full source code listing for the wiki controller:

```
class WikiController < ApplicationController
     def index
          @page = Page.find_by_title( params[:title] || 'HomePage' )
          if @page.nil?
               redirect_to :action => 'new', :title => params[:title]
          else
               @page.body.gsub!(
Regexp.new( '\b((?:[A-Z]\w+){2,})' ), '<a href="/wiki/index?title=\1">\1</a>' )
               render :action => 'show'
          end
     end
  # GETs should be safe (see http://www.w3.org/2001/tag/doc/whenToUseGet.html)
  verify :method => :post, :only => [ :destroy, :create, :update ],
        :redirect_to => { :action => :list }
     def list
          @page_pages, @pages = paginate :pages, :per_page => 10
     end
     def show
          @page = Page.find(params[:id])
          @page.body.gsub!(
```

```
Regexp.new( '\b((?:[A-Z]\w+){2,})' ), '<a href="/wiki/index?title=\1">\1</a>' )
      end
      def new
            @page = Page.new
            @page.title = params[:title] || ''
      end
      def create
            @page = Page.new(params[:page])
            if @page.save
                  flash[:notice] = 'Page was successfully created.'
                  redirect_to :action => 'index', :title => params[:title]
            else
                  render :action => 'new'
            end
      end
      def edit
            @page = (Page.find(params[:id]) ||
Page.find_by_title(params[:title]))
      end
      def update
            @page = Page.find(params[:id])
            if @page.update_attributes(params[:page])
                  flash[:notice] = 'Page was successfully updated.'
                  redirect_to :action => 'show', :id => @page
            else
                  render :action => 'edit'
            end
      end
      def history
            @page = Page.find(params[:id])
      end
      def revert_version
            @page = Page.find(params[:id])
            @page.revert_to!(params[:version])
            redirect_to :action => 'index', :title => @page.title
```

```
      end
      def diff_compare
            @curr_page = Page.find(params[:id])
            @version_page = @curr_page.find_version(params[:version])
            @diff_results = HTMLDiff.diff(@curr_page.body,@version_page.body)
      end
end
```

Using the Wiki

We have implemented all the required features and are ready to start using the wiki. Open http://localhost:3000 in a web browser. The index action of the wiki controller will be called. The HomePage will be displayed. Click on the "Edit this page" link. The edit form will be displayed. Include some wiki markup and then type **"PageTwo"** (see Figure 14.9). Click on the Edit button.

Figure 14.9

Using wiki markup and CamelCasing to insert a page link.

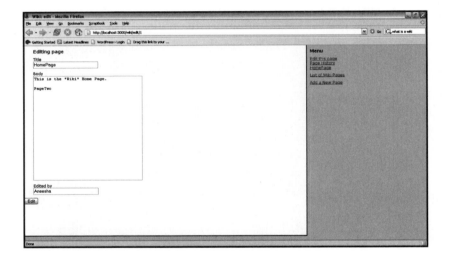

The message in the flash will be displayed. The wiki markup will be rendered. The CamelCasing is converted to a hyperlink. 'PageTwo' does not exist, so when we click on the link, a form to create a new page will be displayed. This is shown in Figure 14.10. The page title is displayed by default.

After the page is displayed, clicking on the "PageTwo" link will display the page (see Figure 14.11).

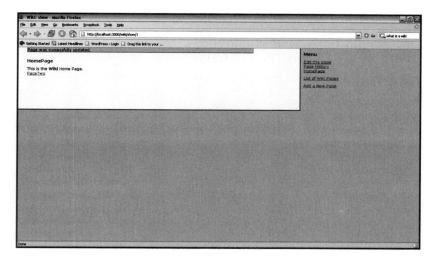

Figure 14.10
Adding a new page.

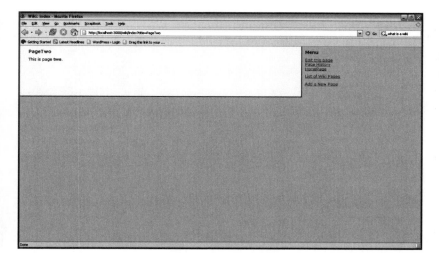

Figure 14.11
Clicking on a CamelCased link will display the page if it exists.

Click on the `"HomePage"` link. As there are multiple versions of `"HomePage"`, we can click on the `"Page History"` link. The `"Page History"` includes links to revert to a previous version or view a comparison (see Figure 14.12).

Click on a `"Diff"` link. The output of the differencing algorithm will be displayed. We can easily see where additions and deletions are made in Figure 14.13.

Figure 14.12
Viewing the versions of
a page.

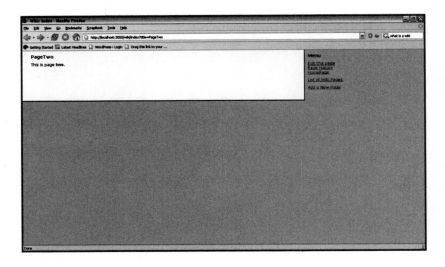

Figure 14.13
A visual comparison of
versions.

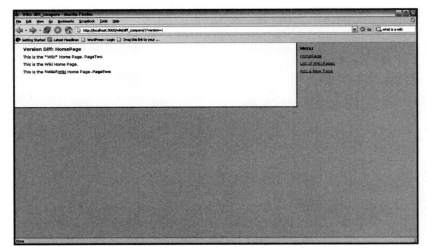

Enhancements

We have implemented all the features we set out to, but there is still room for improvement. Here
are some features that you can implement to enhance the wiki:

* Allow images and file attachments
* Implement a user model and authentication
* Allow pages to be deleted

Designing a Forum

We are going to create a threaded discussion forum. A forum allows users to view and respond to messages or posts. The relationship between messages is stored in a database table. The hierarchy between messages is displayed when the forum is viewed.

Features

The forum will be modeled using `acts_as_nested_set`. In Chapter 4, we used `acts_as_tree`. Both `acts_as_tree` and `acts_as_nested_set` have advantages and disadvantages. The nested set model is more efficient than `acts_as_tree` when you need to retrieve and display a tree. With `acts_as_nested_set`, we are able to retrieve an entire tree with a single query. `acts_as_nested_set` requires more database work behind the scenes when entries are inserted.

The following key features need to be implemented in the forum:

❄ **The ability to display the hierarchical structure of a forum on a single web page.** The relationships between forum messages need to be displayed in a tree-like view.

❄ **The ability to view messages.** A link must be included that allows a message to be viewed.

❄ **The ability to reply to messages.** A link to allow a user to reply to a message.

Setup

Because `acts_as_nested_set` is included with Rails, we don't need to install any plug-ins or libraries.

Create a Rails application called `forum`:

```
$ rails forum
```

Change to the `forum` directory:

```
$ cd forum
```

Create a database called `forum_development` and enter the database password in the `database.yml` file:

```
development:
  adapter: mysql
  database: forum_development
  username: root
  password: secret
  host: localhost
```

Creating the Model and Database

We start by generating a model called `forumpost`:

```
$ ruby script/generate model forumpost
```

The `subject`, `message`, `added_by`, and `created_at` fields are required by each post. The `acts_as_nested_set` requires a `parent_id`, `lft`, and `rgt` fields as well. The `subject` and `added_by` fields are mandatory. We edit the `app/models/forumpost.rb` file and add the validation rule and the `acts_as_nested_set` declaration:

```
class Forumpost < ActiveRecord::Base
    validates_presence_of :subject, :added_by
    acts_as_nested_set
end
```

Next we open the `001_create_forumposts.rb` file and add the code to create the required columns within the `forumposts` table. We also insert a post and a reply in the table:

```
class CreateForumposts < ActiveRecord::Migration
  def self.up
    create_table :forumposts do |t|
      t.column :parent_id, :integer
      t.column :lft, :integer
      t.column :rgt, :integer
      t.column :subject, :string
      t.column :message, :text
      t.column :added_by, :string
      t.column :created_at, :datetime
    end
    parent = Forumpost.create :subject => "My first forum!",
            :message => "This is so cool. Please reply.",
            :added_by => "Aneesha"
    reply = Forumpost.create :subject => "My first forum!",
            :message => "Yes - acts_as_nested_set is quite useful.",
            :added_by => "Celine"
    parent.add_child(reply)
  end
```

```
  def self.down
    drop_table :forumposts
  end
end
```

Tip

Refer to the Rails documentation for more info on `acts_as_nested_set`: http://www.rubyonrails.org/api/classes/ActiveRecord/Acts/NestedSet/ClassMethods.html.

Run the migration:

```
$ rake db:migrate
```

Figure 14.14 shows the `forumposts` **table.** `acts_as_nested_set` **inserts the values for the** `lft` **and** `rgt` **columns.**

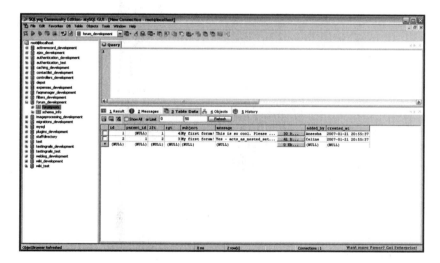

Figure 14.14
The forumposts table.

The Controller and View

The forum controller is the main controller of the application. We change the `config/routes.rb` file so that http://localhost:3000 maps to the forum controller:

```
ActionController::Routing::Routes.draw do |map|
      map.connect '', :controller => "forum"
      map.connect ':controller/service.wsdl', :action => 'wsdl'
```

```
        map.connect ':controller/:action/:id'
end
```

Displaying a Forum Thread

The `index` action of the forum controller retrieves all posts ordered by the `lft` column and stores the result in `@forumposts`:

```
def index
        @forumposts = Forumpost.find(:all,:order=>"lft")
    end
```

The `index.rhtml` template displays all the posts within the `@forumposts` collection. The subject, date, and name of the poster are displayed. Each post also has a View and Reply link.

```
<h1>Threaded Forum</h1>
<% for post in @forumposts %><br/>
<%= post.subject %> (<%= post.created_at.to_s(:short) %> by <%= post.added_by
%>)
[
<% unless post.send(post.parent_column) == nil %>
        <%= link_to "view", :action => "view", :post => post.id %> |
<% end %>
<%= link_to "reply", :action => "new", :parent => post.id %>
]
<% end %>
```

Let's take a look at how the `index` template displays the post and the reply we added to the `forumposts` table within the migration (see Figure 14.15). We were able to retrieve all the posts in the thread, but we still need to format the thread as a tree. We create a `helper` method to help us determine the indentation required (`app\helpers\forum_helper.rb`):

```
module ForumHelper
    def indent(post, i=0)
        $i = i
        if post.send(post.parent_column) == nil
            return $i
        else
            parent = Forumpost.find(post.send(post.parent_column))
            indent(parent, $i += 1)
        end
    end
end
```

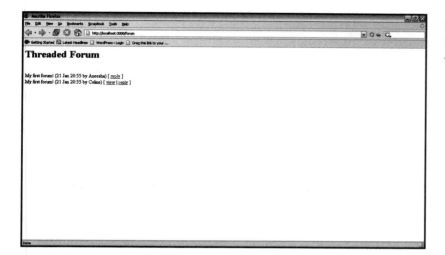

Figure 14.15
Displaying the forum
without indentation.

We use the `indent` helper to insert a dash for each level of indentation required (see Figure 14.16):

```
<h1>Threaded Forum</h1>
<% for post in @forumposts %><br/>
<% indent(post).times do %>-<% end %>
<%= post.subject %> (<%= post.created_at.to_s(:short) %> by <%= post.added_by
%>)
[
<% unless post.send(post.parent_column) == nil %>
    <%= link_to "view", :action => "view", :post => post.id %> |
<% end %>
<%= link_to "reply", :action => "new", :parent => post.id %>
]
<% end %>
```

Viewing Posts

The `view` action simply retrieves a `Forumpost` object by its `id`:

```
    def view
        @post = Forumpost.find(params[:post])
    end
```

369
❋ ❋ ❋

Figure 14.16
Display a threaded discussion forum with indentation.

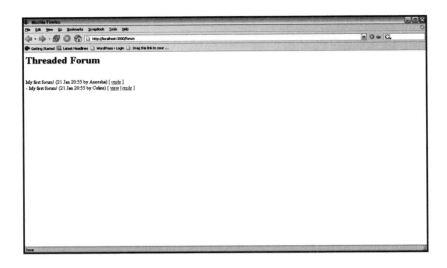

The `view.rhtml` **template displays the** `subject`, `message`, `date`, **and** `added_by` **fields (see Figure 14.17):**

```
<h1>View Post</h1>
<p><strong>Subject:</strong> <%= @post.subject %></p>
<p><strong>Message: </strong> <%= @post.message %></p>
<p><strong>Date: </strong> <%= @post.created_at.to_s(:short) %></p>
<p><strong>Added by: </strong> <%= @post.added_by %></p>
<%= link_to 'Back', :action => 'index' %>
```

Figure 14.17
Display a message.

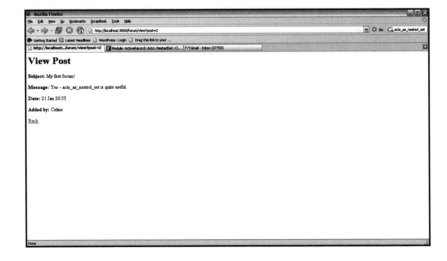

Replying to a Post

The `new` action retrieves the parent post and then sets the subject of the new post to the `parents` subject:

```
def new
      @parent = Forumpost.find(params[:parent])
      @forumpost = Forumpost.new
          @forumpost.subject = @parent.subject
    end
```

The `new.rhtml` file displays a form for a user to reply to a post (see Figure 14.18):

```
<h1>New post</h1>
<%= start_form_tag :action => 'reply', :parent => @parent.id %>
<%= error_messages_for 'forumpost' %>
<p><label for="forumpost_subject">Subject:</label>
<%= text_field 'forumpost', 'subject', :size => 50 %></p>
<p><label for="forumpost_message">Message:</label><br/>
<%= text_area 'forumpost', 'message', :rows => 4 %></p>
<p><label for="forumpost_added_by">Added by:</label>
<%= text_field 'forumpost', 'added_by', :size => 50 %></p>
<%= submit_tag "Reply" %>
<%= end_form_tag %>
<%= link_to 'Back', :action => 'index' %>
```

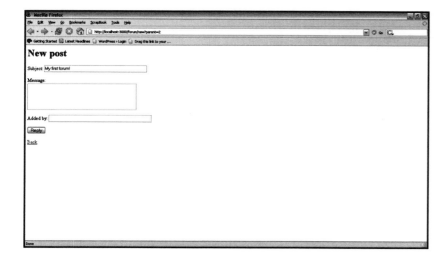

Figure 14.18
Replying to a post.

The `reply` action saves the post and then uses the `add_child` method to associate the post with its parent:

```
def reply
      parent = Forumpost.find(params["parent"])
      @forumpost = Forumpost.create(params[:forumpost])
      parent.add_child(@forumpost)
      if @forumpost.save
            flash[:notice] = 'The post has been added.'
      else
            flash[:notice] = 'The post was unable to be added.'
      end
      redirect_to :action => 'index'
end
```

Source Code for the Forum Controller
Here is the full source code listing for the forum controller:

```
class ForumController < ApplicationController
      def index
            @forumposts = Forumpost.find(:all,:order=>"lft")
      end
      def view
            @post = Forumpost.find(params[:post])
      end
      def new
            @parent = Forumpost.find(params[:parent])
            @forumpost = Forumpost.new
      end
      def reply
            parent = Forumpost.find(params["parent"])
            @forumpost = Forumpost.create(params[:forumpost])
            parent.add_child(@forumpost)
            if @forumpost.save
                  flash[:notice] = 'The post has been added.'
            else
                  flash[:notice] = 'The post was unable to be added.'
            end
```

```
            redirect_to :action => 'index'
      end
end
```

Enhancements

You might consider adding the following features to the forum:

❋ Support for wiki markup within a post

❋ User subscription and authentication

❋ The creation and display of multiple forums

Conclusion

In this chapter, we built a wiki and a forum. The wiki supported wiki markup, stored a new version of a page each time the page was updated, and even allowed changes between versions to be compared. The forum used `acts_as_nested_set` to thread forum posts. I hope you have found learning Rails to be rewarding and are enthusiastic about building your next web application. I wish you all the best. Have fun!

Ruby Quick Reference

This quick reference guide will come in handy as you familiarize yourself with Ruby and start to program database enabled applications using the Rails framework. This reference guide accompanies Chapter 2: "Ruby Essentials."

Command Line Ruby

Start Interactive Ruby (irb):

```
$ irb
```

Start Interactive Ruby with a simple prompt:

```
$ irb --simple-prompt
```

Check Ruby code syntax:

```
$ ruby -cw filename.rb
```

Execute a Ruby program:

```
ruby filename.rb
```

Interpret a Ruby program with warnings displayed:

```
$ ruby -w filename.rb
```

Display the Ruby version number:

```
$ Ruby --version
```

Ruby Code

Comment in code:

```
# This is a comment
```

Variable assignment:

```
# variable begin with a lowercase letter
name = "Aneesha"
```

Constants:

```
# constants begin with an uppercase letter
Pi = 3.14
```

Data types:

```
name = "Aneesha" # a string
no = 20 # an integer
fraction = 0.5 # a float
```

Strings

Repeat a string:

```
>> "Hello " * 3
=> Hello Hello Hello
```

Capitalize a string:

```
>> "hello".capitalize
=> Hello
```

Interpolation (variable substitution):

```
>> name = "Aneesha"
>> puts "Hello #{var}"
=> Hello Aneesha
```

Mathematical Operations

Addition: +

Subtraction: −

Multiplication: *

Division: /

Remainder: %

Exponent: **

Shortcut operators:

+=, −=, *=, /=, **=, %=

Generate a Random Number
Generate a random number between 0 and 1:

```
>> rand
```

Genarate a random number between 0 and 5:

```
>> rand (5)
```

Comparison Operators

```
equal = =
not equal to!=
greater than >
less than <
greater than or equal to >=
less than or equal to <=
```

Conditional Constructs

The if statement:

```
if x == 10
      print "The variable x is equal to 10."
end
```

The if - else statement:

```
if x == 10
      print "The variable x is equal to 10."
```

```
else
    print "The variable x is not equal to 10."
end
```

The `if - elsif - else` **statement:**

```
if x == 10
    print "The variable x is equal to 10."
elsif x==5
    print "The variable x is equal to 5."
else
    print "No match."
end
```

The `case` **statement:**

```
x = 5
case x
when 5
    puts "x is equal to 5"
when 1
    puts "x is equal to 1"
else
    puts "No match"
end
```

Loops

```
# times do loop
5.times do
    puts "Hello World"
end
# do loop
n = 1
loop do
    n = n + 1
    puts "Loop iteration #{n}"
    break if n > 9
end
# while loop
```

```
n = 1
while n < 11
      puts "Loop iteration #{n}"
      n = n + 1
end
puts "Done"
# until loop
n = 1
until n > 10
      puts "Loop iteration #{n}"
      n = n + 1
end
puts "Done"
```

Arrays
Create a new array:

```
numbers = Array.new
```

Or

```
numbers = []
# An array that stores mixed data types
messages = [1,2,"three",4.0]
# An array storing numeric data
numbers = [1,2,3,4,5,6]
# An array that stores Strings
names = ["Madonna", "Aneesha", "Celine"]
# An array that stores decimal values
x_coordinates = [1.0, 3.4, 35.6, 24]
```

Sort an array:

```
>> cities.sort
=> ["adelaide", "brisbane", "cairns", "sydney", "perth"]
```

Reverse the order of an array:

```
>> cities.reverse
=> ["perth", "sydney", "cairns", "brisbane", "adelaide"]
```

Determine the number of items in an array:

```
>> cities.length
```

Add an element at position 0:

```
>>numbers = [1,2,3,4]
>>numbers.unshift(0)
```

Add an element to the end of an array:

```
>>numbers.push(5)
=> [1,2,3,4,5]
>> numbers.push(6,7,8)
=> [1,2,3,4,5,6,7,8]
```

Concatenate arrays:

```
>>[1,2,3].concat([4,5,6])
>>numbers + [4,5,6]
```

Check if an array is empty:

```
>> numbers.empty?
```

Check if an array contains an element with a certain value:

```
>> numbers.include?(1)
```

Remove duplicates:

```
>> [1,2,2,3,4,5,5,6].uniq
=> [1,2,3,4,5,6]
```

Iterate over elements in an array:

```
cities.each do |city|
      puts "City " + city
end
cities.each_with_index do |i,city|
      puts "City index #{i}= " + city
end
```

Hashes

Create a hash:

```
post_codes =
{
```

```
    "Brisbane" => 4000,
    "Mt Gravatt" => 4122,
    "Carindale" => 4152
}
```

Return the value for a key:

```
>> puts post_codes["Brisbane"].to_s
```

Assign a new value to a key:

```
post_codes["Kelvin Grove"] = 4065
List all Keys:
>> post_codes.keys
```

List all values:

```
>> post_codes.values
```

Check if a key exists:

```
>> post_codes.has_key?("Carindale")
```

Determine the number of key value pairs:

```
>> puts post_codes.size.to_s
```

Print each key:

```
post_codes.each_key do |key|
    puts key
end
```

Print each value:

```
post_codes.each_value do |val|
    puts val
end
```

Print key, value pairs:

```
post_codes.each do |key,val|
    puts "#{key} - #{val}"
end
```

Invert a hash:

```
# Swap Key - value pairs
post_codes.invert.each do |key,val|
      puts "#{key} - #{val}"
end
```

Functions

```
# A simple function
def greet_me
      puts "Hello"
end
```

A function that takes an argument:

```
def greet(name)
      puts "Hello #{name}"
end
```

Classes

A class with attr_reader and attr_writer:

```
class Employee
      attr_reader :name
      attr_writer :name
      def initialize
            @name = ""
      end
end
```

A class with att_accessor:

```
class Employee
      attr_accessor :name
      def initialize
            @name = ""
      end
end
```

Appendix B

Ruby on Rails Quick Reference

The Ruby on Rails framework advocates "convention over configuration." Learning the "conventions" in this appendix will help you become a proficient Rails developer.

Create a Rails application	`rails application_name`
Run the interactive Rails console	`ruby script/console`
Start Webrick	`ruby script/server`
Start Webrick on port 80	`ruby script/server -p 80`
Generate a model	`ruby script/generate model non_plural_tablename`
	e.g. `ruby script/generate model employee`
Generate a controller	`ruby script/generate controller plural_table_name`
	e.g. `script/generate controller employee`
Freeze current rails version	`rake rails:freeze:gems`
Generate a scaffolding for a model	`ruby script/generate scaffold modelname controllername`

Appendix A } Ruby on Rails Quick Reference

Generate a migration	`ruby script/generate migration newtablename`
Generate a mailer class	`ruby script/generate mailer registration signup`
Generate a web service API	`ruby script/generate web_service servicename api_one api_two`
Generate an integration test	`ruby script/generate integration_test testname`

Using Rake

Update files in the app, scripts, and public folders	`rake rails:update`
Update the Prototype and Scriptaculous Javascript libraries	`rake rails:update:javascripts`
Update the Rails generators found in the scripts folder	`rake rails:update:scripts`
Delete the log files	`rake log:clear`
Update the database to the latest migration	`rake db:migrate`
Revert or update the database to a migration version	`rake db:migrate VERSION=5`
Display code statistics	`rake stats`
Create a table to store session data in current database	`rake db:sessions:create`
Delete entries from the sessions table.	`rake db:sessions:clear`

Active Record Conventions

Table names must be in plural form	Table name: `employees`
All tables must have a primary key called `id`	Primary key: `id`
Foreign keys must have the name of the parent table with an underscore and `id`	Foreign key: `parent_id`

Timestamps added to fields on update	`updated_at` `updated_on`
Timestamps added to fields on creation	`created_at` `created_on`

Active Record Model Validation

Required fields	`validates_presence_of :field1, :field2`
Numeric fields	`validates_numericality_of :numericfield`
Password confirmation	`validates_confirmation_of :password`

Character range validation	`validates_length_of :password,`
	`:minimum => 6,`
	`:message=>"must be 6 characters in length."`

Unit Testing

Run a single unit test	`ruby unit/test/unitname_test.rb`
Run all tests	`rake test`
Run all unit tests	`rake test:units`
Run all functional tests	`rake test:functionals`
Run an integration test	`rake test:integration`

Rails Plugins

Discover a list of plugin repositories from the Rails wiki	`ruby script/plugin discover`
Display a list of available plugins	`ruby script/plugin list`
Install a plugin by name	`ruby script/plugin install plugin_name`
Install a plugin from a URL	`ruby script/plugin install` `http://somewhere.com/projects/plugins/plugin_name`
Update a plugin	`ruby script/plugin update`
Add a plugin source code repository	`ruby script/plugin source`
List all plugin source code repositories	`ruby script/plugin sources`

Index